Africa

An Encyclopedia
for Students

LANGUAGE FAMILIES

Arabic

Arabic

Berber

Tuareg

Arabic

Berber

Arabic

Arabic

Somali

Amharic

Fulani

Songhai

Wolof

Hausa

Kanuri

Tubu

Kordofanian

Bambara

Mossi

Sara

Oromo

Gur

Fon

Gbaya

Tigrinya

Akan

Ewe

Yoruba

Igbo

Sango

Efik

Mongo

Luo

Ewando

Fang

Ganda

Maasai

Lingala

Kinyarwanda

Kirundi

Gikuyu

Kongo

Luba

Swahili

Chokwe

Bemba

Mbundu

Chichewa

!Kung

Shona

Nama

Sotho

Nguni

Malagasy

LANGUAGES

- NILO-SAHARAN
- AFRO-ASIATIC
- NIGER-KORDOFANIAN
- KHOISAN
- MALAYO-POLYNESIAN

Africa

An Encyclopedia for Students

John Middleton, Editor

Volume 4

Sadat–Zulu

Index

CHARLES SCRIBNER'S SONS

GALE GROUP

THOMSON LEARNING™

*New York • Detroit • San Diego • San Francisco
Boston • New Haven, Conn. • Waterville, Maine
London • Munich*

Developed for Charles Scribner's Sons by Visual Education Corporation, Princeton, N.J.

For Scribners
PUBLISHER: Karen Day
EDITORS: John Fitzpatrick, Brad Morgan
COVER AND INTERIOR DESIGN: Jennifer Wahi
PHOTO RESEARCH: Kelly Quin
PRODUCTION SUPERVISOR: Mary Beth Trimper

For Visual Education
PROJECT DIRECTOR: Darryl Kestler
WRITERS: John Haley, Charles Roebuck, Rebecca Stefoff, Joseph Ziegler
EDITORS: Noëlle Y. Child, Cindy George, Guy Austrian, Charles Roebuck
ASSOCIATE EDITOR: Cheryl MacKenzie
COPYEDITING SUPERVISOR: Helen A. Castro
ELECTRONIC PREPARATION: Fiona Torphy

Contributors
Nancy E. Gratton, Kevin van Bladel, Frank Griffel, Jeremy Raphael Berndt

Library of Congress Cataloging in-Publication Data

Africa: an encyclopedia for students / John Middleton, editor.
    p. cm
    Includes bibliographical references and index.
    ISBN 0-684-80650-9 (set : alk. paper) —ISBN 0-684-80651-7 (v. 1) —
ISBN 0-684-80652-5 (v. 2) —ISBN 0-684-80653-3 (v. 3) —
ISBN 0-684-80654-1 (v. 4)
    1. Africa–Encyclopedias, Juvenile. [1. Africa—Encyclopedias.] I. Middleton,
John, 1921–

DT3 .A249 2001
960'03—dc21
                                                    2001049348

Table of Contents

VOLUME 1
Abidjan—Economic History

VOLUME 2
Ecosystems—Laws and Legal Systems

VOLUME 3
Leakey Family—Rwanda

VOLUME 4
Sadat, Anwar—Zulu

List of Maps

Table of Contents

Color Plates

Volume 1
Peoples and Cultures

Volume 2
The Land and Its History

Volume 3
Art and Architecture

Volume 4
Daily Life

A Time Line of Africa

4 m.y.a.*	Australopithecines *(early hominids) live in northern Rift Valley (Ethiopia, Kenya).*
2.5 m.y.a.*	*Early Stone Age;* Homo habilis *appears (Olduvai Gorge, Tanzania).*
1.5 m.y.a.*– 150,000 B.C.	Homo erectus *appears.*
240,000– 40,000 B.C.	*Middle Stone Age.*
80,000– 20,000 B.C.	*Late Stone Age.*
20,000– 10,000 B.C.	*Farming introduced in lower Nile Valley.*
10,000– 6000 B.C.	*Cattle domesticated in northern Africa.*
	Millet and sorghum grown in western Africa.
6000– 5000 B.C.	*Khoisan hunters of southern Africa create rock paintings.*
3000 B.C.	*King Menes unifies Lower Egypt and Upper Egypt.*
	Agriculture develops in Ethiopian highlands.
2000–1000 B.C.	*Horses introduced in Sahara region.*
	Bananas grown in central Africa.
332 B.C.	*Greeks occupy Egypt.*
200 B.C.	*Romans gain control of Carthage.*
32 B.C.	*Royal city of Meroë flourishes in what is now Sudan.*
A.D. 300s	*Aksum invades Meroë; Aksum king adopts Coptic Christianity.*
530s	*Byzantine empire takes Mediterranean ports.*
600s	*Muslim Arabs invade North Africa.*
ca. 1000	*Shona begin building Great Zimbabwe.*
1200s	*Portuguese voyage to northwest coast of Africa.*
	Sundjata Keïta founds Mali kingdom.

*m.y.a. million years ago

1312–1337	*Mansa Musa rules Mali and makes pilgrimage to Mecca.*
1400s	*Benin kingdom flourishes.*
1498	*Vasco da Gama sails around the southern and eastern coasts of Africa on the way to India.*
1505–1510	*Portuguese seize Swahili towns in eastern Africa and fortify Mozambique.*
	Kongo king Afonso I converts to Christianity.
1517	*Ottoman Turks conquer Egypt and port towns along the Mediterranean.*
1578	*Moroccans defeat Portuguese, remaining free of colonial control.*
1591	*Al-Mansur invades Songhai.*
1600s	*French, English, and Dutch establish trading posts along western coasts to export gold, ivory, and slaves.*
	Akan state emerges.
1650s	*Dutch settle at Cape of Good Hope in southern Africa.*
	Arab traders settle on East African coast.
1700s	*French and British establish network for slave trade in Central Africa.*
	Zanzibar prospers as Arab trading center.
1721	*French colonize Mauritius.*
1787	*British missionaries found Sierra Leone.*
1795	*British seize Cape Colony from Dutch.*
1798	*Napoleon leads French invasion of Egypt.*
1805	*Muhammad Ali takes power in Egypt, breaking free of Ottoman control.*
1807	*Britain and the United States abolish slave trade.*
1817	*Shaka emerges at head of Zulu kingdom in southern Africa.*
1821	*Freed slaves from the United States settle in what is now Liberia.*
1828	*Queen Ranavalona takes throne in Madagascar.*
1830s	*French rule proclaimed in Algeria.*
	Slave trade continues in western Africa.
1835	*Dutch settlers in southern Africa head north in "Great Trek."*
1840s–1880s	*Slave trade flourishes in East Africa.*
1847	*Republic of Liberia is established.*
1852–1873	*David Livingstone explores Central and East Africa.*
1858	*Portuguese abolish slavery in Central Africa.*

1855–1868	*Emperor Téwodros rules Ethiopia.*
1859–1869	*Suez Canal is built.*
1869	*Diamonds are discovered at Kimberley in northern Cape Colony.*
1880–1881	*Afrikaners rebel against Britain in the First Anglo-Boer War, and British withdraw from Transvaal in southern Africa.*
1885	*Mahdist forces capture Khartoum.*
1880s–early 1900s	*European powers colonize most of Africa (present-day names of countries listed):*
	Belgians in Congo (Kinshasa);
	British in Nigeria, Ghana, Sierra Leone, the Gambia, Uganda, Kenya, Somalia, Mauritius, Seychelles, Zambia, Zimbabwe, Malawi, Botswana, Lesotho, and Swaziland;
	French in Mauritania, Niger, Burkina Faso, Mali, Algeria, Tunisia, Morocco, Senegal, Guinea, Ivory Coast, Bénin, Central African Republic, Gabon, Congo (Brazzaville), Chad, Djibouti, Madagascar, Réunion, and the Comoro Islands;
	Germans in Togo, Cameroon, Namibia, Tanzania, Rwanda, and Burundi;
	Portuguese in Guinea-Bissau, São Tomé and Príncipe, Cape Verde, Angola, and Mozambique;
	Spanish in Western Sahara and Equatorial Guinea.
1893–1895	*Africans in King Leopold's Congo revolt.*
1895	*France forms federation of colonies that becomes French West Africa.*
1896	*Ethiopian emperor Menilek defeats Italians, maintaining country's independence.*
1899–1902	*Afrikaners defeated by British in Second Anglo-Boer war.*
1910	*Union of South Africa formed.*
1914–1918	*World War I: French and British capture German Togo; Africans fight on the side of various colonial powers in Africa.*
1922	*Egypt gains its independence.*
1930	*Haile Selassie I crowned emperor of Ethiopia.*
1935	*Italians invade Ethiopia.*
1936	*Union party in South Africa revokes voting rights of blacks.*
1939–1945	*World War II: many major battles fought in North Africa; Africans in French and British colonies drafted to fight in Europe and Asia.*
1940s	*First nationalist political parties are formed in western Africa.*

1944	William Tubman becomes president of Liberia.
1945	Arab League, an organization of Arab states, is founded in Cairo.
	Ethiopia regains its independence.
1948	Policy of apartheid introduced in South Africa.
1950s	Several independence movements against colonial rule develop.
1951	Libya declared an independent monarchy under King Idris I.
1952	Gamal Abdel Nasser seizes power in Egypt.
1953	Northern Rhodesia (Zambia), Southern Rhodesia (Zimbabwe), and Nyasaland (Malawi) join to form the Central African Federation.
1954	War breaks out in Algeria.
1956	Sudan, Morocco, and Tunisia become independent.
1957	Ghana achieves independence, with Kwame Nkrumah as president.
1958	Guinea, under Sékou Touré, becomes independent.
1960	Independence achieved in Cameroon (French Cameroun), Chad, Congo (Brazzaville), Congo (Kinshasa), Dahomey (Bénin), Gabon, Ivory Coast, Madagascar, Mali, Mauritania, Niger, Nigeria, Senegal, Somalia, Togo, and Upper Volta (Burkina Faso).
1961	Rwanda, Sierra Leone, and Tanganyika become independent.
1962	Independence achieved in Algeria, Burundi, and Uganda.
1963	Kenya (under Jomo Kenyatta) and Zanzibar become independent.
	Central African Federation ends.
	Organization of African Unity is founded.
	FRELIMO begins armed struggle for liberation of Mozambique.
1964	In South Africa, Nelson Mandela stands trial and is jailed.
	Tanganyika and Zanzibar join to form Tanzania.
	Malawi and Zambia become independent.
	Hutu overthrow Tutsi rule in Burundi.
1965	Rhodesia declares independence under Ian Smith.
	Mobutu Sese Seko takes power in Congo (Kinshasa) and renames it Zaire.
	King Hassan restores monarchy in Morocco.
	The Gambia gains independence.
1966	Independence achieved in Lesotho and Botswana.

1967–1970	*Biafra attempts to secede from Nigeria.*
1968	*Swaziland becomes independent.*
1969	*Muammar al-Qaddafi seizes power in Libya.*
1970	*Egypt/Sudan: Aswan Dam is completed.*
1974	*Guinea attains independence.*
1975	*Cape Verde and Angola become independent.*
	FRELIMO government gains independence in Mozambique.
1976	*Spain withdraws from Western Sahara; Morocco and Mauritania fight over territory.*
	Residents of Soweto and other South African townships begin violent protests.
1970s–1990s	*War erupts across the continent within the countries of Angola, Chad, Congo (Brazzaville), Congo (Kinshasa), Ethiopia, Guinea-Bissau, Liberia, Rwanda, Sierra Leone, Somalia, Sudan, and Western Sahara, and between the nations of Ethiopia and Eritrea, Ethiopia and Somalia, and Sudan and Uganda.*
1980	*Zimbabwe becomes independent.*
1990	*Nelson Mandela released from prison.*
	Namibia becomes independent.
1993	*Apartheid ends in South Africa.*
	Eritrea gains independence from Ethiopia.
1994	*Rwandan and Burundi presidents assassinated; ethnic violence between Hutu and Tutsi continues.*
	Nelson Mandela becomes first black president of South Africa.
1995	*Outbreak of deadly Ebola virus in Congo (Kinshasa).*
1997	*Laurent Kabila takes power in Zaire and renames it Democratic Republic of the Congo (Kinshasa).*
1999	*Libya hands over two suspects in 1986 airplane bombing over Lockerbie, Scotland.*
2000	*Ghana chooses president John Kufuor in free elections.*
	Paul Kagame is the first Tutsi to become president in Rwanda.
2001	*Congo (Kinshasa) leader, Kabila, is assassinated; Kabila's son, Joseph, succeeds him as president.*

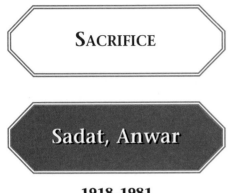

SACRIFICE

See *Religion and Ritual.*

Sadat, Anwar

1918–1981
Egyptian president

* **coup** sudden, often violent, overthrow of a ruler or government

* **Soviet Union** nation that existed from 1922 to 1991, made up of Russia and 14 other republics

The presidency of Anwar al-Sadat was shaped largely by the way he conducted Egypt's relationship with Israel. Sadat won the admiration of Arabs for his war against Israel and then earned international praise for making peace with Israel.

Born in an Egyptian village, Sadat attended school in CAIRO and then joined the army. Dedicated to the goal of ending British control over EGYPT, he sought aid from Germany, Britain's enemy, during WORLD WAR II. The British imprisoned him, but he escaped. Sadat became a follower of Egyptian military officer Gamal Abdel NASSER, who helped lead a coup* against Egypt's British-backed monarchy in 1952. When Nasser became president in 1956, Sadat served as his vice president and took over as head of government on Nasser's death in 1970.

Sadat soon showed that he was not afraid to take decisive action in international affairs. Feeling that Egypt was not receiving proper support from the Soviet Union*, he threw thousands of Soviets out of the country. In 1973 he formed an alliance with the Arab nation of Syria to make a surprise attack on Israel. The war made Sadat a hero in the Arab world because Egypt managed to win back some territory in the Sinai Peninsula from Israel.

After the war Sadat turned toward peace, visiting Israel to propose a treaty between the two nations. Although the Soviet Union and most Arab nations disapproved of this move, Sadat and Israeli Prime Minister Menachem Begin signed a peace agreement in 1979. The two men shared the Nobel Peace Prize for this landmark achievement, but Sadat's actions were unpopular with many in Egypt. Two years later he was assassinated by members of a Muslim group that rejected the notion of peace with Israel. (*See also* **Arabs in Africa, Global Politics and Africa, Islam in Africa.**)

Sahara Desert

* **sub-Saharan** referring to Africa south of the Sahara desert
* **indigenous** native to a certain place

Stretching across northern Africa from the Atlantic Ocean in the west to the Red Sea in the east, the Sahara is the world's largest desert. It forms a natural barrier between two very different geographic and cultural regions: NORTH AFRICA, with its Arab-influenced Mediterranean culture; and sub-Saharan* Africa, where indigenous* African culture is dominant. Yet for centuries people have crossed this dangerous expanse along trade routes, supplying goods to the towns and kingdoms on the Sahara's borders and linking Africa's northern and southern communities. Today the desert supports a population of about 2.5 million people.

Geography. The Sahara desert covers 3.3 million square miles in 11 countries and the territory of WESTERN SAHARA. Two Saharan countries are almost entirely desert—LIBYA and EGYPT.

Sahara Desert

See color plate 15, vol. 2.

About a fifth of the Sahara is covered with sand seas, called ergs. In some places the strong Saharan winds shape the sand into rows of towering dunes. Elsewhere the desert consists mostly of plains covered with gravel or barren rock. Within the Sahara lie two mountain ranges, the Ahaggar in ALGERIA and the Tibesti in CHAD. The highest point in the desert is Emi Koussi, an 11,204-foot peak in Chad. The lowest point, 4,356 feet below sea level, is in Egypt's Qattara depression, one of several Saharan basins.

Two rivers flow all year through the Sahara: the NILE in the eastern desert and the NIGER in the southwest. After the desert's rare rainfalls, smaller streams and rivers appear briefly before drying up and disappearing. The driest parts of the Sahara receive no more than 4 to 6 inches of rain each year. The SAHEL, the zone of transition between the true desert and the rest of Africa to the south, receives up to 24 inches of rain. Occasional springs or pools dot the desert, giving rise to oases, islands of green vegetation amid arid surroundings.

The Sahara was not always as dry as it is now. Before about 3000 B.C., the area experienced cycles of heavier rainfall in which a wide variety of plant and animal life flourished. Prehistoric humans occupied the region during these periods, leaving ROCK ART that shows images of a greener, wetter time when even water-loving hippopotamuses lived in the Sahara.

History. Arab invaders gained control of northern Africa in the A.D. 600s. In the centuries that followed, camel caravans carried gold, slaves, spices, leather, and ostrich feathers from sub-Saharan Africa north across the Sahara and exchanged these goods for weapons, horses, textiles, and paper from the Mediterranean coast. The Saharan people benefited from the trade, providing marketplaces in the oases and collecting tolls and protection money from foreign traders. Cities such as TIMBUKTU (in what is now northern MALI) became thriving centers of commerce.

During the Middle Ages, several kingdoms rose on the fringes of the Sahara. States in the area that is now GHANA and NIGERIA extended their influence into the desert region, but their dominance over the western Sahara ended in 1591, when the sultan of MOROCCO conquered Timbuktu. Saharan groups such as the TUAREG then took control of the region.

Around 1850 Europeans began colonizing Algeria and other parts of the Sahara region. Most of the desert came under French control. When North Africa regained independence in the 1960s, the colonial divisions made by the French became national boundaries. However, the border between Libya and Chad remained in dispute until 1994.

People and Economy. Most of the people who live in the Sahara occupy the oases and the highlands on the desert fringes. Arabic-speaking peoples, including the Bedouin of Libya and the Chaamba of Algeria, live in the northern Sahara. On the northern and western edges of the desert are many groups of BERBERS. The largest Berber-speaking group within the Sahara is the Tuareg, who number between 500,000 and 1 million people. The Berbers and Tuareg have cultural and reli-

Arab culture spread across the Sahara along caravan routes and down rivers such as the Nile. These Muslim tombs near Aswan, Egypt, date from the 1000s.

* **Islamic** referring to Islam, the religion based on the teaching of the prophet Muhammad

gious ties to Islamic*, Arab-speaking northern Africa. To the east, in NIGER and northern Chad, live the Teda or Tubu peoples, whose languages and cultures are closely linked to those of sub-Saharan African groups.

Livestock herding and trade are the main economic activities of the Sahara. Desert dwellers raise camels, goats, and sheep, and in some oases they also grow gardens and date palms. The principal trade good is salt, either mined or obtained from evaporated water. Since ancient times,

Saharans have traded salt for grain and other goods from the agricultural regions south of the desert. The Tuareg salt trade continues today, unlike most of the long-distance trade that once crisscrossed the Sahara. The major economic event of the 1900s in the Sahara was the discovery of mineral resources, particularly oil, phosphate, iron, uranium, and bauxite, the source of aluminum.

Jenne and the Saharan Borderlands. In ancient times, many cities and states flourished in the southern and southwestern borderlands of the Sahara. Before the 1970s historians believed that Arabs and Berbers from North Africa sparked the formation of these states by introducing long-distance trade to the region in the A.D. 800s or 900s.

* **archaeological**   referring to the study of past human cultures and societies, usually by excavating ruins

Recent archaeological* evidence, however, reveals a different history. Excavations show that large, highly organized towns existed before the Arabs arrived and before major trade began across the Sahara. Jenne (or Jenne-jeno) in Mali is one of the best studied of these sites.

Human settlement at Jenne dates from the 200s or 100s B.C. The city reached its height between A.D. 500 and 1000, with a population of at least 10,000. Its citizens exported copper, pottery, and agricultural goods through a local trade network that covered much of the middle course of the Niger River.

Two features show that Jenne was a purely African creation, different from ancient cities built by Arabs and Europeans. First, there is no evidence of a ruling class. Jenne does not have the rich burial sites or monumental public architecture that indicate the presence of nobles or powerful rulers. Second, Jenne was not a dense urban settlement enclosed by a city wall. It was a central town with satellite communities clustered around it. Ruins at other ancient sites in the Niger region suggest that this clustered organization was typical of the African civilizations that arose there. These societies later merged with or developed into the states that joined in the cross-Saharan trade established by Arabs. (*See also* **Climate, Deserts and Drought, Ecosystems**.)

Sahel

* **sub-Saharan**   referring to Africa south of the Sahara desert

* **savanna**   tropical or sub-tropical grassland with scattered trees and drought-resistant undergrowth

The Sahel is a narrow semi-desert region of western Africa. Its name comes from the Arabic word for "shore" or "border," and it is the southern border of the SAHARA DESERT. The Sahel forms a zone of transition between the desert, which extends across the northern part of the continent, and the forests and grasslands of sub-Saharan* Africa. Its dry, desert-like landscape is broken up by thorny trees, bushes, and plants, and during the rainy season grass covers much of the region.

The Sahel is defined by rainfall. It receives an average of 6 to 24 inches of rain a year, more than the desert but less than the savanna* and forest regions farther south. The Sahel usually has a three- to five-month dry season, although in some years this season lasts much longer. From time to time droughts occur, leading to crop shortages and famine in Sahelian nations such as NIGER and Mali.

The boundaries of the Sahel are not fixed. In wet periods, Sahel vegetation moves northward into the Sahara. In dry periods, the Sahel reaches southward and consumes grassland through a process called desertification, in which land loses its fertility and becomes desert-like. Human activities, such as cutting trees for firewood and grazing livestock, are thought to be hastening desertification in parts of the Sahel. (*See also* **Deserts and Drought**.)

Sa'id ibn Sultan

1791–1856
Sultan of Zanzibar

* **coup** sudden, often violent, overthrow of a ruler or government

S a'id ibn Sultan reigned as sultan of Oman and Muscat in the Middle East for some 50 years. During this time he extended his sultanate from Arabia to the east coast of Africa, establishing one of the great trading empires in the region.

Sa'id was the son of the lord of Muscat, who was killed by pirates when Sa'id was 13. One of his cousins seized the throne, but in 1806 Sa'id staged a coup*, killing his cousin and becoming sultan. He then formed an alliance with the British to defeat his rivals in Arabia, including the pirates who had killed his father.

In the early 1820s Sa'id turned his attention to the coast of East Africa. Responding to an invitation from the people of the region, he helped overthrow the Portuguese who dominated the area. By 1837 he controlled the coast from the Persian Gulf to MOZAMBIQUE. Three years later Sa'id moved his capital to the island of ZANZIBAR. He established trade routes into the interior, dealing mostly in ivory and slaves. He exported slaves to plantations in Asia until the British, who had abolished the SLAVE TRADE, prohibited the sale of Omani slaves in Asia.

Sa'id then took up other activities, including sugar refining and growing indigo for dye. However, his greatest success was the introduction of cloves to Zanzibar. He also opened Zanzibar to Western nations that helped modernize its economy. By the time of his death, exports from Zanzibar had doubled and the island had become the world's leading producer of cloves. (*See also* **Arabs in Africa, Ivory Trade**.)

Saint Helena

T he British colonial territory of Saint Helena consists of three small volcanic islands in the southern Atlantic Ocean—Saint Helena, Tristan da Cunha, and Ascension. Saint Helena, the largest of the three, lies 1,150 miles west of ANGOLA. Tristan da Cunha is about 2,500 miles to the southwest, and Ascension is 700 miles northwest of Saint Helena. Jamestown, a small port town on Saint Helena, is the colony's capital.

Rocky cliffs dominate the coast of Saint Helena. The fertile volcanic crater in the island's center is dotted with small farms growing mostly potatoes and vegetables. The islanders also fish and raise LIVESTOCK. Until the mid-1800s the economy was based on hemp, wool, flax, and crafts sold to passing ships. But after the SUEZ CANAL opened in 1869, shipping routes changed and the island has grown steadily poorer. Aid from Britain and money from relatives overseas now supply most of Saint Helena's income.

The two smaller islands have few inhabitants. Tristan da Cunha contains one settlement, and a colonial official and the crews of American and British weather and satellite stations are the only residents of Ascension. Like Saint Helena, Tristan da Cunha relies on money from abroad to supplement its farming income.

All three islands were uninhabited before their discovery by Portuguese navigators between 1501 and 1506. The Portuguese controlled the islands for about 150 years until the Dutch took over briefly. In 1659 the British East India Company gained possession of Saint Helena, using the island as a place to restock ships sailing to and from the Far East.

Saint Helena is most famous as the island to which Napoleon Bonaparte was exiled after his defeat at the Battle of Waterloo in 1815. Since that time the British Crown has assumed responsibility for the island and a British governor has ruled the colony. Over the years attempts to grant the territory independence have met with resistance. The people prefer the islands to remain a colonial possession, and the economy is too weak to support an independent nation. (*See also* **Colonialism in Africa**.)

Samba, Chéri

1956–
Congolese painter

* **apprentice** person being trained in a craft or a profession

Chéri Samba is one of the first modern African painters to receive international recognition for his work. His paintings explore how relations between Africans and Europeans have influenced the way Africans view themselves. Samba has described himself as an explorer of modern Africa and the West. According to some art critics, the main subject of his paintings is the corruption and sin in present-day African and Western society.

Originally named David Samba wa Mbimba-N'zinga-Nuni Masi, Samba was born in the Belgian Congo (present-day CONGO, KINSHASA). At age 16 he moved to KINSHASA, the capital, where he became an apprentice* to a painter. In 1975 he opened his own studio and soon gained the admiration of local art circles. His most popular early paintings were *mbanda* scenes—pictures that show rival wives of the same man quarreling—and images of MAMI WATA. Mami Wata is a mermaid-like figure who represents the temptations of modern life. Often accompanied by a snake, she usually appears holding a mirror and comb.

In 1978 Samba's work was featured at the International Congress of African Studies. The following year he took the professional name Chéri Samba. By the late 1990s his paintings had appeared in more than 30 exhibitions in Europe, North America, and Japan, earning him world reknown. (*See also* **Art**, **Popular Culture**.)

SAN

See *Khoisan.*

São Tomé and Príncipe, which consists of two islands in the Gulf of Guinea, is one of the smallest countries in Africa. However, its strategic location off the coast of West Africa has given it an importance out of proportion to its size and population.

The two islands, São Tomé and Príncipe, are part of a chain of volcanoes that stretch to CAMEROON. Because of this, their terrain is very rugged. The climate of São Tomé, the larger island, varies by altitude. The mountainous interior receives heavy rainfall almost year round, but the climate is drier below about 3,000 feet. The nation's capital, São Tomé, sits on a plain near the coast. The smaller island, Príncipe, lies northeast of São Tomé island.

History and Government. Portuguese sailors discovered the uninhabited islands of São Tomé and Príncipe around 1472. Using slaves from mainland Africa as laborers, the Portuguese established sugar plantations on the islands. These served as models for the sugar plantations in the Americas. Over time, a variety of other immigrants reached the islands. The mix of European and African influences produced a unique CREOLE culture that still exists.

In the 1600s the sugar market declined, and São Tomé and Príncipe became a supply station for slave ships sailing between Africa and the Americas. In the late 1800s the plantations made a comeback with the introduction of coffee and cocoa. The society became strictly divided into groups of free white planters, mixed-race planters known as *forros* and *filhos da terra,* and plantation workers called *serviçais* and *tongas.* Forced to work on the plantations, the laborers had no political rights.

In 1975 São Tomé and Príncipe gained its independence from Portugal. Manuel Pinto da Costa served as the nation's first president from 1975 to 1991. Under his rule the islands became a socialist* state with all businesses under state control. By 1985 the economy was in steep decline. Two years later da Costa agreed to reduce the state's role in the economy in return for aid from the World Bank and the International Monetary Fund.

* **socialist** relating to an economic or political system based on the idea that the government or groups of workers should own and run the means of production and distribution of goods

The results of the economic reforms have been disappointing. The value of the currency has plummeted and prices have shot up, causing occasional food riots. The instability of the government has made these problems worse. Political offices change hands frequently, but they are generally filled only by individuals from the *forro* class. In 1991 Miguel Trovoada, a former colleague of da Costa, was elected president. He faces strong opposition in the legislature (Assembleia Nacional), which has hindered his ability to make changes.

Economy and Peoples. Cocoa dominates the economy of São Tomé and Príncipe. About 60 percent of the arable* land is devoted to cocoa production, which accounts for nearly all of the country's export revenue. Most of the cocoa is grown on large plantations established during the colonial era. However, such heavy dependence on cocoa has caused severe economic problems in years when the price of cocoa fell. São Tomé and Príncipe has also long served as a distribution center for goods moving between Africa and the rest of the world because of its location off the coast of West Africa.

* **arable** suitable for producing crops

São Tomé and Príncipe

Democratic Republic of São Tomé and Príncipe

POPULATION:
159,883 (2000 estimated population)

AREA:
372 sq. mi. (964 sq. km)

LANGUAGES:
Portuguese (official); Fang, Kriolu

NATIONAL CURRENCY:
Dobra

PRINCIPAL RELIGIONS:
Roman Catholic (89.5%), Evangelical Protestant, Seventh-Day Adventist

CITIES:
São Tomé (capital), 43,000 (1993 est.); Trindade, Santana, Neves, Porto Alegre, Santo Antonio

ANNUAL RAINFALL:
Varies from 40 in. (1,000 mm) in northern lowlands to 150–200 in. (3,800–5,000 mm) in highlands.

ECONOMY:
GDP per capita: $1,100 (1999 est.)

PRINCIPAL PRODUCTS AND EXPORTS:
Agricultural: cacao (cocoa), coconuts, coffee, bananas, palm kernels, cinnamon, poultry, pepper, papayas, beans
Manufacturing: textiles, soap, beer, fish processing, timber

GOVERNMENT:
Independence from Portugal, 1975. Republic with president elected by universal suffrage. Governing body: Assembleia Nacional, elected by popular vote.

HEADS OF STATE SINCE INDEPENDENCE:
1975–1991 President Manuel Pinto da Costa
1991– President Miguel Trovoada

ARMED FORCES:
800 (1997 est.)

EDUCATION:
Compulsory for ages 7–14; literacy rate 73% (1991 est.)

---

* **exploit**   to take advantage of; to make productive use of

* **infrastructure**   basic framework of a society and its economy, which includes roads, bridges, port facilities, airports, and other public works

The leaders of São Tomé and Príncipe have been investigating ways to expand the economy by developing new industries. They have recently discovered promising oil reserves beneath the islands, but have not yet begun to exploit* them. Tourism is another possibility. The islands' favorable climate and natural beauty make them an ideal tourist spot. Although a luxury resort recently opened on Príncipe, development of a tourist industry has been hindered by poor infrastructure*, limited overseas transport links, and a lack of trained personnel.

The class structure established in the colonial era still exists to some extent in São Tomé and Príncipe, with the oldest *forro* families controlling the best land. These families also hold considerable power in important local associations. While the different groups no longer live in strict separation, class still plays an important role in defining social relations on the islands. (*See also* **Class Structure and Caste, Colonialism in Africa, Plantation Systems, Tourism.**)

Sarbah, John Mensah

1864–1910
Ghanaian politician

John Mensah Sarbah was the leading African politician in the Gold Coast (modern-day GHANA) in the late 1800s and early 1900s. Born into a wealthy family, Sarbah went to England to study law. At the age of 23, he returned to the Gold Coast to set up a legal practice. He became known for defending the rights of Africans against British colonial authorities. He founded two newspapers, *The Gold Coast People* and *Gold Coast Weekly*, and became an authority on the traditions of the Fante people.

In 1892 Sarbah led the fight against a bill that proposed to transfer administration of public lands from African chiefs to British officials. In

1901 he was appointed to the Legislative Council. There he fought the Native Jurisdiction Bill, which gave Fante chiefs exclusive powers to administer local laws. To Sarbah this went against the democratic traditions of the Fante. In addition to his political achievements, Sarbah wrote two books about the Fante and played an important role in establishing public schools in the colony. (*See also* **Colonialism in Africa, Laws and Legal Systems, Publishing**.)

SAVANNAS

See *Ecosystems.*

SCHNITZER, EDUARD

See *Emin Pasha.*

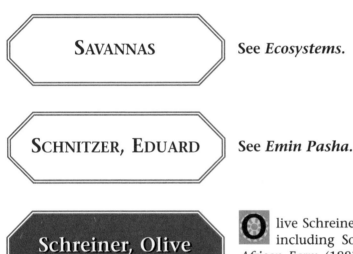

Schreiner, Olive

1855–1920
South African writer

Olive Schreiner wrote various works of social criticism and fiction, including South Africa's first important novel, *The Story of an African Farm* (1883). Her books combine vivid descriptions of life in South Africa, criticism of British colonialism, and support for women's rights and racial equality.

Schreiner was born in Wittebergen, SOUTH AFRICA, where her German father and English mother were missionaries. She spent her childhood at a Lutheran mission and then worked as a governess, caring for children, in the diamond-mining town of Kimberley. In 1881 she moved to London. Two years later she published *The Story of an African Farm,* which tells of a farm girl who seeks independence in a culture that limits opportunities for women. The book was a success and brought Schreiner considerable fame.

In 1889 Schreiner returned to South Africa and married. She and her husband published a book about the country's political and economic problems. Schreiner became increasingly involved in political causes, such as women's rights. She also supported the Afrikaners, Dutch settlers in South Africa, in their war against the British. She wrote a lengthy work of social and economic criticism called *Women and Labour,* but British soldiers burned the manuscript. She rewrote one chapter from memory, which was published in 1911. Two years later Schreiner left her homeland for the second time, returning only in the year of her death. (*See also* **Literature, Women in Africa**.)

SCULPTURE

See *Art.*

Secret Societies

Secret Societies

* **cult** group bound together by devotion to a particular person, belief, or god

* **ritual** ceremony that follows a set pattern

* **anthropologist** scientist who studies human beings, especially in relation to social and cultural characteristics

* **rite** ceremony or formal procedure

* **Islamic** relating to Islam, the religion based on the teaching of the prophet Muhammad

The English term "secret societies" refers to a wide range of traditional cults* in Africa. Members of these groups possess secret knowledge gained through participation in rituals*. Belonging to a secret society gives its members power in the community.

During the colonial era, Europeans in Africa viewed secret societies with alarm. They felt threatened by the involvement of these groups in warfare and politics among the African chiefdoms. Europeans believed that secret societies promoted anti-colonial activity, and some colonies attempted to limit their power. In 1897 British authorities in SIERRA LEONE banned the practice of marking commercial crops and palm trees with symbols—a secret society's way of controlling the size of harvests. As colonial fears grew, many Europeans came to believe that secret societies were widespread, tightly organized groups devoted to rebellion and cannibalism.

Role of Secret Societies. Today, anthropologists* recognize that secret societies are highly diverse and that many of them play a role in political and legal institutions. Among the YORUBA people of western Nigeria, members of the Ogboni society sit on a council with the king. In coastal KENYA, elders belonging to the Vaya society act as judges that determine whether a person is guilty of moral wrongdoing.

Other secret societies have religious or social purposes. Some focus on a single important rite*, such as the INITIATION RITES that mark a child's passage into adulthood. Societies may also be associated with particular skills or activities, such as hunting, blacksmithing, making war, or regulating sexual conduct. In some cases societies address a variety of political and social concerns.

The key element in all secret societies is the "secret," which usually involves the details of a group's initiation rite and other rituals. Other special knowledge may include important historical and political information not possessed by others in the community. Although people outside the society may know its secrets, they do not hold the status or power of members because their knowledge has not come through rites and personal experience.

Poro and Sande Societies. In western Africa the Poro association for men and the Sande or Bondo association for women have wide-ranging activities and interests. Traditionally, all boys in Poro areas must be initiated into the society as part of becoming adults. Elder members generally have higher rank and greater secret knowledge than younger members, whose labor and services they often control. Poro leaders make important community rulings about such matters as land disputes and political succession. The Poro society also controls the timing of certain harvests and passage along trade routes. In some urban or Muslim settings, governmental or Islamic* authorities now hold many of the powers claimed by the Poro, and fewer boys are brought into the association.

The women's Sande or Bondo society continues to flourish even in urban and Muslim locations because its power does not conflict with that of other authorities. The Sande or Bondo association gives the status of adulthood to girls. Its spirit is a river spirit whose powers involve women's secret medicines, including those used for childbirth. The leadership and organization of the women's society are closely linked to those of the Poro. This connection is especially clear in some parts of LIBERIA, where the two societies alternate their "rule" over communities in different years. In Sierra Leone, Muslim Sande has emerged, with Muslim songs replacing the traditional ones. (*See also* **Masks and Masquerades, Religion and Ritual, Witchcraft and Sorcery**.)

Sembène, Ousmane

1923–
Senegalese author and
film director

* **Islam** religion based on the teachings of the prophet Muhammad; religious faith of Muslims

Ousmane Sembène is widely regarded as the father of African CINEMA. Born in SENEGAL, Sembène served in the French army during World War II. He returned to his homeland briefly and took part in a railway strike in 1947–1948. He went back to France and, over the next several years, traveled to Denmark, Russia, China, and Vietnam.

In 1960 Sembène published his best-known novel, *God's Bits of Wood*. Then he went to Russia and studied filmmaking in Moscow for two years. While continuing to write novels and short stories, he began to direct films. He achieved a commercial success with the 1968 film *Mandabi*. This was the first of three films that examined the struggles of Senegalese citizens faced with the social problems of their country. Sembène later directed three historical films, including *Ceddo* (1976), which was banned for years in Senegal because it exposed the role of Islam* in the West African SLAVE TRADE. His most recent film, *Faat-Kine*, tells the story of a Senegalese woman and the sacrifices she makes for her family. Sembène's films and novels have challenged authority and dealt with sensitive issues. He has received many awards for his work. (*See also* **Literature, Popular Culture**.)

Senegal

The West African country of Senegal is one of the few nations in Africa that has enjoyed relatively stable and democratic government since independence. In recent years, however, the nation has faced economic difficulties and an ongoing threat of rebellion in its southern region. These problems have severely tested the strength of Senegalese democracy.

GEOGRAPHY

Located on Africa's Atlantic coast, Senegal is dominated by a series of rivers that cut through its rolling plains. The mighty Senegal River forms the country's northern border, and the Gambia River flows through the southern region. Although Senegal has no real mountains, the foothills of GUINEA's Futa Jallon mountains extend into southeastern part of the country.

The nation is bordered on the north by MAURITANIA, on the east by MALI, and on the south by Guinea and GUINEA-BISSAU. The tiny nation of

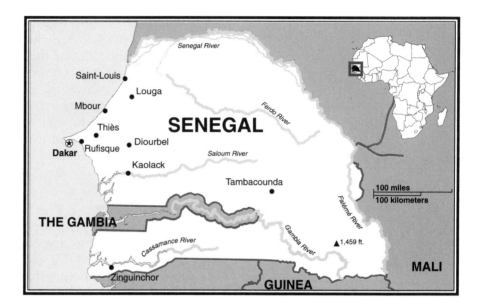

the GAMBIA juts into southern Senegal along the Gambia River, largely separating the southern province of Casamance from the rest of Senegal.

Senegal's climate is warm and dry in the north, but it grows hotter and wetter as one travels south. Vegetation is thin in the far north, where each year the SAHARA DESERT expands southward a few more miles. The barren north gives way to savanna* in the central part of the country, while the more tropical southern region contains mangrove swamps.

* **savanna** tropical or subtropical grassland with scattered trees and drought-resistant undergrowth

HISTORY AND GOVERNMENT

Before the colonial era Senegal was part of a fragmented geographical region that we know today as Senegambia. Located at the crossroads of several cultural traditions and containing diverse groups of people, Senegambia remained a backwater until the 1400s. Developments of the following centuries still have a profound effect on the political atmosphere of modern Senegal.

Precolonial Senegambia. In the 1400s Senegambia saw the rise of various kingdoms that drew their power from control of major rivers. Trade, mostly focused on the great trade routes across the Sahara, enriched the peoples of the interior. The arrival of Portuguese merchants about 1500 led to a redirection of trade to the coast. New kingdoms also arose along the coast, taking advantage of the Atlantic commerce in gold and ivory. Later slaves emerged as the most important part of trade.

The growth of the SLAVE TRADE hastened the decline of the trans-Saharan trade routes. It also increased violence within the region, as rulers raided neighboring lands—as well as one another—to acquire slaves. This led to a centralization of power and to popular uprisings led by Muslim leaders known as marabouts. Nasr al-Din, one of these lead-

* **monopoly** exclusive control or domination of a particular type of business

See color plate 7, vol. 2.

* **indigenous** native to a certain place

ers, controlled the Senegal River valley from 1673 to 1677, when an alliance of kingdoms defeated him.

By the late 1600s the remaining marabout leaders had established their own kingdoms in Senegambia. Although they protected their citizens from the slave trade, they continued to draw power from the sale of slaves and arms. The area remained divided into many small states that existed in an almost perpetual state of war against one another to capture slaves.

European Control. The Portuguese trade monopoly* in the Senegambia region was eventually broken by the arrival of other groups of Europeans, who divided the coastal region into areas of Dutch, English, and French influence. In the 1800s France and Britain emerged as the main powers in the region.

France worked to gain control over the area surrounding the Senegal River, while Britain concentrated on the Gambia River region. Along with Portugal, both nations established forts on offshore islands and seized control over trade from the coastal kingdoms. The forts also enabled Europeans to take over the areas that produced groundnuts, the crop that became the basis of the region's colonial economy after the slave trade ended in the early 1800s.

While Europeans attempted to dominate Senegambia, the region was troubled by internal tensions. African rulers in the north struggled to maintain control over their rural subjects, while militant Islamic forces overran parts of the interior. In the mid-1800s the marabouts launched a series of jihads, or holy wars, but this new movement was eventually put down by African rulers loyal to the European colonial powers. The end of these jihads eliminated one threat to local rulers, but a new danger soon appeared—growing conflict with the European colonizers.

The Colonial Conquest. In time France gained control over most of the region of present-day Senegal, while Britain held power over a narrow strip along the Gambia River. The Europeans faced a complex political and social environment in Senegambia. Most of the region was under the rule of local monarchs who dominated towns and cities but had less influence in rural areas, where the marabout movement had its greatest support. In addition, a number of societies also existed on the edges of the region.

When the French established the colony of Senegal, they divided indigenous* peoples of the region into subjects and citizens. The vast majority of Africans lived in agricultural areas where groundnuts were grown. Although classified as French subjects, these people had limited political rights and were restricted to territorial zones overseen by traditional chiefs. By contrast, the Africans of Dakar and certain other urban market areas were considered French citizens and were represented by a deputy in the parliament in Paris.

When Muslim marabout leaders emerged as Senegal's major groundnut producers, they replaced local chiefs as heads of territorial zones. The French incorporated the marabouts into colonial administration by giving them visible roles in public celebrations and having them serve as official representatives at Muslim religious ceremonies. Identified in this way with colonial power, the marabouts became the main link between the colonial government and the rural populations. Outside of the groundnut-growing areas, however, it was not easy to identify local leaders to bring into the colonial administration. This resulted in a lack of control over remote areas, which developed without a sense of allegiance to a central government.

Independent Senegal. Senegal won its independence from France in 1960, but many of the old political problems remained. Those who controlled groundnut production still exercised the most power and authority, and many rural populations continued to be outside the mainstream of political life. The political system was still based largely on patronage*, with powerful leaders exercising authority over and providing for the needs of weaker clients.

* **patronage** power to appoint people to government positions

Before independence the most powerful political parties in Senegal were the SFIO (the "Reds") and the BDS (the "Greens"). The rivalry between these two parties dominated Senegalese political life from 1948 to 1958, when the two parties merged to form the UPS. A former leader of the Reds, Léopold Sédar SENGHOR, was chosen as the nation's first president. Mamadou Dia, former Green leader, became prime minister.

In 1962 Dia tried to seize control of the country. This attempted overthrow led to the adoption of a single-party system of government headed by a strong president. During the period that followed, Senegal practiced a form of socialism* in which the state controlled the economy and was the main source of jobs and political power. Socialism played a central role in all areas of society as leaders attempted to unify the nation under a single banner. By the early 1970s, however, opposition to the so-called nationalist project was emerging, and groups that had resisted central authority in the past began to challenge the legitimacy of the government.

* **socialism** economic or political system based on the idea that the government or groups of workers should own and run the means of production and distribution of goods

The 1970s were a time of turmoil in Senegal. The economic effects of a drought that began early in the decade were increased by a sharp rise in oil prices and a dramatic decline in prices for Senegal's principal exports, including groundnuts. At the same time, President Senghor agreed to an economic reform plan proposed by international lending agencies, including the International Monetary Fund (IMF), which called for reducing Senegal's national debt and the number of government employees. The result was a steep downturn in the economy and a fiscal* crisis.

* **fiscal** relating to financial matters and revenues

In the midst of these economic difficulties, Senghor embarked on a policy of political reform aimed at liberalizing the government. He allowed the formation of opposition political parties and strengthened the role of the prime minister. In 1980 the ailing Senghor resigned as president and was succeeded by Prime Minister Abdou Diouf.

Senegal Since 1980. Economic reform and the presidency of Abdou Diouf launched what seemed to be a new chapter in Senegalese politics. As government resources declined, the old system of state patronage began to break down, and Diouf looked to a new generation of techni-

* **infrastructure**   basic framework of a society and its economy, which includes roads, bridges, port facilities, airports, and other public works

* **millet**   family of grains

* **gross domestic product (GDP)**   total value of goods and services produced and consumed within a country

cal experts to fill government posts. Diouf was easily reelected in 1983, 1988, 1993, and 1996. However, the economy continued to struggle, and a new political challenge emerged from the Senegalese Democratic Party (PDS) led by Abdoulaye Wade.

The elections of 1998 produced a close race for president, won again by Diouf. But the next election marked the end of his rule. A scandal erupted over the printing of a duplicate set of voter cards, and public outrage led to the election of Abdoulaye Wade as president in February 2000.

Trouble in Casamance. Perhaps the most serious problem facing President Wade is the situation in Senegal's southern province of Casamance. This region is a major source of groundnuts and contains rich FISHING areas off its coast. It also produces cotton for the nation's textile industry and is growing in popularity as a tourist destination for Europeans. The people of Casamance, however, have seen little benefit from these activities.

Since the mid-1980s the Movement of Democratic Forces of Casamance (MFDC) has been fighting for independence from the rest of Senegal. This separatist group is frustrated by economic problems related to the fishing industry and rice growing, and criticizes the lack of government spending on local infrastructure*.

For years Casamance's rebels have received arms from the army of Guinea-Bissau. When Guinea-Bissau's army rebelled against its president João Vieira in 1998, the Senegalese government supported Vieira. The uprising in Guinea-Bissau was put down with the help of Senegal and Guinea. But when the foreign troops left in 1999, the army rose again and overthrew Vieira. Relations between Senegal and Guinea-Bissau have deteriorated since that time.

THE ECONOMY

About 70 percent of Senegal's population works in agriculture, with groundnuts being the most important export crop. Major food crops include rice and millet*, and fishing and cattle-raising are also important economic activities. Despite the large number of people involved in farming, agricultural production is quite low. This is due partly to unreliable weather conditions, which can dramatically affect crop yields from year to year.

Over half of Senegal's gross domestic product (GDP)* comes from trade, transportation, tourism, and service industries. These activities are helped by Senegal's fairly well-developed transportation infrastructure, which includes a busy international airport and extensive road and rail connections. Many service and trade-related activities are performed on an informal basis, so their role in the economy is difficult to determine. Senegalese industry is focused on food processing, mining-based activities, textiles, and CRAFTS.

Set on an island at the mouth of the Senegal River, Saint-Louis was founded by the French as a trading post in 1638. Today this island port relies on fishing and the export of peanuts.

* **hierarchical** referring to a society or institution divided into groups with higher and lower levels

* **caste** division of people into fixed classes based on birth

* **clan** group of people descended from a common ancestor

PEOPLES AND CULTURES

The population of Senegal is very diverse, with the WOLOF being the largest ethnic and language group. About a third of Senegalese are of Wolof ancestry, and Wolof serves as the common language in both Senegal and the Gambia. However, because of Senegal's ethnic diversity, social structure is perhaps the most appropriate way to categorize its people.

Cultures in northern and eastern Senegal traditionally have been based on a hierarchical* social structure consisting of nobles, free persons, occupational castes* (such as blacksmiths), and slaves. Free persons were once mainly farmers, but in recent years many have moved to urban areas in search of other economic opportunities. Although this strict hierarchical social order has broken down in modern times, there is still little intermarriage between descendants of the different groups.

Societies in southern Senegal historically have been less hierarchical and more suspicious of centralized power. Before the colonial era, government in the region came mainly through township councils and small groups of elders associated with various spirit shrines. Different clans* controlled separate shrines, as did men and women on occasion. This type of system helped to avoid the accumulation of power into the hands of a few.

While women in southern Senegal often hold considerable general power, those in northern Senegal frequently act as local political and

Republic of Senegal

POPULATION:
9,987,494 (2000 estimated population)

AREA:
75,749 sq. mi. (196,190 sq. km)

LANGUAGES:
French (official); Wolof, Malinke, Fulani, Pulaar

NATIONAL CURRENCY:
CFA Franc

PRINCIPAL RELIGIONS:
Muslim 92%, Traditional 6%, Christian 2%

CITIES:
Dakar (capital), 2,079,000 (2001 est.); Kaolack, Thiès, Saint-Louis, Zinguinchor

ANNUAL RAINFALL:
Varies from 12–20 in. (300–500 mm) in north to 40–60 in. (1,000–1,500 mm) in south.

ECONOMY:
GDP per capita: $1,650 (1999 est.)

PRINCIPAL PRODUCTS AND EXPORTS:
Agricultural: groundnuts, millet, sorghum, manioc, rice, cotton, corn, green vegetables, poultry, cattle, pigs, fish
Manufacturing: agricultural and fish processing, fertilizer production, petroleum refining, construction materials, textiles
Mining: phosphates, petroleum

GOVERNMENT:
Independence from France, 1960. Republic with president elected by universal suffrage. Governing bodies: Assemblee Nationale (legislative body), elected by universal suffrage; Council of Ministers, appointed by prime minister.

HEADS OF STATE SINCE INDEPENDENCE:
1960–1980 President Léopold Sédar Senghor
1981–2000 Prime Minister Abdou Diouf (president after 1983)
2000– President Abdoulaye Wade

ARMED FORCES:
11,000 (2001 est.)
Education: Compulsory for ages 7–13; literacy rate 33% (2001 est.)

economic leaders. They often have influence in the north's powerful Islamic brotherhoods. This continues the precolonial tradition in which women rulers emerged among the Wolof and Serer peoples. (*See also* **Class Structure and Caste, Colonialism in Africa, Dakar, Ethnic Groups and Identity, French West Africa, Islam in Africa, Ivory Trade, West African Trading Settlements.**)

Senghor, Léopold Sédar

**1906–
President of Senegal**

L éopold Sédar Senghor was both a successful poet and a major political figure. Born in French West Africa (now SENEGAL), Senghor studied to become a Catholic priest. However, he was forced to leave the seminary because he protested against racism. In 1928 he traveled to France to study. He hoped to become recognized as a Frenchman rather than as an African, but he soon decided that this was an impossible goal.

Instead Senghor explored his African roots, writing prizewinning poetry about his identity as an African. While fighting for France in World War II, he was captured by the Nazis. He spent two years in concentration camps, where he continued to write. After the war Senghor entered politics, and in 1946 he became one of Senegal's representatives to the French National Assembly. When Senegal achieved independence in 1960, Senghor was elected its first president.

Throughout his life Senghor balanced political, intellectual, and artistic interests. He developed a theory that the world's civilizations should unite and form a single universal culture. He also helped to create and

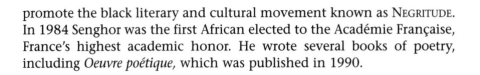

promote the black literary and cultural movement known as NEGRITUDE. In 1984 Senghor was the first African elected to the Académie Française, France's highest academic honor. He wrote several books of poetry, including *Oeuvre poétique,* which was published in 1990.

SENNAR, HISTORY

See *History of Africa.*

Seychelles

See color plate 12, vol. 2.

The Seychelles is a nation consisting of about 115 islands in the Indian Ocean off Africa's east coast. A former British colony, it has been an independent republic since 1976. The country's inhabitants, the Seychellois, are descended from Europeans, Africans, and Asians who settled on the islands.

The heart of the Seychelles is a group of about 40 mountainous, rocky islands. The largest, Mahé, is home to about 80 percent of the country's population and contains Victoria, the nation's capital. Most of the rest of the Seychellois live on the nearby islands of Praslin and La Digue. The country also includes several outlying groups of flat, coral islands.

Arab seafarers may have visited the Seychelles before the 1500s. The first Europeans to explore the islands were the Portuguese, followed by the English and French. Despite these expeditions, the Seychelles remained uninhabited until 1770, when France established a small colony there. In the years that followed, France was at war with Britain and the colony surrendered to the British seven times. Finally in 1814 France formally turned the islands over to Britain. The Seychelles remained under British control, first as a territory of the colony of MAURITIUS and then as a separate colony, until it became independent.

In addition to the original French colonists, groups of people from southern India settled in the Seychelles. The French and Indians settlers brought large numbers of slaves to the islands, mostly from MADAGASCAR and the east African coast. By the early 1800s slaves accounted for more than 85 percent of the colony's population. In the early 1900s additional immigrants from India as well as some from China settled on the islands.

For many years the economy of the Seychelles depended on agriculture. Cotton, coconuts, vanilla, and cinnamon were important export crops. Since the 1970s TOURISM has developed into the islands' major economic activity. The international airport that opened on Mahé in 1971 has made travel to the Seychelles more convenient. Commercial tuna fishing and canning have also become important in recent decades.

The Seychelles' first constitution established a multiparty democratic government. After a 1977 coup* led by France Albert René, the nation adopted a one-party socialist* system and René became president. In 1991, under pressure from Great Britain and France, the Seychelles restored the multiparty system. President René was reelected in 1993 and 1998. (*See also* **Colonialism in Africa.**)

* **coup** sudden, often violent overthrow of a ruler or government

* **socialist** relating to an economic or political system based on the idea that the government or groups of workers should own and run the means of production and distribution of goods

Republic of Seychelles

POPULATION:
79,326 (2000 estimated population)

AREA:
175 sq. mi. (454 sq. km)

LANGUAGES:
English and French (both official); creole

NATIONAL CURRENCY:
Seychelles rupee

PRINCIPAL RELIGIONS:
Roman Catholic 90%, Anglican 8%, other 2%

CAPITAL CITY:
Victoria, 25,000 (1993 est.); Main islands: Mahé, Praslin, La Digue

ANNUAL RAINFALL:
On Mahé varies from 90 in. (2,300 mm) at sea level to 140 in. (3,560 mm) on mountain slopes.

ECONOMY:
GDP per capita: $7,500 (1999 est.)

PRINCIPAL PRODUCTS AND EXPORTS:
Agricultural: vanilla, coconuts, sweet potatoes, cinnamon, cassava, bananas, poultry, fish (especially tuna)
Manufacturing: fish processing and canning, coconut and vanilla processing, boat building, printing, furniture, beverages
Services: Tourism

GOVERNMENT:
Independence from Britain, 1976. Republic with president elected by universal suffrage. Governing bodies: 35-seat Asemblee Nationale and Cabinet of Ministers.

HEADS OF STATE SINCE INDEPENDENCE:
1976–1977 President James R. Mancham
1977– President France Albert René

ARMED FORCES:
200 (2001 est.)

EDUCATION:
Compulsory for ages 6–15; literacy rate 84% (2001 est.)

1909–1962
Tanzanian poet and writer

Sheikh Shaaban Robert is regarded as one of the greatest poets and writers in the SWAHILI language. He developed a new style of Swahili writing that combined traditional storytelling with the techniques of modern poems and novels. He also introduced the essay into Swahili literature.

Born near the port city of Tanga in Tanganyika (present-day TANZANIA), Shaaban Robert was educated in DAR ES SALAAM. After completing his studies he went to work as a civil servant in Tanganyika's British colonial government, serving as a customs clerk and in the Veterinary Department, the Provincial Commissioner's Office, and the Department of Land Survey. In addition to his work as his civil servant, he was also active in a number of government and other organizations. He was a member of the East African Swahili Committee, the East African Literature Bureau, the Tanganyika Language Board, and the Tanga Township Authority, which later became the Tanga Town Council. Meanwhile, he began to write, publishing many of his poems in a newspaper run by the colonial government. He also translated great works of literature, such as the *Rubaiyat* by the Persian poet Omar Khayyam, into Swahili.

In his later years, Shaaban Robert wrote realistic novels. In works such as *The Day of Reckoning* and *Utubora the Farmer* (both published in 1968), he examined the problems of his land and its people. He belonged to various literary organizations, such as the East African Literature Bureau and the Tanganyika Languages Board, and won honors for his writing. Today Shaaban Robert's poems, novels, and essays are widely read by students of Swahili literature. (*See also* **Literature**.)

Shaka Zulu

ca. 1790–1828
Ruler of the Zulu

* **tribute** payment made by a smaller or weaker party to a more powerful one, often under the threat of force

Shaka Zulu founded the Zulu kingdom, which once controlled sections of present-day South Africa. In 1816 Shaka succeeded his father as ruler of the Zulu, a small ethnic group in southern Africa. Shaka soon expanded his chiefdom. He created a fierce army, providing his troops with long-bladed spears that were ideal for stabbing enemy soldiers in close combat. He also developed effective battle strategies that enabled him to defeat rival armies.

Several neighboring chiefdoms accepted Shaka's rule and became part of the Zulu state. His troops raided and conquered other nearby peoples. Shaka forced the surviving males of defeated groups to join the Zulu army. He also required conquered people to pay tribute*, which greatly increased his wealth and made the Zulu the most powerful group in the region. Shaka's wars and invasions were a disaster to those he conquered. His rule also brought violence and hardship to his own people, and in 1828 several Zulu leaders murdered Shaka. (*See also* **Southern Africa, History of; Zulu.**)

Shembe, Isaiah

1870–1935
South African church leader

* **indigenous** native to a certain place

Isaiah Shembe was a ZULU prophet who founded his own church in the early 1900s. As a young man Shembe experienced a dramatic conversion that led him to give up worldly things and become a wandering preacher and healer. He joined the African Baptist Church in 1906 and eventually became an ordained minister. However, he broke away in 1911 to establish the Church of the Nazaretha.

Based on Old Testament teachings, Shembe's church incorporated elements of indigenous* Zulu religion. According to his followers, Shembe performed miracles of healing and was able to foresee the future. After his death he was buried in the village near Durban, SOUTH AFRICA, where his church was based. Shembe's tomb became a place of pilgrimage for his followers and the area around the burial site became known as "paradise." Two of his sons took over leadership of the church, which still exists. (*See also* **Christianity in Africa, Prophetic Movements, Religion and Ritual.**)

SHIPS AND SHIPPING

See *Transportation.*

Shona

* **clan** group of people descended from a common ancestor

The Shona are a cluster of peoples who have lived for about 2,000 years in the Zimbabwean Plateau, a region of southern Africa that includes most of ZIMBABWE and part of MOZAMBIQUE. The Shona divide themselves into clans* that are associated with particular chiefdoms and areas. Although most Shona identify with a clan rather than with the Shona group as a whole, most Shona communities contain a mixture of clans.

Over the centuries a number of Shona states have developed. The

See
color plate 1,
vol. 3.

Shona kingdom of ancient Zimbabwe flourished in the 1300s and 1400s and was part of a gold trade network that extended as far as China. At the heart of the kingdom, the Shona built the impressive stone city of Great Zimbabwe—its ruins are now a major tourist attraction. After Zimbabwe lost power, the Shona formed smaller kingdoms, including Monomatapa and Rozvi Mambo. In the 1800s neighboring peoples weakened Shona authority in the region. By the time the British and Portuguese colonized Shona territory in the late 1800s, the Shona had divided into many small, independent chiefdoms.

In the past the Shona farmed and herded livestock. Today most of them combine farming with work in the cities, maintaining strong links between town and country. The Shona are known internationally for two art forms: stone sculpture and the music of the *mbira,* an instrument made of a hollow gourd with metal reeds that the player plucks. Although many Shona practice Christianity, they often turn to traditional religions to solve personal problems, such as illness, and to improve the fertility of the land.

Sierra Leone

Established as a haven for former slaves, Sierra Leone was for many years one of Africa's success stories. When it gained independence in 1961, this resource-rich nation had a prosperous merchant class and a long history of representative government. Its recent history, however, has been filled with political instability and violence. Since 1991 a devastating civil war has reduced the nation to a state of chaos.

GEOGRAPHY

Sierra Leone is located on the Atlantic coast of West Africa between the countries of GUINEA and LIBERIA. Its broad coastal belt, covered by dense mangrove* swamps, gives way to wooded hills and gently rolling plateaus in the interior. The mountainous southeastern portion of the country features peaks up to 6,000 feet high. The climate of Sierra Leone is extremely hot and humid, with average rainfall of about 200 inches along the coast. Dense tropical rain forest covers portions of the country's land area.

HISTORY AND GOVERNMENT

Europeans first visited Sierra Leone in 1460 when Portuguese explorer Pedro de Cintra landed on the coast. He named the area Sierra Leone, meaning "Lion Mountains," because of the beauty of its mountains. At that time the region was thinly settled by indigenous* Mende and Temne people. Contact between local peoples and coastal traders was frequent throughout the period before European rule.

Refuge for Slaves. In 1787 a British abolitionist* named Granville Sharp persuaded his government to establish a colony in Sierra Leone for people of African descent living in Britain. The first settlers to arrive

* **mangrove**   tree found in coastal areas that grows in dense clusters

* **indigenous**   native to a certain place

* **abolitionist**   person committed to ending slavery

21

angered a local Temne chief and were driven away. Four years later a private London firm called the Sierra Leone Company reestablished the settlement. The company hoped to introduce "civilization" and replace the local trade in slaves with trade in vegetables grown in the region.

The Sierra Leone Company recruited about 1,200 colonists from Canada, who founded the coastal settlement of FREETOWN in 1792. The group included American blacks, loyal to Britain, who had been freed during the American Revolutionary War. The Sierra Leone Company and its colonists disagreed about the purpose of the colony. The settlers viewed Sierra Leone as a haven of freedom in which to start a new life; the company regarded it as a moneymaking venture. These disputes led to an armed uprising of settlers in 1800 that was put down by the company.

Growing Pains. The Sierra Leone Company had problems not only with settlers but also with local Temne rulers. In the past the Temne had leased land to European slave traders but had kept control over it. However, in the treaties they signed with the Sierra Leone Company the Temne unknowingly surrendered control of the land to the company. This led to arguments that resulted in war. In 1801 and 1802 Temne forces attacked Freetown, but the British eventually drove the Temne away from the area.

The Temne were not the only threat to the colony. Britain and France went to war in 1793, and the following year French forces burned Freetown to the ground. Because of continuing losses, the Sierra Leone company could not make a profit, and in 1808 it yielded control of the colony to the British Crown. In the following years, Sierra Leone became a naval base from which the British conducted raids on ships that violated Britain's ban on the SLAVE TRADE. Enslaved Africans who were picked up on the ships were resettled in Freetown.

Sierra Leone Flourishes. During the early 1800s, some 80,000 freed slaves were settled in Sierra Leone. Under the guidance of missionaries and British officials, most converted to Christianity, learned English, and adopted Western names and lifestyles. The mixing of people from different backgrounds and races produced a Creole society that combined elements of both African and European culture. In time the members of this mixed population became known as Krio.

With little European competition, Krio traders in Sierra Leone established profitable import-export businesses dealing in timber, palm oil, and palm kernels. A Krio middle class emerged that invested in land and built large houses for themselves. Prosperous Krio business leaders contributed generously to the building of churches and schools. Christian missions provided schooling for children, and in 1827 the Church Missionary Society founded Fourah Bay College for higher education. With these educational opportunities, new generations of Krio became doctors, lawyers, and government officials.

* **Islam** religion based on the teachings of the prophet Muhammad; religious faith of Muslims

The majority of the Krio population were originally YORUBA people from NIGERIA who kept many of their cultural traditions, such as belief in Islam* and membership in SECRET SOCIETIES. Over time, many people from surrounding areas moved to Freetown. Although the Krio worked alongside these newcomers, they tended to separate themselves from non-Krio groups. Some Krio even considered them a threat.

By the 1840s lack of employment opportunities forced many Krio to leave Sierra Leone. Some returned to their Yoruba homeland, while others decided to start new businesses elsewhere. This migration took many educated Krio to neighboring colonies such as the Gold Coast (present-day GHANA), the GAMBIA, Nigeria, and Liberia, where they became missionaries, traders, businesspeople, and government workers. The stream of emigrants from Sierra Leone formed the nucleus of an African middle class in British West Africa during the late 1800s.

The Road to Independence. During the 1800s tensions arose and intensified between the Krio and local British businessmen. To protect their commercial interests against Krio competition, Britain annexed* the interior of Sierra Leone in 1896 and established a protectorate*. Two years later the British imposed a Hut Tax on Africans to help pay the cost of colonial government. This led to an armed uprising in 1898, and resistance to British rule increased over the following years.

* **annex** to take over or add a territory to an existing area

* **protectorate** weak state under the control and protection of a strong state

At about this same time, the British began expanding the political rights of Sierra Leoneans. In 1882 the colonial council appointed its first black member, and regular elections were held in Freetown beginning in 1895. Outside Freetown, however, few people had the right to vote. Furthermore, despite Sierra Leone's history as a haven for former slaves, its first antislavery law was not passed until 1926. By this time tensions existed not only between the Krio and the British but also between the Krio and the colony's growing Lebanese population. Social tensions sometimes erupted in protests, violent riots, and forms of guerrilla* warfare.

* **guerrilla** type of warfare involving sudden raids by small groups of warriors

By the 1950s events were rapidly moving toward independence for Sierra Leone. A constitution adopted in 1951 called for a black majority in the Legislative Council, and within six years all residents in Sierra

Sierra Leone

* **coup** sudden, often violent, overthrow of a ruler or government

Leone had the right to vote. By the time independence came in 1961, Sierra Leone had a long history of participatory government marked by free and fair elections.

Civilian Rule. The country's first prime minister, Sir Milton Margai, ensured that Sierra Leone enjoyed a free press, open debate in government, and effective participation in the political process by people throughout the land. When he died in 1964, his half-brother Albert was elected prime minister. However, the second Margai lost support when he tried to set up a one-party state. In the 1967 elections the ruling Sierra Leone People's Party (SLPP) was defeated by the opposition party, the All People's Congress (APC). Shortly after the APC candidate Siaka Stevens became the new prime minister, the military staged a coup*. But military rule met with considerable opposition, and Stevens was returned to power a year later.

Stevens and the APC took the coup as a warning against weakness and quickly moved to establish stronger control over the government. Political corruption and violence increased, and by 1978 Sierra Leone had become a single-party state under APC leadership. Although Stevens was popular at first, growing corruption combined with a declining economy undermined his support. Faced with political defeat, Stevens resigned in 1986 and turned the government over to a hand-picked successor, Major General Joseph Momoh.

In his first years Momoh took steps to reform politics and create a more open system of government. He set up a commission to explore a return to multiparty politics and draft a new constitution. He also addressed the nation's growing economic problems by creating a program designed to control government expenditures and increase revenue. Momoh's plans were disrupted in 1991 when Liberian rebel leader Charles Taylor invaded Sierra Leone.

Descent Into Chaos. Joining Taylor in his invasion was a Sierra Leone rebel group known as the Revolutionary United Front (RUF). Together, these forces quickly overran the countryside and captured Sierra Leone's diamond mining areas. Nigeria and Ghana sent troops to support the Sierra Leonean army, but they had little success against Taylor's guerrilla soldiers. Amid growing turmoil, a military coup led by Captain Valentine Strasser overthrew Momoh in 1992.

Despite initial victories against Taylor and the RUF, Strasser was no more effective than Momoh at ending the civil war. By 1994 rebel forces controlled the interior of Sierra Leone, and within a year they held major mining facilities, cutting off a crucial source of the nation's income. By 1995 the country was overrun by independent warlords and bandit groups in addition to the RUF. The government controlled only Freetown, and the economy was devastated. A 1996 coup toppled Strasser, and despite the continued fighting, elections were held in March of that year.

Only six months later, however, another coup ended the rule of the new civilian president, Ahmed Tejan Kabbah. The leaders of the coup freed from prison Major Johnny Paul Koroma, who was awaiting trial for an earlier coup attempt against Kabbah. Koroma ruled Sierra Leone

* **anarchy** state of lawlessness or political disorder

* **amnesty** official pardon granted to individuals for past offenses against the government

Civil war in Sierra Leone began in the early 1990s. These Kamajor hunters banded together in defense units to protect villages against attacks by rebels and groups of roving soldiers.

for a year as head of an armed forces council. During this time the country slipped into anarchy*. Freetown was engulfed in violence, including looting by soldiers and rebels.

After ten long months of fighting, troops provided by the Economic Community of West African States (ECOWAS) drove Koroma out of Freetown and restored Kabbah as president. Still, the fighting continued, and in January 1998 Freetown suffered another devastating attack that destroyed a fifth of the city's buildings. The international community finally intervened, pressuring both sides to find a solution, and peace talks were scheduled for the spring of 1999.

The Lomé Accord. In July 1999 the RUF and the government of Sierra Leone signed a peace treaty in Lomé, the capital of Togo. According to the terms of the agreement, Kabbah ruled as president but shared power with RUF leader Foday Sankoh and Johnny Paul Koroma.

The Lomé Accord also called for rebel soldiers to turn in their arms and return to civilian life. All who had taken part in the fighting were granted amnesty*. Since the signing of the agreement, United Nations forces have replaced ECOWAS troops as peacekeepers, and there have been plans for a war crimes trial to prosecute rebels for atrocities against civilians. Meanwhile, RUF forces continue to hold parts of the country,

Sierra Leone

 Republic of Sierra Leone

POPULATION:
5,232,624 (2000 estimated population)

AREA:
27,699 sq. mi. (71,740 sq. km)

LANGUAGES:
English (official); Krio, Temne, Mende, Limba

NATIONAL CURRENCY:
Leone

PRINCIPAL RELIGIONS:
Muslim 60%, Traditional 30%, Christian 10%

CITIES:
Freetown (capital), 669,000 (1990 est.); Bo, Koindu, Kenema, Makeni

ANNUAL RAINFALL:
Varies from 200 in. (5,000 mm) on the coast to 85 in. (2,160 mm) in the north.

ECONOMY:
GDP per capita: $500 (1999 est.)

PRINCIPAL PRODUCTS AND EXPORTS:
Agricultural: coffee, cocoa, palm kernels, rice, palm oil, peanuts, livestock, fish

Manufacturing: mining, beverages, textiles, cigarettes, footwear, petroleum refining
Mining: diamonds

GOVERNMENT:
Independence from Britain, 1961. Republic with president elected by universal suffrage. Governing bodies: 80-seat House of Representatives (legislative body), with 68 members elected by popular vote; Ministers of State, appointed by the president.

HEADS OF STATE SINCE INDEPENDENCE:
1961–1964 Prime Minister Sir Milton Margai
1964–1967 Prime Minister Sir Albert M. Margai
1967 Brigadier David Lansana
1967–1968 Brigadier Andrew T. Juxon-Smith
1968–1986 Prime Minister Siaka Stevens (president after 1971)
1986–1992 President Joseph Saidu Momoh
1992–1996 Captain Valentine Strasser
1996 Bridadier Julius Maada Bio
1996–1997 President Ahmed Tejan Kabbah
1997–1998 Major Johnny Paul Koroma
1998– President Ahmed Tejan Kabbah

ARMED FORCES:
5,000 (2001 est.)

EDUCATION:
no universal and compulsory education system exists; literacy rate 31% (2001 est.)

and Liberia's president Charles Taylor continues to be a destabilizing force in the region.

THE ECONOMY

See map in Minerals and Mining (vol. 3).

Before the outbreak of war in 1991, the economy of Sierra Leone was based on agriculture and mining. Agriculture employed most of the population, with coffee and cocoa being the main export crops. The bulk of the nation's export revenues came from the mining of diamonds, iron ore, and the mineral rutile, a form of titanium.

The civil war has ravaged Sierra Leone's economy. Fighting in rural areas drove many people off the land and into the cities. As a result most of the best farming land remains unplanted, leaving major agricultural areas out of production. Rebel forces control the mining industry and earn money from smuggling diamonds and mineral ores to Liberia and other neighboring countries. The prospects for economic improvement in the short term are dim.

PEOPLES AND CULTURES

* **subsistence farming** raising only enough food to live on

The majority of the people of Sierra Leone are rural dwellers who depend on subsistence farming* for a living. Some 60 percent belong to the Mende and Temne ethnic groups, and about 10 percent are Krio. The rest of the population consists mostly of other West African groups.

* **tribute**   payment made by a smaller or weaker party to a more powerful one, often under the threat of force

Political relations in Sierra Leonean society have traditionally revolved around who receives and who provides tribute*. The tribute takers have usually been those in power, who are also responsible for distributing wealth and ensuring the fertility of the land and people. This social relationship has broken down in recent years, largely as a result of widespread government corruption and the violence unleashed by the civil war. A small educated group continues to control Sierra Leone and most of the nation's wealth, while the rural population struggles just to survive. The result is a massive social and economic divide within the country. (*See also* **Colonialism in Africa, Creoles, Genocide and Violence, Lebanese Communities, Slavery, United Nations in Africa, Warfare.**)

Slave Trade

Throughout history SLAVERY has been a feature of many societies in all parts of the world, including Africa. Some Africans were enslaved within their own homelands. Far more, however, were carried off as slaves to other parts of Africa or around the world through the slave trade. The slave trade was a type of commerce in which enslaved humans were bought, sold, or traded as goods or property.

It is impossible to know for certain how many millions of Africans suffered the brutality and cruelty of the slave trade before it came to an end in the 1800s. In terms of forcible relocation, the greatest number of people were taken from western and central Africa and shipped across the Atlantic Ocean to European colonies in the Americas. However, slave traders had carried off people from other parts of Africa for centuries before the transatlantic slave trade began.

To those enslaved, the slave trade brought profound suffering. To some of the slave trade operators, it brought great wealth. The slave trade also had various long-term effects, including the establishment of African populations on other continents, the weakening of African societies that were robbed of many productive young people, and warfare among African states, some of which supplied captives to foreign slave traders.

REGIONAL FEATURES OF THE SLAVE TRADE

Slave trading occurred in most parts of Africa. However, distinctive forms of the trade developed in the northern, western, central, and eastern parts of the continent. Each of these regions was also the source of slaves for specific foreign markets.

Northern Africa. The northern branch of the African slave trade arose after Arabs invaded and conquered North Africa in the A.D. 600s. Slavery became a feature of the Islamic* civilization established by the Arabs along Africa's Mediterranean coast and in the Near East. At first, most of the enslaved people brought to Islamic areas came from central and eastern Europe. They were supplied by Italian agents, who undertook the trade despite the Catholic church's ban on the selling of Christian slaves to Muslims

* **Islamic**   relating to Islam, the religion based on the teaching of the prophet Muhammad

27

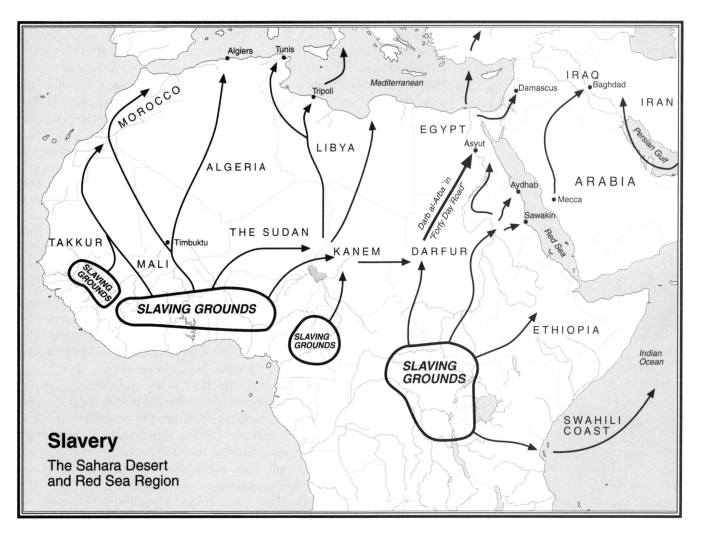

Slavery
The Sahara Desert
and Red Sea Region

After about the year 1000, the states of Europe became stronger and better able to protect their citizens from slavery. As a result the supply of European slaves to Muslim traders dwindled. To replace these slaves, North African merchants, who were already engaged in commerce across the SAHARA DESERT with western Africa, began acquiring more and more black captives from that region, along with such goods as gold, ostrich feathers, and ivory.

The largest part of the northern African slave trade involved camel caravans organized by the BERBER and Arabic-speaking peoples of North Africa and the Sahara region. Some of these caravans crossed the western Sahara, carrying enslaved black Africans from what is now MALI, NIGER, NIGERIA, GHANA, and other parts of western Africa to settlements in Arab North Africa.

Other caravans began farther east in Darfur in what is now SUDAN. They carried captives from the southern NILE RIVER valley, ETHIOPIA, and southern Sudan north to EGYPT along a route called the Forty Day Road. Most of the slaves who traveled these desert routes had to walk, and many died along the way. Another branch of the northern African slave trade took captives on foot eastward through Ethiopia to ports on the

Red Sea. From there they were shipped to the Arabian peninsula and places farther east.

Historians estimate that 3.5 to 4 million captives crossed the Sahara and another 2 million crossed the Red Sea between the 700s and the 1900s. Most of these victims of the Saharan and Red Sea slave trades were settled in North Africa, Arabia, the lands around the Persian Gulf, or southern Asia. Others, however, remained within the Sahara region, northern Sudan, or Ethiopia. Among the slaves were many women, destined to become domestic laborers or concubines*. Enslaved men were acquired to work in agriculture, mining, shipping, fishing, and for other manual labor. In addition, some rulers in Egypt and elsewhere in North Africa used black male slaves as soldiers.

Western Africa. Beginning in the 1400s European powers established colonies in a number of areas, first on islands in the Atlantic Ocean, later in the Americas, and finally in Africa. In order to exploit* the vast resources of these new colonies, especially those in the Americas, Europeans needed many workers. They turned to slave labor to meet this need.

Colonizers in the Americas first tried to enslave the native peoples, but their attempts ended in failure. Overworked and infected with European diseases, the Native Americans were nearly wiped out in many places. As a result, the colonizers had to bring in labor from other regions. European traders were already familiar with western Africa as a source of goods such as gold, pepper, and copper and had even acquired some black slaves there. With the colonization of the Americas, the trickle of black slaves grew into a flood, and a slave trade developed that involved both Africans and Europeans.

Europeans rarely ventured inland on slave raids, leaving that part of the business to Africans based on the coast of western Africa. Many of the captives came from interior regions, and nearly all were acquired by violence—through war, raids by organized groups of slave-takers, and kidnappings by individuals or small groups. Those taken were marched to the coast and held in captivity until a European slave ship arrived.

African slaves became part of a highly profitable commercial network that is often called the triangle trade. On the first leg of the triangle, ships carried European manufactured goods such as cloth and cheap guns to Africa to be exchanged for slaves. The second leg of the triangle, known as the Middle Passage, took the enslaved Africans to the Americas. The majority of them ended up on sugar plantations on the island colonies of the Caribbean. Others went to sugar and coffee plantations in Brazil and to tobacco and cotton plantations in Britain's southern American colonies. The third leg of the trade carried sugar, rum, tobacco, and other plantation crops to Europe.

The Middle Passage was a fearful ordeal for captive Africans. Chained slaves were jammed into crowded, poorly ventilated cargo holds for the voyage, which lasted from three to six weeks. On average, 15 to 30 percent of the human cargo died of disease, abuse, or exhaustion during the trip. Of the enslaved people who survived the journey, many died of overwork or malnutrition within a few years of their arrival in the Americas.

* **concubine** woman maintained by a man in a sexual relationship other than marriage

* **exploit** take advantage of; to make productive use of

See color plate 7, vol. 2.

Slave Trade

The transatlantic slave trade lasted from the 1440s to the 1860s and was at its peak from 1700 to 1850. Historians estimate that at least 13 million people were shipped from Africa to the Americas as slaves. Most of them were between 15 and 30 years old. About two thirds of the captives were male—slaveholders in the Americas preferred men for field labor.

Of the 13 million Africans forced to make the overseas journey to the Americas, the great majority came from the coastal region of western Africa, between Senegal and Cameroon. So many captives were taken from the lands between the Volta River in Ghana and the Niger River in Nigeria that Europeans called that region the Slave Coast.

Central Africa. Central Africa also contributed a steadily increasing share of the captives sent to European colonies in the Americas. In the 1500s about one out of five slaves in the transatlantic trade came from the west-central African coast between Congo and Angola. After 1800 nearly half of the slaves shipped from Africa originated in that region.

The Portuguese began exporting slaves from central Africa in the 1500s, when they established sugar plantations on the island of São Tomé off the western coast of Africa. By the 1560s the Portuguese had brought 30,000 slaves to the island, mostly from Angola. In the century that followed, they developed a large-scale slave trade south of the Congo River, aided by bands of young African warriors who conducted raids to gather slaves.

By the 1600s Brazil had replaced São Tomé as the principal market for Portuguese slave traders. The vast sugar plantations of Brazil required ever larger numbers of African slaves, and the discovery of gold and diamonds in Brazil in the 1700s increased the demand for labor even more. In the late 1600s English, French, and Dutch slavers also began operating along the Atlantic coast of central Africa, shipping enslaved people primarily to sugar plantations in the West Indies.

As the demand for slaves grew, some groups of central Africans became more deeply involved in the trade, opening new territories in the interior as sources of slaves. Warlords led raids into the population centers of these territories and sent caravans of captives back to the coast. The slave trade eventually included enslaved Africans from regions as distant as the center of the continent, 900 miles from the coast.

By the 1700s nearly all societies in central Africa owed their power either to their control of slaving routes or to the defensive strengths they had developed to protect themselves from slave raids. African kingdoms near the coast gave up raiding and became go-betweens, buying slaves from the zones of violence in the interior and selling them to buyers on the coast. To profit from the commerce in slaves, some local rulers in central Africa forced their subjects into debt and then condemned them to slavery when they could not repay what they owed.

Eastern Africa. Enslaved people from eastern Africa were shipped out of ports on the Indian Ocean coast for centuries. The first evidence of a significant slave trade in the region dates from after the rise of Islam

* **caliphate** state in the Muslim empire

in the A.D. 600s. The Abbasid Caliphate* that formed in what is now Iraq and Iran imported African slaves for use as soldiers, farm laborers, and domestic workers. Muslim traders also sent Africans farther east, to Indonesia and China.

In the centuries that followed, slaves may have been exported from eastern Africa, but the Arabs who established trading communities along the coast were mainly interested in gold and ivory. After the Portuguese arrived in the area and gained control of the coast in the 1500s, they carried some enslaved Africans to Portuguese colonies in Asia. However, slave raiding and slave trading did not become major economic activities in eastern Africa until the mid-1700s, when new demands for labor appeared.

Beginning in the late 1600s, the state of Oman on the Arabian coast expanded its cultivation of date palms and also started plantations along the coast of KENYA. In the early 1700s the French established Caribbean-style sugar plantations on the Indian Ocean islands of MAURITIUS and RÉUNION. These developments created a growing demand for slave labor. To meet the demand, new slave markets arose in eastern Africa. The largest were in the southern part of the coast, but by the 1800s virtually every port on the eastern coast was involved in the slave trade to some degree. From these bases, Arab, SWAHILI, and African slave traders conducted raids and buying expeditions into the interior.

From the 1500s to the mid-1800s, Europeans brought millions of enslaved Africans to the Americas to work in agriculture and mining. This print shows the "passengers" of the slave ship *Gloria* in 1850.

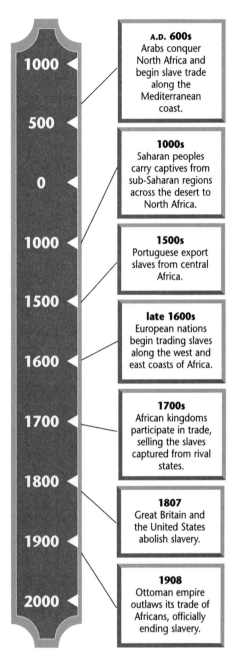

A.D. 600s
Arabs conquer North Africa and begin slave trade along the Mediterranean coast.

1000s
Saharan peoples carry captives from sub-Saharan regions across the desert to North Africa.

1500s
Portuguese export slaves from central Africa.

late 1600s
European nations begin trading slaves along the west and east coasts of Africa.

1700s
African kingdoms participate in trade, selling the slaves captured from rival states.

1807
Great Britain and the United States abolish slavery.

1908
Ottoman empire outlaws its trade of Africans, officially ending slavery.

Most victims of the eastern African slave trade came from MOZAMBIQUE, TANZANIA, the region around Lake Malawi, eastern Congo, and MADAGASCAR. Some of those who passed through the coastal slave markets were sent overseas or to the offshore islands; others went to Arab-operated plantations in ZANZIBAR, Kenya, and southern SOMALIA. During the first half of the 1800s, slave traders from Brazil also appeared in the slave markets of eastern Africa, seeking labor for Brazil's booming plantation economy. The African rulers of Madagascar and Dutch settlers in SOUTH AFRICA also imported slaves from eastern Africa. This slave trade in this region reached its height between 1770 and 1870, with exports perhaps reaching 30,000 people a year.

THE END OF THE SLAVE TRADE

Although every age had some compassionate or just-minded individuals who opposed the traffic in human beings, putting an end to this ancient and widespread evil required broad public support. Abolition—the movement to end slavery—began to attract support among Europeans in the late 1700s, largely because of moral outrage against slavery. In the late 1800s the Ottoman Empire, which controlled Islamic North Africa and the Near East, also moved toward abolishing the slave trade as a result of internal reform movements and pressure from European powers. In the end the slave trade was eventually stamped out partly for religious or moral reasons and partly for economic ones. Four hundred years of violent slave trading, however, had left deep marks on the African population.

Abolition. The late 1700s saw the growth of European political philosophies that stressed the rights of all people to freedom and equality. At the same time Africans themselves fought against slavery and the slave trade, both through resistance in Africa and efforts to sway public opinion in Europe. Africans such as Olaudah EQUIANO and Ottobah Cugoano, former slaves from western Africa who lived in England, spoke and wrote about the cruelties of the slave trade and urged that it be outlawed. Other Africans performed the same role in France and the Americas. The personal stories of such individuals, told with eloquence and conviction, helped swell the ranks of the growing abolition movement.

While the abolition movement was gaining strength, far-reaching changes in industry and trade were reducing the economic rewards of slavery. The prices of raw materials such as sugar began to fall on world markets, but African traders and rulers were raising the price of slaves. These factors meant that slaveholders had to pay more for slaves whose output in labor was worth less in the marketplace. At the same time the rise of the Industrial Revolution encouraged bankers and other investors to put their money into factories, not plantations. British and European business leaders began to believe that the economic value of Africa in the future would be as a source of raw material for industry and a market for mass-produced factory goods rather than as a source of labor. From an economic point of view, abolition involved transforming Africans from slaves into customers for European goods.

In 1805 Denmark became the first country to make it illegal for its citizens to participate in the slave trade. Great Britain did the same two years later. The United States banned the slave trade in 1808, followed by the Netherlands in 1814 and France in 1817. In addition to abolishing the slave trade, Britain took on a policing role, sending naval vessels to the Atlantic coast of western Africa to seize slave ships. Britain did not succeed in stopping the trade immediately—in fact, the number of slaves shipped from western Africa rose during the 1820s and 1830s. In time, however, the combination of enforcement and reduced demand caused the slave trade to decrease significantly.

Outlawing the slave trade was only the first step in ending slavery. Great Britain abolished the institution of slavery and freed all slaves in 1834. By the time Brazil ended slavery in 1888, the institution had been outlawed throughout the Western world. Meanwhile, within the Ottoman Empire the period from the 1830s to the 1880s was a time of reform when upper-class, educated people began questioning slavery on moral grounds. During that time Ottoman rulers also came under increasing pressure from Great Britain and other European nations to abolish slavery. Britain took steps to choke off the trade routes that supplied the Ottoman empire with slaves. As a result, the Ottomans passed a series of laws between 1847 and 1908 ending the trade in both African and white slaves and officially abolishing slavery.

Even after the slave trade was outlawed, the traffic in slaves continued in some places, though on a greatly reduced scale. In addition, people remained in various forms of bondage in Africa and elsewhere. Such practices, however, had not only become illegal—they were internationally recognized as profoundly wrong and violations of HUMAN RIGHTS.

Long-Term Effects. The trade in African slaves brought about the largest forced movement of people in history. It established the basis for black populations in the Caribbean and in North and South America. At the same time, it disrupted social and political life in Africa and opened the door for European colonization of the continent.

The effects of the slave trade are well illustrated in western Africa, the source of most enslaved people in the transatlantic trade. When Europeans first began exchanging goods for gold, pepper, and other items along the western African coast, such commerce encouraged peaceful relations and trade among indigenous* societies. Everyone benefited as these trade goods flowed smoothly among African groups and between Africans and Europeans.

* **indigenous**   native to a certain place

The shift in European demand from gold, foodstuffs, and such products to slaves changed the relations among African groups and states. The prices Africans received for slaves made it more profitable for them to take captives from their neighbors than to establish networks for producing and selling other goods. In this way the slave trade encouraged strong states to raid weaker states for slaves. As a result, many African societies were torn by organized slave wars and general banditry. Successful slave-raiding and trading societies formed new states that were dominated by military groups and constantly at war with their neighbors.

Slave Trade

While the abolition movement achieved tremendous victories and did much good, in one way it had a negative effect on Africa. Abolition and the Christian reform movement with which it was closely linked gave Europeans a strong interest in the internal affairs of African states and an excuse to become involved in those affairs. Eventually the mission to stamp out slavery became, in the eyes of many Europeans, a justification for bringing African territory under their control. During the late 1800s they divided the continent into colonies.

Another legacy of the slave trade was the loss, in generation after generation, of young Africans who would play a productive role in the economic or political development of their homelands. Some parts of Africa were severely depopulated* by the taking of captives and the flight of people trying to avoid capture. It is impossible to say what Africa could be like today had it escaped the widespread and long-lasting ravages of the slave trade. (*See also* **Colonialism in Africa; Diaspora, African; Economic History; History of Africa.**)

* **depopulated** referring to a greatly reduced number of inhabitants

Slave Exports from Central Africa

Years	Total Exports	Central Africa	Percentage from Central Africa
1450–1600	367,000	50,000	13.6%
1601–1700	1,868,000	500,000	26.8%
1701–1800	6,133,000	2,058,000	33.6%
1801–1870	3,274,000	1,517,300	46.3%
Total	11,642,000	4,125,300	35.4%

Source: Lovejoy, Paul E. "The Volume of the Atlantic Slave Trade: A Synthesis," *Journal of African History*, 23, no. 4 (1982). All figures are estimates.

Slavery

Slavery involves treating human beings as property that people can own. In the past, when slavery was legal or customary in many places, some slaves were granted certain rights and privileges. However, no slave ever had true liberty or freedom, and the institution of slavery rested on force or the threat of force that could be used against the enslaved.

In Africa, as in other parts of the world, forms of slavery have existed since the beginning of recorded history. The SLAVE TRADE forcibly removed millions of Africans from the continent, and many other individuals remained enslaved within Africa. In numerous African societies, slavery and the institutions and conditions related to it had economic, political, and cultural significance. Although slavery was abolished during the 1800s, variations of it have continued to exist in some groups in Africa into modern times.

FORMS OF SLAVERY

* **servile** relating to a slave or a person in lowly position

* **Islam** religion based on the teachings of the prophet Muhammad; religious faith of Muslims

* **medieval** referring to the Middle Ages in western Europe, generally considered to be from the A.D. 500s to the 1500s

* **cult** group bound together by devotion to a particular person, belief, or god

* **creditor** one to whom money is owed; lender

Various type of servile* institutions developed in Africa. Under systems of formal slavery, enslaved persons were considered property. Ownership gave masters the right to sell slaves and use them and their labor without regard for the slaves' wishes. Such slavery existed in some traditional African societies as well as in the Muslim societies that developed in North Africa after Islam* entered the continent in the A.D. 600s. Islamic law permitted slavery but included rules governing the relationship to prevent extreme cruelty and abuse. The law also defined categories of people who could or could not be enslaved. The categories varied. Muslims did not always agree, for example, on whether or not other Muslims could be enslaved.

Concubinage was a special category of slavery in which masters maintained female slaves called concubines as sexual partners. Concubines and their children sometimes had certain rights, especially under Islamic law. If a concubine bore a child fathered by her master, he could not sell her or the child. In non-Muslim areas, children born to concubines were usually treated as equal to the children of free women.

In some African societies, certain slaves belonged not to individuals but to a particular political position. They lived on land that was controlled by the individual who held that position at a given time. This form of slavery, in which people were bound to the land rather than to a particular master, has been compared to the condition of peasant workers called serfs in medieval* Europe. Sometimes the bondage was religious rather than political. Along the coast of western Africa, for example, cult* slavery was common. Slaves were presented to a shrine, and the priests of the shrine had access to their labor and their bodies. These slaves could not be sold because they belonged to the shrine, but they and their children were outcasts.

Debt peonage, also called pawnship, was a servile condition based on a relationship between a debtor and a creditor*. Under this system a creditor held an individual—a "pawn"—as a guarantee that a debt would be repaid. Often the pawn was not the actual debtor but one of the debtor's relatives. The pawn had to work for the creditor until the debtor paid off the debt, ending the pawn's period of servitude. If the debt was not repaid, or if the creditor himself fell into debt before the pawn was released, the creditor could sell the pawn into slavery. In business arrangements, one side sometimes held individuals as commercial hostages. If the other side failed to complete the transaction, the hostages became slaves. In certain societies pawnship sometimes served as a way for men to acquire additional wives. Slave wives or concubines were captured or purchased, but pawn wives were gained in return for canceling debts.

Practices associated with pawnship and other forms of enslavement suggest that there were various stages between freedom and slavery in Africa. For example, not all war captives, political prisoners, and kidnapping victims became slaves immediately. Often they entered a form of servitude from which they could be released by payment of a ransom. If the ransom was not paid, they became slaves. Although in some cases

35

Slavery

individuals succeeded in moving out of slavery, countless other people were enslaved through kidnappings, raids, wars, or violations of safeguards that were supposed to protect pawns and servants.

FACTORS INFLUENCING SLAVERY

Slavery occurred in both large and small societies in Africa and in various political settings. Economic conditions played a major role in the kinds of servile arrangements that developed and the number of people who were enslaved.

Economic Factors. Slavery became especially important in areas where large-scale agriculture, with its high demand for labor, developed into a major economic activity. Many slaves, for example, worked as agricultural laborers in the SAHEL, the region south of the SAHARA DESERT. One ruler of the Songhai Empire in Nigeria in the 1500s is said to have owned about 20 plantations along the NIGER RIVER, most of them producing rice and all of them worked by slaves. The importing of slaves into the Sahel continued into the late 1800s.

Along the Atlantic coast, slaves played a large role in the economy, working in agriculture and carrying goods to market. During the 1800s, thousands of slaves worked on plantations along the coasts of SENEGAL and the GAMBIA, producing groundnuts for export. Although the Jola people of the southern Senegal coast had resisted the slave trade for years, as the trade in groundnuts increased they began selling each other into slavery. The Jola slaves cultivated rice plantations that fed the groundnut producers.

During the 1800s European and Arab colonies in southern and eastern Africa made extensive use of slaves, especially in producing goods for export. On the island of ZANZIBAR and along the coast of eastern Africa, Arabs and SWAHILI established plantations where slaves cultivated cloves. The Portuguese used slave labor to grow sesame in MOZAMBIQUE, and cotton, coffee, and other crops in ANGOLA. These developments were part of a trend also seen in tropical areas of the Americas and Asia—the effort to capture export markets through the use of slave labor on plantations and in mines.

Enslaved persons from Africa had another economic role as well—as exports in the international slave trade. States of western Africa that supplied captives to the trade, such as ASANTE in present-day GHANA and Dahomey in BÉNIN, became the dominant powers in that region during the 1700s and early 1800s, when slave exports from Africa were at their peak.

Political Factors. Slavery and servile conditions existed in a variety of cultures in Africa. Slavery was present in some small communities in which the difference between groups or social classes was not great. In larger, more complex societies, it occurred on a larger scale. Such societies had many roles that slaves could fill. Some served as bureaucrats*, soldiers, commercial agents, or wives and mothers of rulers; others labored in mines, plantations, or agricultural slave villages.

* **bureaucrat** one who works in a bureaucracy, a large departmental organization within a government

By the 1700s slaves and servile pawns were concentrated in Africa's most centrally organized states and most economically developed areas. Political and commercial groups—rulers, nobles, and merchants—had acquired the majority of slaves. In many places rulers maintained their hold on political power by collecting a large personal following, which often included slaves and people in other servile conditions as well as relatives. Many male slaves were placed in their masters' armies as soldiers, while female slaves generally lived and worked in the households of their masters.

In a number of African states, including Ghana, ancient EGYPT, and some Nigerian societies, slaves were killed when royal or noble masters died so that they could accompany the masters into the afterlife. Some groups sacrificed slaves into the 1800s. A funeral for a wealthy master was not the only occasion for such sacrifices—slaves might also be killed in religious ceremonies. Such events took place most often in societies where slaves had become very numerous. They had various purposes—to decrease slave populations, to terrorize slaves and make them easier to control, to punish criminals, and to frighten rival societies by killing captives.

Abolition—the movement to end the slave trade and slavery itself—became a powerful political force in Europe during the 1800s. Although the abolition movement grew out of the sincere belief that slavery was wrong, it also provided Europeans with a reason to invade and conquer the African continent. In the late 1800s and early 1900s, the European powers established firm control over most of Africa. Together with the spread of Christianity, their rule undermined slavery and other servile institutions.

These institutions did not disappear overnight. In some regions reform was gradual, and slavery and pawnship died out slowly. Colonial administrations themselves established new servile institutions, such as forced labor for road-building projects or plantations. They also introduced taxation, which often required Africans to take whatever wage labor they could find in order to pay their taxes. As a result, many Africans labored in conditions not very different from servitude. In addition, local African rulers who cooperated with the new colonial administrations usually were allowed to keep some degree of power over those who had been slaves or pawns. Finally, although Europeans made the buying and selling of slaves illegal, the laws were not always easy to enforce. Traffic in slaves continued for years in parts of Africa. In some areas it survived even after the colonies gained independence in the mid-1900s.

CHARACTERISTICS OF AFRICAN SLAVERY

* **anthropologist** scientist who studies human beings, especially in relation to social and cultural characteristics

Some anthropologists* believe that African slavery is best understood in relation to African culture. African slavery, they argue, differed in key ways from the slavery practiced by Europeans and Americans who obtained slaves as laborers through the international slave trade.

Western slavery was an economic institution—slaves were property whose value lay in the work they could perform. In Africa, on the other

Slavery

Slave traders lead a group of African captives to the coast, where the captives will be sold as slaves and loaded onto ships.

hand, slavery involved not only economic but also social and political factors. People acquired slaves for reasons other than economic usefulness. Ownership of a large number of slaves, for example, was a sign of power and importance.

African slavery was also closely related to issues of KINSHIP, the network of extended family relationships that form the primary social unit in most African cultures. Forcibly torn from their kinship groups or their lines of ancestry, slaves and pawns were stripped of their social identities. They became nonpersons in cultures that traditionally defined existence as membership in a social group rather than in terms of individuality.

Slaves who were intended for sale or sacrifice remained nonpersons. Once acquired by a master, however, slaves and pawns became part of the master's social network, which could include immediate family members, more distant relatives, persons in various types of servile relationships, and other slaves. Although slaves occupied the outer rim of this network, they were still recognized as part of it. Generally they were given new names to mark the fact that their old identities had ceased to exist.

The main characteristics of Western slavery were the loss of freedom and the possibility of regaining it. In African societies, however, people placed a very high value on belonging to a kinship group. For them slavery also involved the loss of kinfolk. Newly acquired slaves in Africa possessed none of the rights or benefits of kinship, but in time they or their descendants could receive some of those rights and benefits as they gradually became part of the master's kinship group.

Sometimes slaves were adopted outright and transformed into family members rather quickly. In other cases, the process occurred slowly, as succeeding generations came to be regarded more and more as part of the group, until eventually the boundaries between those of free descent and those descended from slaves became blurred. In this sense, the Western notion of slavery—the ownership of people as property—was very different from the realities of the institution of slavery in Africa. (*See also* **Class Structure and Caste; Diaspora, African; Economic History; Ethnic Groups and Identity; Plantation Systems.**)

Smuts, Jan Christiaan

1870–1950
Prime Minister of South Africa

* **League of Nations** organization founded to promote international peace and security; it functioned from 1920 to 1946

Jan Christiaan Smuts spent most of his life trying to unify SOUTH AFRICA, first as a soldier and later as a politician. The son of Afrikaners, South Africans of Dutch ancestry, Smuts lived in Cape Colony before studying law at Cambridge University. After returning to South Africa, he fought on the side of the AFRIKANER REPUBLICS during the South African (Boer) War (1899–1902) against Britain. Following peace negotiations, Smuts helped to unite South Africa—then a self-governing British territory—under largely Afrikaner leadership.

During World War I Smuts fought with British forces that conquered German Southwest Africa (now NAMIBIA). In 1916 he went to England where he held a cabinet post in the government of Prime Minister Balfour. During that time he helped to draft the declaration that proposed founding a Jewish state in Palestine. At the end of the war, he attended the peace conference, where he supported the decision to create a League of Nations*.

In 1919 Smuts was elected prime minister of South Africa. He tried to strengthen the country's ties to Britain—a move that many Afrikaners opposed. Smuts was defeated in the elections five years later. He won office again in 1939 and brought South Africa into World War II against the wishes of his political opponents.

Smuts dedicated his career to achieving a peaceful union of British and Afrikaner settlers in a South Africa governed by European principles. Although he did not believe in sharing power with Africans, he opposed the racist APARTHEID policies introduced by the National Party in 1948. (*See also* **World Wars I and II.**)

Sobhuza I and II

Kings of Swaziland

* **clan** group of people descended from a common ancestor

Sobhuza I (ca. 1780–1839) founded the Swazi kingdom of southwest Africa by uniting various Nguni-speaking clans* in southern SWAZILAND. To accomplish this, he used techniques of persuasion that included arranging alliances through marriage and granting titles and choice lands to neighboring chiefs. Sobhuza then moved his people into central Swaziland, defeating rival clans and expanding his holdings as far north as the Transvaal. He defended his territory against attacks by ZULU and Ndwandwe forces and was negotiating with missionaries to consolidate the kingdom at the time of his death.

Sobhuza II (1899–1982), a descendant of Sobhuza I, was named heir to the throne as an infant. By the time he was crowned in 1921, the Swazi kingdom had grown considerably weaker. However, Sobhuza II was skilled in diplomacy* and managed to restore the kingdom's power by playing off settlers, colonial officials, and local rivals against one another. When Swaziland achieved independence in 1968, he became its first ruler. Five years later he canceled the nation's constitution. Extremely popular, Sobhuza II continued as king without opposition until his death. (*See also* **Kings and Kingship; Southern Africa, History.**)

* **diplomacy** practice of managing relations between nations without warfare

SOCIAL STRUCTURE

See *Class Structure and Caste.*

Somalia

* **clan** group of people descended from a common ancestor

Since the beginning of its civil war in 1991, Somalia has served as a grisly example of what can happen when an African state collapses. Once a relatively prosperous nation, Somalia turned to ruins when independent warlords—representing various Somali clans*—battled viciously for turf and power. The fighting disrupted all services, and famine took thousands of lives. In the year 2000, a peace conference selected a president to head a new central government. But many people still live in areas outside the government's control.

GEOGRAPHY

Somalia occupies a strategic position on the Horn of Africa, the region of eastern Africa where the Red Sea and the Indian Ocean meet. The country consists mostly of a large plateau broken by a chain of mountains in the far north. Its extremely hot and dry climate includes two rainy seasons alternating with two dry seasons. During the hottest part of the year, temperatures can climb to over 120°F. Rainfall in the north averages only about 3 inches per year, but the far south of the country can receive up to 20 inches.

Somalia has two rivers that carry water all year round, the Juba and Shabeelle, both in the far south. The area between the rivers is virtually the only place in the country that can support commercial agriculture. Banana and sugar plantations are located here, along with acacia and aloe trees (also grown in the north). Most of the remaining plant life consists of scrub brush and grasses. In the north, such vegetation and the area where it grows are called the *guban,* meaning "burned." Mangrove* swamps line the coast, which has a cooler and more humid climate than the interior.

* **mangrove** tree found in coastal areas that grows in dense clusters

The Haud Plateau and the Ogaden Plains, important features of Somalia's geography, stretch out across the nation's northwestern border with ETHIOPIA. Both the Haud and the Ogaden have served as grazing lands for pastoralists* for hundreds of years. Until recently, Somalis

* **pastoralist** someone who herds livestock

40

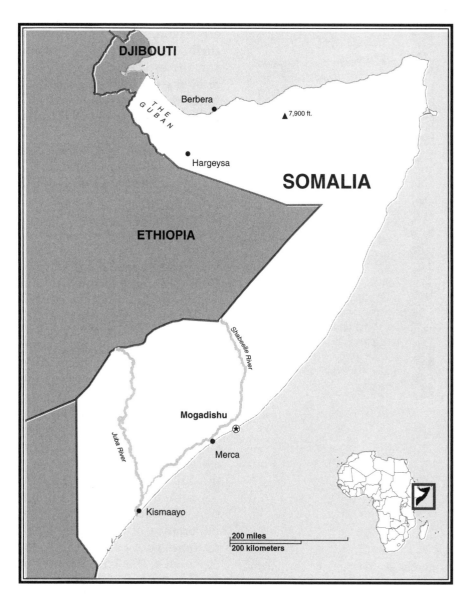

crossed into Ethiopia on a seasonal basis in search of good pastureland. However, since the late 1970s this territory has been the subject of disputes between the two countries, and the movement of the herders has been disrupted. Tension over the Haud and Ogaden continues, and even fighting has occurred.

HISTORY AND GOVERNMENT

Ancestors of the Somali peoples inhabited the Horn of Africa as long as 2,000 years ago. Some clans trace their occupation of the area back to the A.D. 1100s. But while the Somalis forged a common culture based on agriculture, pastoralism, and Islam*, they never united under a single political ruler.

Colonial Somalia. In the late 1800s, Britain and Italy both established colonies in what is now Somalia. The British occupied the north-

* **Islam** religion based on the teachings of the prophet Muhammad; religious faith of Muslims

41

Somalia

A Tale of Two Flocks

Somali pastoralists traditionally divide their flocks of animals into two separate herding units. One unit is based on the needs of goats and sheep, which require frequent watering. The other is based on the needs of camels, which need water much less often. Grazing camels, which provide milk, are usually put in the care of young unmarried men. Sheep and goats, on the other hand, travel with families. The families also use camels to carry their tents and other belongings. Thus, while a married herder with his sheep and goats may be in one place, his main herd of camels may be far away under the care of a younger kinsman.

* **nationalist** devoted to the interests and culture of one's country

* **coup** sudden, often violent, overthrow of a ruler or government

ern region, called Somaliland, but used it mainly as a base to supply their port of Aden on the Arabian Peninsula. British officials allowed the Somalis to keep their local clan councils and left them in charge of resolving conflicts among the local population. However, they transferred the traditional Somali grazing lands of the Haud and Ogaden to Ethiopia. This move laid the groundwork for the later conflicts between the two countries.

The Italians controlled the central and southern regions that make up the bulk of modern Somalia. In Somalia Italiana, colonial officials followed a policy of eliminating local authority and forcing Somalis to adopt Italian law. Southern Somalis reacted to Italian rule with armed resistance that continued until the 1920s.

By the late 1950s, the drive for Somali independence had gained momentum. The most important political parties in both the north and south called for all Somali territories to unite under a single flag. By June 1960, both Somaliland and Somalia Italiana had won independence, and in the following month they joined to form the Somali Republic. Its first elected president was Aden Abdullah Osman Daar.

Civilian Rule. Although united as a nation, the two former colonies remained far apart in many ways. In the north, British colonial policies had produced a highly educated group of Somalis, many of whom attended British universities. In the south, the Italians had provided much less education. The only real tie between the peoples of the two regions was a vague sense of shared identity. When the new state took shape, the south gained most of the benefits of government. The greatest number of political offices went to southerners, even though far more northerners were qualified to fill them.

Northerners and southerners typically had different ideas about what type of policies to pursue. The northern politicians emphasized the importance of developing the nation's economy and fostering good relations with neighboring countries. However, the southerners who dominated the government were generally passionate nationalists*. They pushed for the idea of a "greater Somalia" that incorporated those areas of KENYA and Ethiopia where Somalis lived. This program led to ongoing border clashes with Ethiopia and poor relations with Kenya.

The Barre Regime. On October 15, 1969, Somalia's president Abdirashid Ali Sharmarke was assassinated, and one week later, the military seized control of the government. The leader of the coup* was the army's commander in chief, Major General Muhammad Siad Barre. Along with the other military leaders, Barre formed the Supreme Revolutionary Council to run the country and was selected as the council's chairman. He quickly dismantled Somalia's democratic institutions, banned political parties, and arrested his political opponents. He set up a series of councils, with himself at the head of each, to run the various affairs of state.

Barre moved to eliminate the clan and KINSHIP ties that formed the traditional routes to political power in Somalia. In an effort to unify the nation, his government introduced the first written form of the Somali language and aggressively promoted LITERACY programs. At the same

* **Soviet Union**   nation that existed from 1922 to 1991, made up of Russia and 14 other republics

* **socialist**   relating to an economic or political system based on the idea that the government or groups of workers should own and run the means of production and distribution of goods

* **secede**   to withdraw formally from an organization or country

* **autonomous**   self-governing

time, Barre signed an agreement with the Soviet Union* and established a socialist* dictatorship. He also brought most parts of the economy under state control and prohibited private trading activities.

With Soviet help Barre expanded the military. In 1977 he sent Somali troops into Ethiopia to back a rebel group sympathetic to Somali territorial claims. However, this action angered the Soviet Union, which also supported the Ethiopian government. The Soviet Union sent arms and supplies to Ethiopia, and with the help of Cuban troops the Ethiopian army drove the Somalis out. REFUGEES fleeing the fighting poured into Somalia in large numbers. Barre sought assistance from the United States.

By this point Barre had made many enemies. In 1981 northern clans rose against him, and he turned the military against them. The Somali army destroyed the northern city of Hargeisa, killing some 50,000 people. The fighting devastated the northern economy, and civil unrest spread throughout the country. By the late 1980s, several southern clans had established their own militias led by local warlords. In 1990 rebel forces entered the capital of MOGADISHU. Barre fled early the next year.

Civil War and Anarchy. One faction of the United Somali Congress, the group that captured Mogadishu, named General Muhammad Farah Aideed to head the government. However, other groups rejected Aideed, and civil war broke out. Central government in Somalia collapsed entirely. In its place, a dozen or more clans controlled their own regions of the country, supported by their own militias.

Fighting was especially fierce in Mogadishu. The battles destroyed most of the once-beautiful seaside city and created tens of thousands of refugees. A crippling drought struck from 1991 to 1992, creating a famine in which between 300,000 and 500,000 people died. This enormous tragedy led the UNITED NATIONS (UN) and other international agencies to mount an emergency relief operation.

International relief efforts soon gave way to frustration. The UN saw most of its aid taken by the warlords and given to their followers rather than to the starving population. The organization sent troops from several nations—mostly from the United States—to protect the shipments of food, medicine, and other aid. But the operation soon changed its focus to trying to restore peace and order in the country. This ambitious goal meant disarming the warlords, who refused to cooperate. The United States and its allies sought to capture General Aideed. But when Aideed's forces shot down an American helicopter and killed several U.S. troops in a gun battle, the Americans pulled out of the operation. By 1995, the UN had also abandoned relief efforts in Somalia.

While the south was being torn apart by war, the leaders of the northern clans met to discuss the future of their region. In 1991 they decided to secede* and form a separate state called Somaliland. Another region called Puntland also declared itself autonomous*. Local northern militias turned in their weapons and some order began to return to the north. But so far, other countries have refused to recognize Somaliland as an independent nation, preferring that all of Somalia reunite.

Somalia

Somalia Today. In 1996 General Aideed was killed in fighting and was succeeded by his son Hussein, who refused to attend peace talks in 1996. Negotiations continued in several countries, but little came of them. Then, in May 2000, President Ismail Omar Guelleh of Djibouti hosted a conference to try to find a solution.

The conference agreed to create an assembly of 245 members, including seats reserved for women and for members of less powerful clans. The assembly chose Abdikassim Salad Hassan as Somalia's new president, to head a government for three years before holding national elections. However, most of the warlords did not take part in the conference, and they remained cool to Salad Hassan's presidency. In addition, Somaliland and Puntland refused to rejoin a united Somali state.

Salad Hassan faces the formidable challenges of restoring peace, disarming the warlords, and rebuilding a nation from the destruction of civil war. The capital lies in ruins and the economy is in tatters. Clan rivalries are as strong as ever. In a more positive development, tensions with Ethiopia have died down, thanks to the diplomatic intervention of Libya's ruler, Muammar al-Qaddafi. But Somalia's road ahead appears long and filled with dangerous obstacles.

More than 50,000 refugees of Somalia's civil war have fled to Yemen. In 2000 many of these Somalis lived in camps such as the one pictured here.

The Somali Democratic Republic

POPULATION:
7,253,137 (2000 estimated population)

AREA:
246,000 sq. mi. (637,660 sq. km)

LANGUAGES:
Somali (official); Arabic, Italian, English

NATIONAL CURRENCY:
Somali shilling

PRINCIPAL RELIGIONS:
Sunni Muslim

CITIES:
Mogadishu (capital), 1,219,000 (2001 est.); Hargeisa, Kismayu Merca, Berbera, Boosaaso, Borama, Giamama

ANNUAL RAINFALL:
Less than 3 in. (77 mm) overall, but up to 20 in. (550 mm) on high ground

ECONOMY:
GDP per capita: $600 (1999 est.)

PRINCIPAL PRODUCTS AND EXPORTS:
Agricultural: livestock, bananas, incense, sugarcane, cotton, cereals, corn, sorghum, mangoes, beans, fish

Manufacturing: sugar refining, textiles, limited petroleum refining
Mining: gypsum; unexploited deposits of uranium, iron ore, bauxite, gold, tin

GOVERNMENT:
Independent Somali Republic formed in 1960, the union of British and Italian Somaliland protectorates. Since 1991, the government has been in transition.

HEADS OF STATE SINCE INDEPENDENCE:
1960–1967 President Aden Abdullah Osman Daar
1967–1969 President Abdirashid Ali Sharmarke
1969–1991 Major General Muhammad Siad Barre (president after 1976)
1991–1997 Several presidents elected for same period by different groups: Ali Mahdi Mohamed (1991–1997); Abdurahman Ahmed Ali "Tur" (1991–1993); Mohamed Ibrahim Egal (1993–); Mohammed Farah Aideed (1995–1996); Hussein Mohammed Aideed (1996–)
1997–2000 41-member National Salvation Council
2000– President Abdikassim Salad Hassan

ARMED FORCES:
225,000 (2001 est.)

EDUCATION:
Compulsory for ages 6–14; literacy rate 24% (1990 est.)

ECONOMY

Before the civil war, livestock and agriculture formed the base of Somalia's economy. Livestock was the country's leading export, followed by bananas. Frankincense and myrrh, aromatic gums used in the manufacture of incense and perfume, also provided sources of income. But a series of droughts in the 1980s, combined with the effects of the war, have ravaged Somalia's livestock herds and crippled its agriculture.

The early rulers of independent Somalia tried to develop manufacturing. Between the 1960s and the mid-1970s the country built food processing, textile, and pharmaceutical plants and a petroleum refinery. The economy fared relatively well. But the situation began to deteriorate when the government took over most areas of the economy in the 1970s. Droughts and the ongoing border struggle with Ethiopia made the situation worse.

In the early 1980s Somalia agreed to an economic restructuring plan proposed by the International Monetary Fund (IMF). The program, which included plans to return companies and resources to private ownership, made little headway. In 1984, the economy suffered a severe blow when a cattle disease called rinderpest struck Somali livestock, and Saudi Arabia refused to import any Somali animals. Somalia's exports earnings fell by almost half, and Somalia could no longer make payments on its debts to the IMF. The IMF and other donors cut off aid in

1988, and three years later the civil war began. Since that time, the nation's economy has been in shambles.

PEOPLES AND CULTURES

The Somalis form a single ethnic group related to peoples in the neighboring countries of Ethiopia and Kenya. They traditionally practice a pastoral lifestyle, moving from pasture to pasture with their herds of livestock. However, some Somalis in the more fertile areas of the country have adopted farming.

See color plate 7, vol. 4.

Most Somalis follow Islam, which provides a further cultural connection with peoples in the lands surrounding Somalia. As Muslims, Somali men may have up to four wives, whom they may divorce.

The Somalis have long lived in a very decentralized society without hereditary chiefs or kings. Instead, councils of elders run the affairs of the country's six major clan families. Political decisions between clans occur during council meetings, long gatherings in which people discuss matters in great detail before reaching a decision.

Somalia has a distinguished tradition of oral poetry. The Somalis use poetry to preserve history, comment on current events, and express public and personal feelings. The country's first female pop star, Maryam Mursal, turned to poetry to criticize the government of Muhammad Siad Barre. Poetry also plays an important role in the large clan meetings that are the basis of Somali politics.

SONGHAI EMPIRE

See *Sudanic Empires of Western Africa.*

South Africa

The modern state of South Africa includes former British and Dutch colonies in which white settlers brutally dominated the region's black African population. As an independent nation, South Africa expanded and strengthened this pattern of racial discrimination under a policy known as APARTHEID, meaning "separateness." Suffering greatly under the rule of the white minority government and police, black South Africans continued their resistance. The dramatic defeat of the white government in 1994 signaled an end to apartheid and the beginning of a new era of black majority rule. It did not, however, mark the end of the country's political and economic troubles.

GEOGRAPHY

South Africa occupies the southernmost tip of the African continent and includes several small offshore islands. It is bordered on the north by NAMIBIA, BOTSWANA, ZIMBABWE, MOZAMBIQUE, and SWAZILAND. The small independent nation of LESOTHO lies within South African territory. South Africa's terrain can be divided into three major regions: the coast,

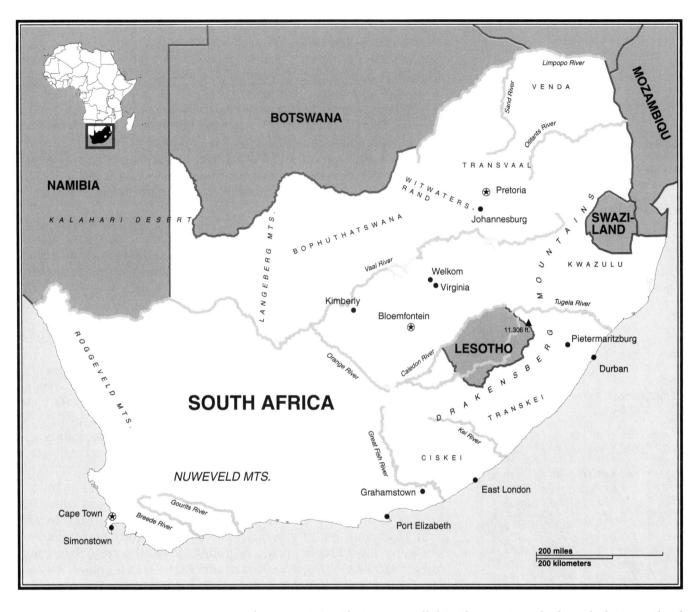

the mountains that run parallel to the coast, and a broad plain north of the mountains.

Along the westernmost part of the coast, the climate is generally warm and dry with a long rainy season. Just inland, several small mountain ranges divide the coast from the KALAHARI DESERT. Some plants and animals do live in the Kalahari, which receives a small amount of precipitation. Flanked by the Drakensberg range, South Africa's highest mountains, the eastern coast is hot and humid.

Beyond the central and eastern mountains lie the veld, made up of high plateaus. Grassy hills roll across the north central plateau known as the highveld. It includes the Witwatersrand (or Rand), a rocky ridge that is the source of several rivers and enormous deposits of gold and diamonds. The bushveld, a grassy plain dotted with trees and bushes, stretches north of the Rand. To the west, the Cape Middleveld includes the basin of the Orange River.

See map in Archaeology and Prehistory (vol. 1).

* **discrimination** unfair treatment of a group

* **indigenous** native to a certain place

Making Music

With roots in many different African musical traditions and African American jazz, South African popular music includes an impressive variety of styles. Some stars produce slick dance tunes known as bubblegum music that feature electric drums and synthesizers. In other popular bands, a male "groaner" sings in a deep voice, accompanied by a soft female chorus singing in close five-part harmony.

Since the 1990s, South Africa has encouraged the popular music industry, hosting many national and international music festivals. Several South African bands, including the acclaimed male a cappella group Ladysmith Black Mambazo, enjoy worldwide fame.

South Africa's climate does not have many extremes, with an average temperature of about 60°F. The western part of the country averages less than 20 inches of rain per year. The eastern part receives more precipitation and is the site of most of the country's major agriculture. However, the Western Cape province in the far southwest does enjoy enough rainfall in winter to grow wheat, fruit, and wine grapes.

South Africa has only one true lake but several large rivers. The Orange, Vaal, and Limpopo Rivers form a major river system in the central and northern areas. Several other rivers drain the southern and eastern coasts into the ocean. However, water is scarce in some areas, and people must use water transported from other parts of the country.

HISTORY AND GOVERNMENT

Issues of race and segregation have dominated South African history and politics. While informal at first, discrimination* against nonwhites eventually became enshrined in law. It reached a peak after 1948 in the state policy of apartheid, which denied blacks even the most basic of civil rights. Years of resistance to apartheid finally bore fruit in 1994 with the election of Nelson MANDELA, the country's first black president.

History Before 1910. Western South Africa was originally inhabited by HUNTING AND GATHERING peoples known as the San and nomadic herders called Khoi. BANTU-speaking farmers dominated the eastern part of the region. In the mid-1600s Dutch farmers settled the area that is now CAPE TOWN. They eventually expanded north and east, killing and enslaving the Khoi and San and fighting with the XHOSA and other indigenous* groups.

The British took over the Cape Colony in 1806. They drove indigenous people off much of the land and gave it to British colonists. The Dutch settlers, known as Boers or Afrikaners, resented British rule, and in the 1830s and 1840s thousands of them moved north and east across the Orange River into lands where groups such as the ZULU, Sotho, and NDEBELE had been warring with each other. The Dutch colonists established several independent states including the Orange Free State and Transvaal.

The situation changed quickly when gold and diamonds were found on Afrikaner lands. Settlers and investors rushed to the Afrikaner republics, founding boom towns such as JOHANNESBURG. They soon built a huge mining industry on the labor of black workers. Increasing conflicts between Afrikaner and British interests led to war in 1899. Winning the war, Britain created a new state in which white colonists—Dutch as well as British—held power over a large population of black Africans.

The Union of South Africa, established in 1910, was part of the British Empire. Louis Botha and James Hertzog led the largest political party, the South African Party, which adopted moderate policies based on the shared interests of the Europeans. However, Hertzog and his supporters, mainly rural Afrikaners, split off to form the Nationalist Party.

During the colonial era, Europeans developed enormously successful gold and diamond mines in South Africa. The Big Hole Mine in Kimberley was once the world's richest diamond mine.

The Rise of Black Politics. In 1912 the South African government passed laws to restrict the areas where blacks could own or purchase land. These laws also limited the movement of other nonwhites, including Asians and the mixed-race population known as CAPE COLOURED PEOPLE. Mohandas K. Gandhi, a leader of the Indian community in the Transvaal and Natal provinces, protested these laws with a strategy of nonviolent resistance. He later used this strategy to great effect in leading India to independence.

The tensions caused by these laws were typical of the social and political atmosphere in South Africa. Afrikaners rose up in arms several times, and other white workers loudly protested labor conditions. Black workers also began to organize, staging a series of strikes just after World War I. In the 1920s Clements KADALIE formed the first mass African political movement, the Industrial and Commercial Worker's Union (ICU), with over 100,000 members at its height.

Political parties emerged as well. The African Native Convention (ANC), formed in 1912, represented the political hopes of black people, and changed its name to the African National Congress in 1925. The African Political Organization fought for the rights of the Coloured population. The Communist Party of South Africa also became involved in politics, and by the late 1920s it had formed close ties with the ANC and called for black majority rule.

By the end of the 1920s, however, most of these labor and political movements were fading. The great labor campaigns of the ICU lost steam, while internal bickering nearly destroyed the Communist Party. The ANC spoke only for the black middle class, a small group, and had few supporters among the mass of poor and rural Africans.

The Road to Apartheid. In the 1930s, the worldwide Great Depression brought new hardships. The main white parties chose to cooperate in a new United Party. But in 1934 the Afrikaner politician Daniel Malan left the organization to form the National Party (NP). The NP worked to bring together Afrikaners of all social classes by emphasizing their common ethnic identity, skin color, and language—Afrikaans, a version of Dutch. The NP campaigned on a platform of white supremacy that called for total racial segregation and discrimination.

Many English-speaking conservatives supported the NP's proposals. The government passed laws that forced black people to move into specially created "native reserves" and gave their land to white settlers. Black people were not permitted to live in some areas of cities or have certain jobs.

South Africa recovered from the Depression thanks to a dramatic rise in the price of gold and an increase in industry during World War II. Blacks looking for work flocked to the cities in large numbers, leading to housing shortages and slums. White people, who controlled all the businesses and resources, grew richer while their black workers and servants stayed poor. More and more black people joined unions, strikes, and demonstrations.

By this time younger elements in the ANC forced the party to take a more aggressive position toward the government. In 1949 the ANC adopted a program of "national freedom" that called for black autonomy* and an end to white domination. The National Party responded with an openly racist program, designed to put an end to black political activity. Campaigning on proposals for a system of apartheid, the NP won a narrow victory in the elections of 1948.

* **autonomy** independent self-government

The Apartheid Era. The NP passed a series of laws that made segregation a part of every public institution. Residential and business districts were classified as white or black, and many blacks were forcibly removed from neighborhoods where their families had lived for generations. Public places and services were segregated to prevent the mixing of races.

At birth, each South African was classified as white, black, Asiatic, Coloured, or other. This racial identity determined where an individual could live, work, and go to school. It also affected whether people could vote, where they could own property, and even where they were allowed to stand. Pass laws required all citizens to carry passbooks identifying them by name and race. Police could demand to see passbooks at any time and arrest anyone caught in a forbidden area.

In 1960, 69 people were killed in Sharpeville, South Africa, when police opened fire on a crowd of unarmed protestors. The event resounded around the world. Here on the tenth anniversary of Sharpeville, students in London re-enact the shooting.

Under apartheid, each race had separate schools. While the nation's Department of Education focused only on white schools, the government drastically cut funding for black schools. While white students were trained for technical and professional careers, black students were expected to take unskilled jobs.

In 1958, under Prime Minister Hendrik VERWOERD, the South African government changed the name of the native reserves to "black homelands." It assigned each of these desperately poor rural areas to a different African ethnic group and gave them some degree of autonomy. The government promised independence to any homeland that requested it. But many black people, including the ANC, saw the plan as a way to ignore the needs of the black population while keeping the best land in white hands. Moreover, the millions of black people who lived in slums around white cities had no voice in either the white government or the black homelands.

The ANC Fights Back. The ANC responded to apartheid with massive protests and resistance campaigns. The party allied itself with other organizations, including the South African Indian Congress, the Coloured People's Congress, the South African Congress of Trade Unions, and a group of white liberals called the Congress of Democrats. But in the late 1950s, a group of black members refused to accept white allies and formed an "Africanist" organization called the Pan-African Congress (PAC).

In 1960 both the ANC and PAC sponsored demonstrations against the pass laws. In the town of Sharpeville, police officers fired on an unarmed crowd of demonstrators, killing 69. The government declared a state of emergency, banned the ANC and PAC, and arrested over 2,000 activists.

The leaders of the ANC and PAC went underground to avoid arrest. The ANC and the Communist Party formed a military group called Umkhonto we Sizwe, or "Spear of the Nation," also known as MK. This organization carried out armed guerrilla* attacks. The government increased the powers of the police: anyone suspected of a crime could be arrested and held for up to ten days; those suspected of terrorism could be jailed without a trial or a time limit. In 1963 the police caught MK leaders including Nelson Mandela and Walter Sisulu. They were sentenced to life in prison without parole.

* **guerrilla**   type of warfare involving sudden raids by small groups of warriors

For the next ten years, the apartheid system enjoyed its greatest success. White industry owners made huge profits, and foreign investment poured into the country. Segregation increased in all spheres of life. The police stepped up arrests under the pass laws, keeping black people out of the cities except to work.

Apartheid in Crisis. By the early 1970s, events both inside and outside of South Africa increased the pressure for changes in the system. A worldwide economic slowdown led to inflation* and unemployment. The country depended on goods and technology imported from abroad, and its own exports could not keep pace. Meanwhile, black trade unions, banned since the 1950s, began to reassert themselves in the form of strikes and protests.

* **inflation**   increase in prices

Active opposition to apartheid spread throughout black society. Steve BIKO's Black Consciousness Movement swept through schools and colleges. In 1976, teachers in the black township of Soweto led schoolchildren in a protest against a rule that English and Afrikaans be used equally in classes, although most black schools operated entirely in English. Police opened fire on the protesters, and the resulting deaths sparked a week of rioting and revolt. The police cracked down with overwhelming force, killing over 174 blacks and wounding over 1,200.

The Soweto Massacre generated a wave of protest both at home and abroad. In South Africa, it sounded the call for a younger generation of black activists to take up the struggle. Overseas, officials of the ANC pressed foreign governments to boycott South African goods and refuse to sell weapons to the South African police and military. Archbishop Desmond TUTU issued a powerful moral message.

Meanwhile, events in neighboring African countries also spelled trou-

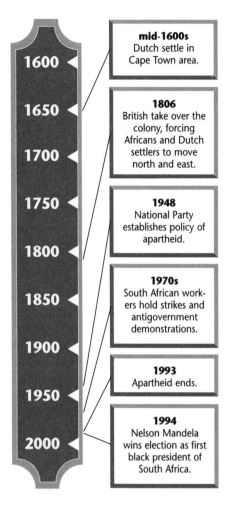

mid-1600s
Dutch settle in Cape Town area.

1600

1650

1806
British take over the colony, forcing Africans and Dutch settlers to move north and east.

1700

1750

1948
National Party establishes policy of apartheid.

1800

1850

1970s
South African workers hold strikes and antigovernment demonstrations.

1900

1993
Apartheid ends.

1950

1994
Nelson Mandela wins election as first black president of South Africa.

2000

* **communist** relating to communism, a system in which land, goods, and the means of production are owned by the state or community rather than by individuals

* **Soviet Union** nation that existed from 1922 to 1991, made up of Russia and 14 other republics

ble for the NP government. In the mid-1970s, communist* guerrilla movements won independence for black Africans in two Portuguese colonies, ANGOLA and Mozambique. Shortly afterward, black guerrillas overthrew the white supremacist government of Ian Smith in Rhodesia (now Zimbabwe). White South Africa found itself surrounded by independent, hostile black nations.

The Total Strategy. In response to these pressures, President Pieter W. Botha adopted a policy known as "Total Strategy." He hoped to preserve apartheid through compromise and force. He increased spending on black education and eased rules governing black labor and residency. But at the same time, he gave the police, army, and intelligence services a larger role in the government. More than ever, South Africans lived in a police state.

The NP also tried to form alliances with prosperous Indians and Coloured people against the black groups. It created a new National Assembly with three bodies—one for whites, one for Indians, and one for Coloureds—but still with no black representation. The white upper house had the authority to impose laws without the consent of the other houses and could veto any law those houses proposed.

Botha's plan failed to satisfy black South Africans. In the 1980s they organized against apartheid as youths, as women, as workers, as students, and as neighbors. The MK staged several astonishing military attacks, and the ANC returned from exile to center stage in South African politics. Strikes, protests, and riots shook the nation, and the state responded with massive detentions, trials, police brutality, and army troops sent into the black townships. Abroad, ANC leaders and their supporters convinced other nations and corporations to withdraw economic support from South Africa. In return, wealthy Western nations pressured the ANC to abandon its communist goals. As the economy staggered, the NP replaced Botha with a new president, F.W. DE KLERK.

The Beginning of the End. By 1990 both the state and the ANC were facing a crisis. The declining economy and deteriorating social situation sapped the government's strength. Meanwhile, the ANC lost its bases in Angola and Mozambique, while the Soviet Union* dramatically reduced its funding for communist groups such as the ANC. In February Mandela wrote to President de Klerk from prison, and the two leaders met. De Klerk freed Mandela and other political prisoners and proposed negotiations.

Not everyone was excited about this turn of events. Some white South Africans opposed any real equality for black citizens. Meanwhile, the ANC faced a stiff challenge from the Inkatha Freedom Party (IFP), which had been created in the early 1970s when the ANC was officially banned. The ANC had always had its base in the Xhosa, Sotho, and Tswana ethnic groups; the IFP has strong ties with the Zulu people. While many ANC supporters came from urban slums, Zulu members of the IFP generally had a fairly stable lifestyle and hoped to avoid widespread violence by cooperating with the white government.

With the release of Mandela, the ANC once again became a legal party—as well as a rival of the IFP for black power. The IFP deeply resented a government measure, passed under pressure from the ANC, that banned the Zulu practice of carrying spears and other traditional weapons. The IFP's leader, Gatsha Buthelezi, called for a separate Zulu state, and clashes between IFP and ANC supporters became commonplace, leading to thousands of deaths.

The End of Apartheid. Despite increasing chaos and uncertainty, plans for a new constitution went forward. After three years of negotiation, elections were set for early 1994. On May 10, 1994, the results were announced, with the ANC winning nearly two-thirds of the votes. Mandela took office as the first black president of South Africa. The ANC abandoned its earlier communist ideals. It called for a capitalist* market economy in which state-owned business would be sold to private and foreign investors.

Mandela's victory did not end black discontent. The ANC made many election promises, most of which it could not possibly keep due to the condition of the nation's economy. Efforts to privatize* industries and reduce the size of government led to layoffs that angered the unions and the Communist Party. Labor strikes, protests, and political violence remained common.

Despite these difficulties, Mandela managed to steer a middle course, balancing the demands of his supporters with the needs of the nation's economy and international relations. He set up a Truth and Reconciliation Commission to take testimony about the violence and injustice of South Africa's past. A new constitution went into effect in 1996, adding a Bill of Rights that guarantees broad freedoms. Elections in 1999 took place fairly peacefully, and the ANC remained the dominant party. Mandela retired, and his vice president, Thabo Mbeki, was elected president.

However, Mbeki inherited a country still struggling to deal with an ailing economy and a history of racial injustice. He and the ANC face formidable challenges in returning the country to the prosperity it once enjoyed without exploiting* black workers. Mbeki has eased the process of privatizing industries and allowed investors to buy and sell freely in the country's markets. His policies have become more practical, but he does not speak with the moral voice of Mandela. Even so, the end of apartheid offers black citizens the freedom to participate in their government and to hope for peaceful change and progress.

ECONOMY

Compared to its neighbors, South Africa has a large and diverse economy, but one that has grown slowly. Manufacturing now employs more than 25 percent of the workforce. The main industries are steel production, clothing, textiles, and food processing.

Mining, once the mainstay of the economy, has declined heavily in recent years. Although gold and diamonds are still important exports, the low price of gold threatens to close many mines. In addition, a financial crisis in Asian countries in the 1990s reduced the export of South African diamonds. However, coal has become a more important export, and it supplies most of South Africa's energy needs.

* **capitalist** referring to an economic system in which businesses are privately owned and operated and where free markets coordinate most economic activity

* **privatize** to transfer from government to private ownership

* **exploit** to take advantage of; to make productive use of

 See map in Mining and Minerals (vol. 3).

54

Republic of South Africa

POPULATION:
43,421,021 (2000 estimated population)

AREA:
471,008 sq. mi. (1,219,912 sq. km)

LANGUAGES:
English, Afrikaans, Ndebele, Pedi, Sotho, Swazi, Tsonga, Tswana, Venda, Xhosa, and Zulu (all are official)

NATIONAL CURRENCY:
Rand

PRINCIPAL RELIGIONS:
Christian 68%, Traditional and animistic 28.5%, Muslim 2%, Hindu 1.5%

CITIES:
Pretoria (administrative capital), 1,508,000 (2001 est.); Cape Town (legislative capital), 2,993,000 (2001 est.); Bloemfontein (judicial capital), 300,150 (1991 est.); Johannesburg

ANNUAL RAINFALL:
Varies from 40 in. (1,000 mm) on east coast to only 2.4 in. (61 mm) in the extreme west.

ECONOMY:
GDP per capita: $6,900 (1999 est.)

PRINCIPAL PRODUCTS AND EXPORTS:
Agricultural: corn, wheat, sugarcane, wine grapes, macadamia nuts, vegetables, livestock, wool, dairy
Manufacturing: automobile assembly, metalworking, machinery, textiles, iron and steel, chemicals, fertilizer, food processing
Mining: gold, diamonds, chromium, and coal
Services: tourism

GOVERNMENT:
Granted self-governing power from Britain, 1910. Became part of British Commonwealth in 1931. Declared an independent republic in 1961. Republic with president elected by the National Assembly. Governing bodies: 400-seat National Assembly, elected by universal suffrage; 90-seat National Council of Provinces, with 10 members elected by each of the nine provincial legislatures.

HEADS OF STATE SINCE DECLARED INDEPENDENT REPUBLIC:
1961–1967 President Charles Robberts Swart
1967–1968 President Jozua Francois Naude
1968–1975 President Jacobus Johannes Fouché
1975–1978 President Nicholaas Diederichs
1978–1979 President Balthazar J. Vorster
1979–1984 President Marais Viljoen
1984–1989 President Pieter W. Botha
1989–1994 President Frederik W. de Klerk
1994–1999 President Nelson Mandela
1999– President Thabo Mbeki

ARMED FORCES:
82,400 (2001 est.)

EDUCATION:
Compulsory for ages 7–16; literacy rate 82% (2001 est.)

Less than 15 percent of the land in South Africa has fertile soil, and agriculture plays a small role in the country's economy. The main crops are wheat, corn, wine grapes, and macadamia nuts. South African farmers are among the world's leading producers of cannabis—the plant that produces marijuana and hashish—and it has an important role in the country's illegal economy.

The healthiest economic sector seems to be the TOURISM industry. Over 500,000 people work in the tourism industry, serving over five million visitors each year. Most of the tourists are fellow Africans who come to enjoy the country's stunning mountains and sparkling beaches. However, South Africa's crime rate, among the highest in the world, continues to discourage prospective visitors.

HEALTH AND EDUCATION

Like all developing countries, South Africa struggles to provide adequate HEALTH CARE and EDUCATION for its citizens. The country's greatest health challenge is undoubtedly AIDS.

South Africa's HIV infection rate is the highest in the world—one out of every five South Africans is HIV-positive. Unfortunately, AIDS drugs are very expensive, and the Western companies that produce them are only now beginning to take steps to make the drugs available at greatly reduced prices. Past government policies have aggravated the problem, researching ineffective solutions and even denying medical care to some.

Education is in as desperate condition as health care. In 1976 the ANC called for a boycott* of schools, which resulted in a generation of young South Africans who cannot read and write. Although more than 90 percent of children are now enrolled in school, many do not attend classes, and schools face a critical shortage of teachers. The school system has not produced enough qualified graduates to fill jobs that demand skilled workers, and the economy has suffered for it. Education and job training are high priorities for South Africa's government.

PEOPLES AND CULTURES

South Africa includes a tremendous variety of ethnic groups and cultures. Most South Africans belong to Bantu-speaking groups such as the Nguni (which includes the Xhosa, Swazi, and Zulu peoples), Sotho, Venda, and Tsonga. The main difference among these groups is in their languages, although some cultural differences exist among them as well. Bantu groups were traditionally led by chiefs who inherited their position from older relatives. Councils assisted the chiefs at all levels of government. These power relationships were expressed by the saying, "A chief is chief by his people." All Bantu groups worshiped ancestors and showed a great respect for the elderly. However, as Africans moved to the cities, their traditional beliefs and practices weakened.

Non-Bantu populations in South Africa include remnants of the San and Khoi, as well as white descendants of Dutch and English settlers. Since the mid-1970s the Inkatha Freedom Party has worked to establish a strong separate identity for the country's Zulu population. Indians, originally brought over as slaves in the late 1800s, have grown into an important urban population. They now total some one million people, located mostly in the southeastern portions of the country. The Cape Coloured population, descended from the mixing of whites, Asians, and Africans, numbers over three million. (*See also* **Colonialism in Africa; Global Politics and Africa; Independence Movements; Indian Communities; Khoisan; Minerals and Mining; Southern Africa, History; Unions and Trade Associations.**)

* **boycott** refusal to participate or buy goods, as a means of protest

 See map in Humans, Early (vol. 2).

Southern Africa, History

* **indigenous** native to a certain place

The arrival of Europeans in southern Africa in the 1600s set in motion a long period of upheaval that transformed the region. A series of violent conflicts pitted Dutch settlers against indigenous* peoples, the Dutch against the British, the British against indigenous peoples, and various African groups against each other. After white settlers discovered gold and diamonds in the 1800s, they established a booming industry that relied on white control of black labor. This system set the stage for APARTHEID—the policy of racial segregation in SOUTH AFRICA.

In the South African (Boer) War (1899-1902), Afrikaners and British colonists fought for control of the region's rich gold reserves. More than 60,000 people—civilians as well as soldiers—lost their lives in the struggle.

---

* **barter** exchange of goods and services without using money

The Period of Settlement. Around 1600, BANTU-speaking farmers known as the Nguni dominated the eastern part of southern Africa. The west was home to the San, a people who hunted and gathered food. Along the southwestern coast, the Khoi tended to herds of livestock. The borders between their lands were not rigid, and the groups apparently lived side by side without major conflicts.

In the early 1600s, British and Dutch ships bound for Asia were making regular stops at Table Bay, the future site of CAPE TOWN. There they took on fresh water and bartered* with the Khoi for cattle. In 1652 the Dutch East India Company ordered Commander Jan VAN RIEBEECK to establish a permanent supply base at the cape. The company granted land and supplies to poor Dutch and French Protestant settlers, who spread into the countryside.

The Khoi and San resisted the European takeover, but bands of settlers attacked Africans and their livestock, and death and disease took their toll. By the late 1700s the Dutch settlers, known as Boers, had displaced or killed many of the Khoi and San and taken their lands. Those who survived were often forced to work on the settlers' farms. Owning slaves became a measure of wealth for the Boers.

* **annex**   to take over or add a territory to an existing area

By 1780 the Dutch Cape Colony had grown to about 10,000 settlers. But the colonists' expansion eastward was halted by the XHOSA, a farming people who fought fiercely for their land. For the next hundred years, the colony's eastern frontier became a bloody battleground.

In 1795 Britain annexed* the Cape Colony, returning it briefly in 1803 before taking control again three years later. British military forces defeated Xhosa armies and gave Xhosa land to white settlers. The British brought in thousands of new settlers and created a strong central government in Cape Town, headed by a governor-general. The missionaries who came to convert Africans to Christianity brought more change, and some missionaries criticized the way Europeans treated Africans.

The Mfecane and the Great Trek. During the early 1800s, as white settlers were fighting the Xhosa in the east, the NGUNI and other peoples of the region were building stronger states. In a competition for land and control of the IVORY TRADE, powerful chiefs led their warriors against other peoples, driving weaker groups north and west. The region's upheavals—conquests and population shifts—were known as the Mfecane, or "the crushing." Meanwhile, Britain's Cape Colony demanded slave labor and other goods, intensifying the conflicts of the Mfecane.

The most famous figure of the Mfecane was SHAKA ZULU, who ruled a powerful ZULU kingdom from 1816 to 1828. Zulu attacks forced some African peoples to migrate, causing confrontations with others. The great leader MZILIKAZI took the NDEBELE people farther north. SOBHUZA led the Ngwane to form a new kingdom that became the basis for the modern state of SWAZILAND. MOSHOESHOE conducted the Sotho people to a mountainous region farther south, founding a nation that still exists today as LESOTHO.

News of the Mfecane reached the Cape Colony. Frustrated with British rule, many Boers decided to move northward and settle the lands Africans were fleeing. Between 1834 and 1845, several thousand Boers undertook this journey, later known as the "Great Trek," which carried them beyond the boundaries of the British colony. The Boers also came to call themselves Afrikaners and their language Afrikaans.

Diamonds and Gold. The Afrikaners conquered the Africans who remained in the region known as the highveld, and they established several independent states. The Afrikaners and the British maintained an uneasy truce until diamonds were discovered in Boer territory in 1870. Britain tried to annex some of the diamond areas but was beaten back by Afrikaner forces. Around the same time the British succeeded in crushing the last traces of indigenous resistance, including a major conflict with the Zulu and their king CETSHWAYO.

In 1886 prospectors in Afrikaner territory discovered a huge area of gold-bearing rock, near what is now the city of JOHANNESBURG. But the gold was deep underground, and great quantities of rock had to be mined to produce small amounts of gold. Large companies began

Voting Rights

In the late 1900s South Africa followed a policy known as apartheid, which segregated black people and denied them the right to vote. Ironically, blacks had enjoyed broader legal rights under British colonial rule. In 1853 all adult males who owned property, regardless of color, received the right to vote. Unfortunately, few blacks had property. Under the constitution of 1910, blacks could vote in some areas but not others. Where they had the right, though, various restrictions kept the black vote to a minimum. In 1936 the white government of South Africa removed all blacks from the voting rolls.

58

employing thousands of laborers and expensive equipment to recover the precious metal.

The companies created a racist system of mine labor that set a pattern for discrimination* in all aspects of life in what later became South Africa. Some 90 percent of the mine workers were blacks, and they received one-ninth of the white workers' salaries. The companies promoted white employees to skilled and supervisory positions, while keeping black workers in backbreaking, unskilled jobs. Many blacks were forced to live in compounds owned by the companies, where they paid high prices for rent, food, and other needs. Most workers were migrants who had traveled many miles from home and spent months separated from their families.

* **discrimination** unfair treatment of a group

War and Union. As mining in Boer lands became a major industry, Britain feared that the Afrikaners would dominate the region. The British tried several schemes to create conflict with the Afrikaners and their leader, Paul KRUGER. One such scheme forced Cecil RHODES, the prime minister of the Cape Colony, to resign. In 1899 the two main AFRIKANER REPUBLICS, Transvaal and the Orange Free State, declared war on the British Cape Colony and Natal. Both sides used black Africans as workers and soldiers in the South African (or Boer) War. Although the British troops outnumbered the Afrikaners by about five to one, the Afrikaners won several early victories under capable leaders such as General Jan Christiaan SMUTS.

The British troops countered by destroying Boer farms and imprisoning civilians in concentration camps, where 20,000 Afrikaners and 13,000 Africans died. After three years of bitter fighting, the Afrikaners gave in. The two sides agreed to a union as a white minority in control of the black majority. In 1910 an all-male, all-white convention drew up a constitution for a new state called the Union of South Africa, a part of the British Empire. It became fully independent in 1961, but the black majority did not overthrow the white minority until 1994. (*See also* **Colonialism in Africa, Khoisan, Nongqawuse.**)

Soyinka, Wole

1934–
Nigerian writer

Wole Soyinka is a noted Nigerian writer and political activist. He was born in Ijebu-Isara in western NIGERIA, the son of a schoolteacher. After studying at a university in the city of Ibadan, he traveled to England, where he attended the University of Leeds and earned a degree in English literature.

In 1957 Soyinka moved to London and wrote scripts for the British Broadcasting Corporation. He also wrote plays, several of which were produced in London theaters. His play *The Lion and the Jewel* concerns two African men competing for a beautiful woman. One is a young schoolteacher who foolishly "Westernizes" himself. The other, an older but wiser man, wins the woman by drawing on African cultural traditions. The play's lesson—the importance of developing new ideas within a framework of traditional culture—has been a recurring theme in Soyinka's work.

After returning to Nigeria in 1960, Soyinka wrote *A Dance of the Forests* in honor of Nigerian independence. The play celebrates the end of the colonial era but warns its audience of the dangers of other forms of oppression*. It shows Soyinka's mastery of the English language and his commitment to social and political criticism. That commitment later brought trouble to Soyinka, who was imprisoned in the late 1960s for criticizing the government. After his release in 1969, Soyinka traveled abroad, writing prison memoirs, plays, fiction, poetry, and essays.

In 1976 Soyinka returned to Nigeria as chairman of the department of dramatic arts at the University of Ife. He continued to write, founded several theater groups, and expanded his political role. He championed campaigns to improve everyday life in Nigeria, such as by insuring safety on the nation's roads. In 1986 he became the first black African to receive the Nobel Prize for literature. Since that time Soyinka has been an important voice on behalf of individual liberty and human rights in Nigeria. His 1989 novel *Isara: A Voyage around "Essay"* is a tribute to his family and community. (*See also* **Literature, Theater**.)

* **oppression** unjust or cruel exercise of authority

SPANISH COLONIES

See *Colonialism in Africa.*

Spirit Possession

In spirit possession, nonhuman forces or entities are believed to enter a person's body and affect his or her actions. Western cultures usually view possession as a sign of madness or evil. But in Africa, spirit possession is considered a form of communication between people and spirits that has important religious, social, and political meaning.

Although it is believed that the spirits that possess people have greater powers than humans, they are not considered gods. In some cultures they are ancestors or mythical heroes; in others they are foreign beings. The spirits signal their presence through illness, dreams, sudden avoidance of certain items or practices, or the appearance of several distinct personalities in one person (the host). Spirits considered harmful may be exorcised, or removed. However, in many cases the spirit's host accepts possession.

* **ritual** religious ceremony that follows a set pattern

When possession is accepted, a ritual* of accommodation is usually performed in which the spirit is summoned and invited to take over the host's body. The host enters a trance followed by a period of total or partial amnesia. The spirit may demand that the host wear certain clothes, eat certain foods, or perform certain activities on a regular basis. Afterwards, the possessed individual often becomes a medium* through which the spirit communicates on certain social or religious occasions.

* **medium** person called upon to communicate with the spirit world

There are several theories about the meaning and purpose of spirit possession. Among some groups, possession is an important religious activity that uses spirits to uphold the moral order of society. An official priesthood, typically male, interprets the communication between the spirit and human worlds. Other cultures see it as a way to deal with personal problems such as illness or infertility.

Ultimately, spirit possession provides a powerful form of communication within African societies. Through possession, the spirits of heroes or ancestors pass on cultural knowledge that unifies members of a group. Spirits representing outside forces, such as different religious or political systems, express new ideas and discuss new practices. Possession can serve as a force of resistance—encouraging people to avoid new ideas— or a force of change—encouraging them to adopt or adapt new ideas. (*See also* **Death, Mourning, and Ancestors; Healing and Medicine; Mythology; Religion and Ritual; Taboo and Sin; Vodun; Witchcraft and Sorcery.**)

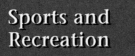

Sports and Recreation

See
color plate 4,
vol. 4.

Traditional African cultures valued play and recreation. Africans enjoyed board games and took part in organized activities such as wrestling, dancing, and canoe racing. When Europeans introduced Western sports during the colonial era, Africans found aspects of those sports familiar. Since then Africans have incorporated Western sports into their cultures, won prizes in international sports competitions, and continued to enjoy traditional African pastimes.

Development of Sports in Africa. Europeans introduced Western sports to Africa both by playing themselves and by teaching sports to young Africans. At first, missionaries and other Europeans trained Christian converts and the upper level of African society in Western-style sports. By the 1920s—often in response to African demands—colonial educators and social workers encouraged investment in playing fields and equipment for the general population. Only after the African nations gained their independence in the 1960s, however, did sports facilities become more widely available.

Some young Africans became involved in sports through organized instruction in schools or youth clubs. Others learned by watching. In SOUTH AFRICA, for example, crowds watched British soldiers play soccer in their free time during the Boer War (1899–1902). Soon barefoot boys were playing the game in dusty streets, using makeshift balls of rags or paper. Teams sprang up in African townships and competed in matches. Soccer became extremely popular in the cities because it filled urban players' and fans' need to create new identities and social networks. Teams could represent ethnic groups, neighborhoods, religious denominations, or occupations such as railroad workers or police.

By the 1930s, organized sports in Africa had taken on the characteristics of the games that were played around the world. Teams competed in leagues in stadiums before large, enthusiastic, sometimes uncontrollable crowds, supported by specialists such as coaches and referees.

Even international sports, however, have had distinctive characteristics in Africa. One African twist is the use of magic in sporting contests. Boxers have worn armbands containing special magical preparations to bring them victory, and soccer teams have planted charms in the mid-

Sports and Recreation

African athletes have won many medals and set new records in international competitions. Here Kenyan runner Catherine Ndereba arrives triumphantly at the finish line of the Boston Marathon in 2001.

dle of playing fields to cause difficulty to their opponents. Such practices still occur, and soccer teams preparing for important matches often employ team magicians in the hope of improving their chances.

Another feature of organized sports in Africa is the broad role of sports clubs. Such clubs became centers of social activities, and their administrators took on the role of village elders to young players. They gave advice, collected dues, helped club members with family expenses, and assisted young men in finding jobs.

Africans in International Sports. Many African governments view sports as an opportunity to promote national unity, community among African nations, and international recognition of African achievement. The first All-African Games took place in the city of BRAZZAVILLE, Republic of Congo, in 1965, with more than 3,000 athletes from 30 countries. African nations then established the Supreme Council for Sport in Africa. Based in CAMEROON, the council promotes and coordinates continent-wide sporting events.

Africans have enjoyed growing success in the major events of the international sports calendar. They have competed in the Olympic Games since 1908, and their participation has grown dramatically since they have gained independence. Some African customs have discouraged girls from participating in sports—such as the early age of marriage for women. However, girls and young women are increasingly active in athletic competitions and have won gold medals in track and other Olympic events. Kenyan, Ethiopian, Moroccan, and Nigerian runners have had great success around the world.

Soccer remains the most popular sport in Africa, and teams from African countries have begun to attract attention in the World Cup, the international soccer championship. Members of some African soccer teams play professionally for European clubs, which offer higher salaries than African clubs. In addition, African basketball players have had successful careers with American professional teams.

African Games. Africans have a board game called *mancala* or *bao* in which players try to capture game pieces dropped in cups or holes on a board. *Mancala* is ancient. People in sub-Saharan* Africa were playing versions of it centuries ago, along with other strategy games similar to checkers, chess, and backgammon. Introduced to the Americas by enslaved Africans, *mancala* is the basis for commercially marketed board games such as Pitfall and Oh-Wah-Ree.

In earlier times *mancala* was more than recreation. Associated with rulers, shrines, and temples, it could be played only by kings and their relatives in some countries. In the Buganda kingdom of UGANDA, the game was kept in the court hall, where the prime minister played it while deciding court cases. In GHANA, the ASANTE kings played *mancala* on golden boards, and it was said that even the gods enjoyed the game. Today people of all ages and classes play versions of *mancala*. Equipment varies from lines or holes dug in the ground, with stones or seeds as counters, to beautifully carved and decorated sets found in art collections. The playing ground may have two, three, or four rows with as many as 50 holes in a row, but games of two or four rows with six to eight holes per row are most common.

Other African games include KENYA's *shisima*, similar to tic-tac-toe; SIERRA LEONE's chess-like *kei*, which uses a board divided into squares and game pieces called black men and white men; and *nigbe*, a western African game of chance that uses cowrie shells as dice. When played in public, these games draw crowds of onlookers, who cheer on the players and follow each move closely—African games are generally a community affair.

See color plate 13, vol. 1.

* **sub-Saharan** referring to Africa south of the Sahara desert

Children learn counting, concentration, and the art of interacting with others through games and play, often accompanied by singing and dancing. Many Africans still consider the old games important for developing children's mental and physical skills, and the games are sometimes included in coming-of-age ceremonies. (*See also* **Dance, Festivals and Carnivals, Popular Culture.**)

Stanley, Henry Morton

1841–1904
British explorer and author

Henry Morton Stanley made several extensive journeys in Africa in the second half of the 1900s. The books he wrote about his adventures were widely read. Stanley was born John Rowlands in Wales, where he grew up in an orphanage. In 1859 he traveled to the United States and changed his name to that of a merchant who had befriended him. Drifting from place to place, Stanley fought on both sides in the American Civil War and served on naval and merchant ships. In the late 1860s he became a journalist reporting on the Indian Wars of the American West.

Stanley went to Africa as a correspondent for the *New York Herald*. In 1871 the newspaper sent him to search for David LIVINGSTONE, the British missionary and explorer who was missing in central Africa. Stanley found the explorer and uttered the now famous greeting, "Dr. Livingstone, I presume?" His accounts of the journey received wide attention. When Livingstone died a few years later, Stanley decided to continue the explorer's work. Between 1874 and 1877 he led an expedition across Africa from east to west by way of Lake Victoria and the CONGO RIVER—a journey described in his book *Through the Dark Continent* (1878).

Stanley next spent five years working for King Leopold II of Belgium, overseeing the construction of a railroad in the Congo colony. In the late 1880s he led a third and final expedition, crossing Africa from west to east to rescue EMIN PASHA, a European working as a provincial governor for Egypt. Emin was reportedly stranded in the center of the continent. Stanley wrote *In Darkest Africa* about that expedition. He spent his remaining years in England, serving as a member of the British Parliament. (*See also* **Travel and Exploration.**)

STORYTELLING

See *Oral Tradition.*

Sudan

Sudan is the largest country in Africa and one of the most troubled. Almost from the moment it won independence in 1956, political violence and civil war have torn the nation apart. In part, these difficulties reflect longtime divisions between the various ethnic and religious groups that occupy the region. In part, they are the result of colonialism and conquest by the British, Turks, and Egyptians. Global

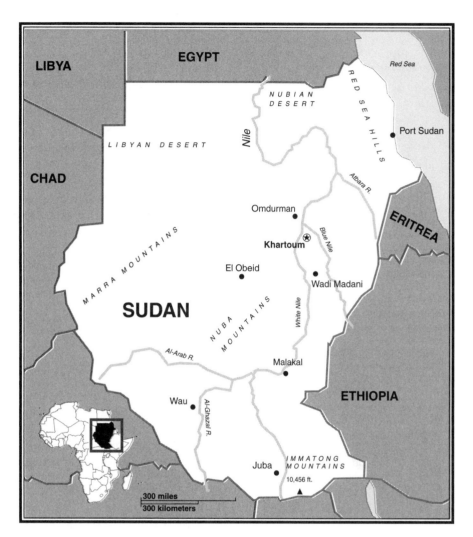

politics and struggles over resources such as oil have continued to trouble Sudan's complex political life.

GEOGRAPHY

Sudan occupies almost a million square miles of highly diverse terrain in northeastern Africa, an area greater than that of the United States east of the Mississippi River. Stretching nearly 1,200 miles from north to south, the country straddles three distinct environmental zones: the desert, the SAHEL, and the tropics.

Environments. The SAHARA DESERT dominates the northern third of the country, from the border with EGYPT to the Sudanese capital of KHARTOUM. South of Khartoum lies the Sahel region, a semiarid zone that covers most of the country. This region receives just enough rainfall to support short grasses, scrub trees, and crops such as sesame and sorghum* that need little water. In the eastern Sahel, many people use water irrigation to grow crops; in the western Sahel, most Sudanese are pastoralists*, raising herds of animals. The most southerly portion of

* **sorghum** family of tropical grasses used for food

* **pastoralist** someone who herds livestock

65

Sudan

* **cash crop**   crop grown primarily for sale rather than local consumption

* **tributary**   river that flows into another river

* **dynasty**   succession of rulers from the same family or group

* **tribute**   payment made by a smaller or weaker party to a more powerful one, often under the threat of force

* **exploit**   to take advantage of; to make productive use of

Something for Everyone

One of Sudan's greatest natural resources is a thorny tree called Acacia senegal. The Sudanese use its wood for fuel and construction, weave strong ropes from its root fibers, and dry its seeds for food. But the tree's most significant product is its sap, known as gum arabic. For thousands of years, local people have collected the gum for use in medicine, crafts, and food.

Today, companies around the world buy nearly all of the gum arabic Sudan can produce. This versatile ingredient keeps ice creams smooth, prevents cakes from crumbling, and makes sodas more flavorful. It also coats pills for easy swallowing, makes skin lotions feel silky, and provides the adhesive for postage stamps.

Sudan has a tropical climate, with about twice as much rainfall as in the Sahel. In times of peace, the country's most important cash crops* are grown in the south. However, the ongoing civil war has disrupted agriculture in this part of the country.

Rivers and Mountains. Settlement in Sudan, as in Egypt, depends for its life on the NILE RIVER. The White Nile River rises in UGANDA and flows north across the Sudanese border into the Sudd, the world's largest permanent swamp. Half of the river's water evaporates in the swamps before the remaining stream continues north. The Blue Nile has its source in ETHIOPIA, which borders Sudan on the southeast. The Blue Nile and White Nile Rivers meet at Khartoum and flow as one toward Egypt. Over half of Sudan's population lives along the Nile or its tributaries*.

For the most part, Sudan consists of a large, rolling plain, broken occasionally by baobob trees and formations of volcanic rock. Several mountain ranges rise from the landscape, including the Nuba, Marra, and Immatong ranges. The country's highest point, Mount Kinyeti, looms 10,456 feet above the border with Uganda. A line of hills and low mountains also lie inland from the Red Sea coast.

HISTORY AND GOVERNMENT

The area occupied by Sudan has historically been home to a many ethnic groups with various languages, social customs, and political structures. Its ancient history includes the kingdom of NUBIA, which had close relations—and conflicts—with the pharaohs of Egypt. But Sudan was not united politically until about 1500, when a series of major powers began competing to control the region.

The Funj Sultanate. Around 1504 Muslim immigrants from Arabia united with the local Funj dynasty* of northeastern Sudan to form the Funj Sultanate. This Islamic kingdom was ruled by noblemen whose rank depended on their blood relation to the monarch. Diverse groups of people lived within the kingdom, growing crops and raising livestock in small settlements. They paid tribute* and taxes for the right to live and work on the land.

Throughout the 1500s the sultans of Funj successfully fought off attacks by the powerful Ottoman Empire, which had its bases of power in Turkey and the Middle East. During the 1600s the Funj expanded their kingdom and opened trade routes to the Red Sea and Arabia. Their capital city, Sennar, grew large and prosperous. However, by the mid-1700s internal divisions weakened the sultanate.

Turkish and Egyptian Rule. In 1821 the Ottoman ruler of Egypt, Muhammad Ali conquered the tottering remains of the Funj Sultanate. His main goals were to capture slaves to build up his army and to exploit* Sudan's natural resources. He took thousands of captives during his raids, but many died on the journey through the desert to training camps in Egypt. Because his plan to obtain soldiers from the Sudan failed, Muhammad Ali focused on exploiting resources, growing cash

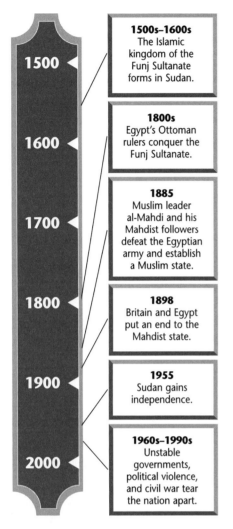

1500s–1600s
The Islamic kingdom of the Funj Sultanate forms in Sudan.

1800s
Egypt's Ottoman rulers conquer the Funj Sultanate.

1885
Muslim leader al-Mahdi and his Mahdist followers defeat the Egyptian army and establish a Muslim state.

1898
Britain and Egypt put an end to the Mahdist state.

1955
Sudan gains independence.

1960s–1990s
Unstable governments, political violence, and civil war tear the nation apart.

crops such as cotton. He earned money through the sale of these crops and through the heavy taxes imposed on the people who grew them.

The Ottomans divided Sudan into provinces ruled by Islamic governors appointed by the Egyptian government. However, the governors had little control over the rural areas of their provinces. The rulers who followed Muhammad Ali introduced administrative changes to the system. They named some Sudanese to government posts, and Arabic gradually replaced Turkish as the language of government.

By the mid-1800s the Ottoman rulers expanded their authority to include southern Sudan because of its natural wealth. Traders and merchants from Europe and the Middle East saw the opportunities for profit, and they created a thriving trade in slaves and ivory. The SLAVE TRADE reached such devastating levels that European countries put pressure on the Egyptian government to end it. The Egyptians sent several expeditions to fight the slave traders but had limited success. In most cases the expeditions were led by Europeans.

The Revolt of the Mahdi. Many Sudanese complained bitterly under the burden of high taxes, foreign rule, and the violent campaign against the slave trade. Large numbers of people supported the rebellion launched in 1881 by Muhammad Ahmad ibn Sayyid Abdullah, a holy man who proclaimed himself al-MAHDI, meaning "the expected one." According to legend, the Mahdi would appear in order to restore the purity of Islam and liberate the people from Ottoman rule.

Supported by pastoralists from the north, al-Mahdi and his followers defeated the Egyptian armies and captured Khartoum in 1885. He established a Muslim state ruled according to religious principles and laws. Al-Mahdi himself died a few months after his victory, and the task of running the new state fell to his successor Khalifa Abdullahi. Controlling most of what is now Sudan, the Mahdists fought constantly with their neighbors. In 1898 a British-Egyptian expedition led by Herbert Horatio Lord Kitchener captured the Mahdist capital and put an end to the Mahdist state.

Anglo-Egyptian Rule. By that time, several European powers had become well established in northeastern Africa. In Sudan, the British and Egyptians jointly ruled the country in an arrangement known as the Condominium. Under the Condominium, a British governor-general had final authority over civil and military matters. The Egyptian government appointed this official based on recommendations from the British—Lord Kitchener himself served as the first governor-general of Sudan.

The Condominium administration divided Sudan into provinces ruled by governors. Until World War I most of these governors were, like Kitchener, army officers. However, in the mid-1920s the British began a program of turning the Sudanese against themselves. They began to choose governors from among the indigenous* Sudanese leaders. They also began to treat the country's northern section, where most of the people were Muslim, quite differently from the southern areas, where

* indigenous   native to a certain place

most people followed traditional religions. In separating the north from the south, the British hoped to prevent Islam from spreading southward.

The British provided education and economic opportunities in the north, while neglecting the south. The two halves of Sudan also grew apart in their culture and language. The so-called Southern Policy has had devastating effects on Sudan and has been a factor in the civil wars that have raged in Sudan since its independence.

Independence and Civil War. From the 1930s to the 1960s fervor for national independence swept across Africa, and Sudan was no exception. Though the movement started among a small group of intellectuals in Sudan, it soon split along religious lines into two main political parties. The National Unionist Party (NUP), allied with the Khatmiyya religious sect, wanted a union of Sudan with Egypt. The Umma Party, allied with the Mahdists, called for independence. These parties were joined in their struggle by the Sudanese Communist Party and several labor unions.

In 1953 Britain agreed to grant the Sudanese self-rule for three years, followed by a vote on the future of the country. In an election for a new parliament, the NUP won the majority of seats, but it soon changed its position and announced that it favored independence for Sudan. In

More than half of Sudan's population lives along the Nile River or one of its tributaries. Shown here is a section of the Nile north of Khartoum.

* **autonomy** independent self-government

* **coup** sudden, often violent, over-throw of a ruler or government

* **socialist** relating to an economic or political system based on the idea that the government or groups of workers should own and run the means of production and distribution of goods

* **secede** to withdraw formally from an organization or country

December 1955 the parliament voted unanimously for independence, effective the following month. But northern Muslims dominated the whole process, ignoring southerners' demands for local autonomy*. Just five months before independence, army units in the south rebelled and killed hundreds of northern traders and officials.

The NUP and the Umma Party formed a government together, but the political situation remained so unstable that the prime minister invited the military to take power. General Ibrahim Abboud suspended the constitution and outlawed political parties, trade unions, and strikes. The government pursued brutal policies to promote Islam and Arabic culture in the south, where the violent rebellion continued. In 1964 a popular uprising forced the military to surrender control of the state.

The new civilian government lasted just four years before being overthrown by another military coup*. Colonel Ja'far Nimeiri took over as head of government and, supported by the Communist Party, declared Sudan a socialist* state. However, the Communists soon split with Nimeiri and attempted a coup of their own in 1971. Nimeiri held onto power, but he found himself with few remaining allies. He signed a peace treaty with the southern rebels that gave the south some autonomy.

A Brief Peace. To strengthen his hold on power, Nimeiri joined forces with the militant Muslim Brotherhood. At the same time, he repeatedly violated the agreement he signed with the rebels. He declared that Sudan would be ruled by Shari'a, Islamic law. The discovery of oil in the south made him determined to regain control of the region. The south rebelled yet again, this time led by the Sudan People's Liberation Army (SPLA). A coup drove Nimeiri from power in 1985.

In 1989, another military coup brought General Umar Hasan Ahmad al-Beshir to power, supported by the Muslim Brotherhood and a new party, the National Islamic Front (NIF). Beshir promised a return to civilian rule but declared that Sudan would be an Islamic state ruled by Shari'a. The southerners could not accept this policy, and they forced the government to abandon Shari'a in the south two years later.

John Garang, leader of the SPLA, demanded self-rule for the south. But some southern groups signed peace agreements with Beshir, and rebel leader Riek Machar joined the government. Other groups called for the south to secede*. Some of these splits were caused by friction between two ethnic groups, the Nuer and the Dinka—Garang and most the SPLA belonged to the Dinka.

Garang utterly rejected any deal, and the SPLA combined with Beshir opponents from both the south and the north in the new National Democratic Alliance (NDA). The NDA launched armed attacks on dams that supplied electric power to Khartoum, as well as on the pipeline that carried oil from southern oil fields to the Red Sea.

The Wunlit Covenant and After. In 1999, many of the Dinka and Nuer rebel groups met at the city of Wunlit and signed a treaty called the Wunlit Covenant. Faced with the threat of a reunited southern opposi-

Republic of the Sudan

POPULATION:
35,079,814 (2000 estimated population)

AREA:
967,244 sq. mi. (2,505,813 sq. km)

LANGUAGES:
Arabic (official); Nubian, Ta Bedawie, English, dialects of Sudanic and Nilotic languages

NATIONAL CURRENCY:
Sudanese pound

PRINCIPAL RELIGIONS:
Sunni Muslim 70%, Animist 25%, Christian 5%

CITIES:
Khartoum (capital), 2,731,000 (2001 est.); Port Sudan, Wad Medani, El Obeid, Atbara, Juba, Malakal, Renk

ANNUAL RAINFALL:
From 5 in. (130 mm) in the central region to 50 in. (1,270 mm) in the south

ECONOMY:
GDP per capita: $940 (1999 est.)

PRINCIPAL PRODUCTS AND EXPORTS:
Agricultural: cotton, gum arabic, sesame, sorghum, millet, wheat, sheep, groundnuts

Manufacturing: textiles, cement, cotton ginning, edible oils, soap, distilling, sugar, footwear, petroleum refining
Mining: oil, iron ore, chromium, copper, zinc

GOVERNMENT:
Independence from Britain and Egypt, 1956. Republic with president elected by universal suffrage. Governing bodies: 400-seat National Assembly (legislative body), with 275 members elected by popular vote and 125 elected by National Congress.

HEADS OF STATE SINCE INDEPENDENCE:
1956–1958 Council of State (civilian)
1958–1964 General Ibrahim Abboud
1964–1965 Supreme Council (military)
1965–1969 Isma'il al-Azhari
1969–1985 Colonel Ja'far Muhammad Nimeiri (president after 1971)
1985–1986 Lieutenant General Abd al-Rahman Siwar al-Dahab
1986–1989 Supreme Council (civilian)
1989– General Umar Hasan Ahmad al-Beshir (president after 1993)

ARMED FORCES:
94,700 (2001 est.)

EDUCATION:
Compulsory for ages 7–12; literacy rate 46% (2001 est.)

* **secular**   nonreligious; connected with everyday life

tion, Beshir signed a separate peace with the leader of Sadiq al-Mahdi, an influential Islamic politician who had been part of the NDA. With al-Mahdi's support, Beshir forced a leading Islamic militant, Hassan al-Turabi, from the government. Beshir tried to sell himself as a champion of secular* rule. This policy pleased the governments of neighboring states, which were also struggling against fundamentalist Islamic movements. Beshir signed agreements to end hostile relations with Egypt, Uganda, LIBYA, ERITREA, and ETHIOPIA.

But while achieving peace with other nations, Beshir launched a new offensive to take over the southern oil fields. International agencies have accused the Sudanese government of killing and enslaving civilians in an attempt to drive all non-Arabs from the area. Meanwhile the civil war with the south continues. The war has had a ruinous effect on the region, with at least 1.5 million dead and 5 million displaced. With food supplies and health care disrupted, starvation and disease are common. Few observers see prospects for peace anytime soon.

ECONOMY

For many years Sudan has relied on agriculture as the main pillar of its economy. Cotton accounts for more than half of all export earnings.

The main cotton-growing region is the area between the White and Blue Niles called the Gezira. In the 1920s the colonial government established a huge irrigation project in the Gezira to grow crops for export.

Other important cash crops include coffee, tea, tobacco, and gum arabic. Gum arabic has many uses in candy, cosmetics, and medicines, and Sudan produces more than three quarters of the world's supply. A terrible drought in 1984 and 1985 took a serious toll on agriculture, and over 250,000 people died in a famine.

Oil reserves were discovered in the south in the late 1970s, and the government has fought since that time to exert control over the oil fields. Several foreign companies have significant stakes in Sudan's oil industry. However, Beshir's actions in the south have led HUMAN RIGHTS groups to put pressure on these nations to withdraw their investments in the country.

PEOPLES AND CULTURES

Sudan's geographic diversity is matched by its cultural diversity. The Sudanese speak an estimated 400 different tongues, although Arabic serves many as a common language. While the government has vigorously promoted Islam, about one fourth of the people follow traditional religions. Most non-Muslims live in the southern part of the country.

The peoples of northern Sudan share historical connections to the Arab world, but few of these cultures are purely Arabic. The Islamic Funj Sultanate, for example, had links to the black Africans of the Nuba Hills and the Ethiopian border. Most of the people who live along the rivers trace their ancestry to Arab sources and speak Arabic, but their traditions often reveal a Nubian heritage.

See color plate 4, vol. 3.

In many parts of northern Sudan, the word "Arab" simply means a nomadic herder of the desert. Some nomadic Arab populations of Sudan are light-skinned because they have not intermarried much with black Sudanese. However, most northern populations, such as the Baggara, have done so. While these societies usually moved from place to place with their herds of animals, they settled in farming villages and grew crops when conditions for pastoralism were poor.

In recent times, West African peoples such as the HAUSA and FULANI from NIGERIA have settled in Sudan. Some were drawn by a desire to establish farms in the Gezira region; others came on their way to Islamic pilgrimages to Arabia.

The most numerous peoples of southern Sudan are the Dinka and Nuer herders. These people, particularly the Nuer, have often valued their autonomy and resisted authority. Other groups of this region include the Azande, Shilluk, and Nuba. (*See also* **Arabs in Africa, Colonialism in Africa, Deserts and Drought, Ethnic Groups and Identity, Genocide and Violence, History of Africa, Hunger and Famine, Islam in Africa, Livestock Grazing, Warfare.**)

Sudanic Empires of Western Africa

Sudanic Empires of Western Africa

* **sub-Saharan**   referring to Africa south
of the Sahara desert

The Sudanic empires of Western Africa were a group of powerful states that developed south of the SAHARA DESERT between the A.D 700s and 1500s. The most prominent of these states were GHANA, MALI, and Songhai. The Arabs called the whole stretch of land south of the desert *bilad al-sudan* ("the land of the blacks"). Thus the term "Sudan" came to mean the area ranging from the present-day nation of SUDAN through western Africa. The Sudanic empires developed vast commercial networks, trading grains and gold from the SAHEL and sub-Saharan* Africa for salt from the Sahara.

History and Government. Ghana, the first great Sudanic trading empire, was founded by Soninke peoples. By about 800 Ghana was a wealthy kingdom, and it reached its peak in the mid-1000s. Soon afterward the empire began to decline as the Almoravids, a Muslim group from North Africa, gained control of the Saharan trade routes and parts of the Sudan. Although Ghana survived until the 1200s, it never regained its former power.

In the early 1200s a group of southern Soninke peoples known as the Susu began gaining influence in the region. However, they were con-

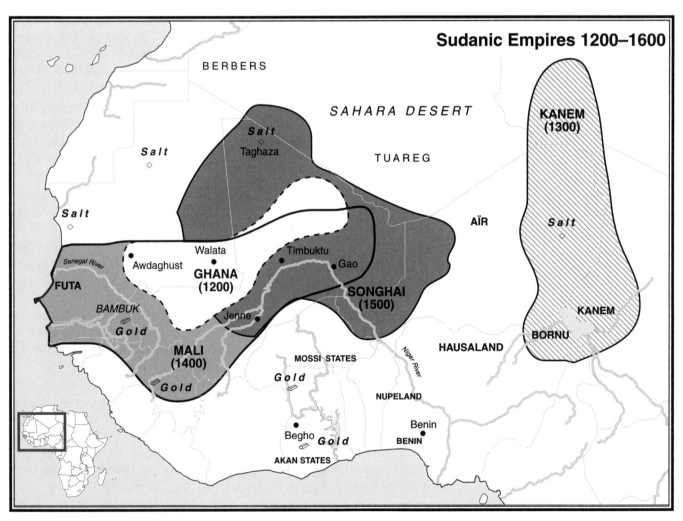

Sudanic Currency

Traders in the Sudanic empires used various types of money, including gold, copper, iron, shells, and strips of cloth. One of the most important currencies was gold, either in the form of dust or coins. Merchants weighed the dust against gold coins to determine its value. By the 1000s gold coinage had been adopted throughout the Muslim world. At about the same time, cowrie shells from the Maldive Islands in the Indian Ocean appeared in markets in Mali. Only in areas without access to cowrie shells did traders use cloth money.

* **tribute**   payment made by a smaller or weaker party to a more powerful one, often under the threat of force

* **pilgrimage**   journey to a shrine or sacred place

* **dynasty**   succession of rulers from the same family or group

* **succession**   determination of the person who will inherit the throne

* **monopoly**   exclusive control or domination of a particular type of business

* **Islam**   religion based on the teachings of the prophet Muhammad; religious faith of Muslims

quered in the mid-1200s by SUNDJATA KEÏTA, the king of the Malinke. Sundjata took over the remnants of Ghana and founded the empire of Mali. At its height in the 1300s, Mali stretched from the Atlantic coast in the west into the Sahara in the northeast. The BERBERS of the Sahara region paid tribute* to Mali and served in its armies. The most famous of Mali's rulers, MANSA MUSA, shaped the Islamic character of Mali and expanded the empire to its greatest size. In 1325, during a pilgrimage* to the holy city of Mecca in Arabia, he passed through EGYPT, where the people of CAIRO marveled at his wealth and generosity.

By the late 1300s Mali had lost its political influence over the Sahara. The TUAREG people of the desert took advantage of the empire's weakness and captured the trading city of TIMBUKTU. In the 1400s Songhai, the last of the great Sudanic empires, rose in power. SUNNI ALI, a Songhai ruler, chased the Tuareg from Timbuktu and gradually gained control of a large area around the middle NIGER RIVER. Songhai enjoyed its greatest power in the 1500s under the members of the Askiya dynasty*, who formed alliances with the Tuareg and extended the empire over large portions of the western Sudan. In 1591 MOROCCO conquered Songhai, bringing the 800-year history of the Sudanic empires to an end.

The Sudanic monarchs had great power, wealth, and dignity, and a wide social distance separated them from their subjects. Kings never spoke directly to their subjects, but used spokespersons, such as griots, the oral historians of the empire. The griots also served as counselors and settled legal disputes.

When a monarch died, there were often no clear rules about who should take over the throne. As a result, disputes over succession* were common. Dynasties survived primarily because they were not challenged by others. The Keita dynasty of Mali, for example, held power from the 1200s to 1500s and continued to rule over small chiefdoms after the break up of the empire.

Economy. Agriculture, fishing, and cattle raising were all important to the economies of the Sudanic empires. These activities produced a variety of products that stimulated trade. Women tended to dominate local trade and men generally controlled the long-distance Saharan routes. Merchants established a network of branches off the main commercial routes, and used relatives and slaves to help conduct their businesses.

Trade strengthened the power of the Sudanic rulers by bringing them wealth, connections with foreign merchants, and a near monopoly* over important products, such as metals and horses. As the empires grew, the trade routes became more well-established. The Arabic traveler IBN BATTUTA praised the safe trade routes he found in the Sahara and throughout the empire of Mali.

Religion. The Sudanic rulers were the first people in their kingdoms to convert to Islam*. They were drawn to the faith because they thought that Muslims represented a higher, more prosperous civilization, and Islam was seen as a powerful religion. Chiefs and kings adopted Muslim names, learned how to pray, and celebrated Muslim festivals. They asked Muslim religious leaders for blessings and gave them official roles in

* indigenous native to a certain place

state ceremonies. However, most rulers did not abandon their traditional beliefs. Instead, they attempted to add the spiritual protection of Islam to that offered by their indigenous* religions.

Most common people continued to follow their ancestral beliefs while adopting some aspects of Islam. Generally, Islam became the dominant faith only in certain market towns. Merchants often converted to Islam more readily because their life of constant travel separated them from the traditional culture at home. While some Sudanic rulers attempted to incorporate Islamic practices in their states, others did little to encourage the spread of Islam. (*See also* **Arabs in Africa, History of Africa, Islam in Africa, Kings and Kingship, North Africa: History and Cultures.**)

Suez Canal

The Suez Canal is an artificial waterway in EGYPT that links the Mediterranean and the Red Seas. Cut across the Isthmus of Suez, a strip of land connecting Africa and western Asia, the canal made it possible for ships to travel from Europe to Asia and back without sailing all the way around Africa.

The Suez Canal was not the first waterway built across part of Egypt. In ancient times, the Egyptians dug a channel that ran from the NILE RIVER to the Red Sea. The Romans later lengthened the canal, but in A.D. 775 the Arab rulers of Egypt destroyed it.

As trade between Europe and Asia increased in later centuries, various European nations considered building a canal across Suez to shorten trade routes. Each time the project was considered too difficult. Finally, in 1854, Egypt authorized a French engineer named Ferdinand de Lesseps to construct a canal. Work began two years later under the management of the Suez Canal Company, an association of European and Egyptian shareholders that owned the rights to operate the canal for 99 years. At first, the company forced unpaid or poorly paid Egyptian peasants to dig the canal by hand. Later, in response to international criticism, the company hired European workers with heavy machinery to complete the job.

When it was completed in 1869, the canal measured 100 miles long, 30 feet deep, and 100 feet wide. Its route passed through four lakes and had eight major bends. Several hundred ships used the Suez Canal during its first year of operation. In following decades both cargo and passenger traffic steadily increased, especially after 1950, when oil was first shipped from Persian Gulf oilfields to Europe by way of the canal. In 1956 the Egyptian government took control of the canal, and it has been managed since that time by the Egyptian Suez Canal Authority. Egypt closed the canal twice, from 1956 to 1957 and again from 1967 to 1975, because of conflicts with nearby Israel. The canal's busiest year was 1966, with 21,250 transits, or passages.

Today, usage of the Suez Canal has declined somewhat. Although engineers widened and deepened the canal several times to a final measurement of 590 feet wide and 53 feet deep, many modern tankers are too large to travel through the canal. In addition, a pipeline now carries great quantities of oil across the Suez Peninsula. Still, the Suez Canal remains an important route for ships transporting agricultural products from North America and Europe to Asia and for carrying petroleum products from the Middle East to European refineries. Other common cargoes include cement, metals, and fertilizers. (*See also* **Trade, Transportation.**)

Sufism

* **Islam** religion based on the teachings of the prophet Muhammad; religious faith of Muslims

* **indigenous** native to a certain place

* **nationalism** devotion to the interests and culture of one's country

Sufism, the mystical tradition of Islam*, has had a profound influence on the beliefs and practices of Muslims in Africa. Arabs from the Arabian Peninsula first brought Islam to Africa in the A.D. 600s. By the early 1200s various orders, or schools, of sufism had emerged in North Africa, based on the teachings of influential religious leaders.

Sufism reached its peak in Africa during the 1800s. At that time many new Sufi orders sprang up in northern and eastern Africa, such as the Sanusiyya founded by Muhammad ibn Ali-Sanusi. The new orders, led by the families of their founders, adopted different ideas and patterns of organization from the older ones. Instead of being based on a local tribe, the new orders drew members from various groups. They were the first to teach Islam in indigenous* languages instead of Arabic. They insisted on strict faithfulness to the Qur'an—the Islamic holy scriptures—and devotion to the prophet Muhammad.

During the colonial era some Sufi orders helped organize local resistance to foreign rule. The Sufi leader Umar al-Mukhtar led the forces fighting Italian power in LIBYA until his death in 1931. Two Sufi orders of SUDAN, the Mahdists and the Khatmiyya, formed political parties that supported Sudanese nationalism*. But not all Sufi leaders opposed the colonial powers. The Muridiyya in SENEGAL worked with colonial officials, despite government mistrust of the group.

Over time the Sufi brotherhoods grew more urbanized and became active in business. They valued Western education, and today a large percentage of educated Sudanese are members of Sufi families. Since independence Sufi groups such the Wahhabis in MALI and the Izala in NIGERIA have emerged to challenge the dominance of the established orders. The growth of African cities and the spread of modern systems of communication have helped new forms of Sufism to replace the traditional Sufi orders in many parts of the continent. (*See also* **Islam in Africa, Religion and Ritual.**)

Sundjata Keïta

**ca. 1205–1255
Founder of the Empire of Mali**

A brilliant military leader and skilled administrator, Sundjata Keïta founded the empire of MALI, one of the great SUDANIC EMPIRES OF WESTERN AFRICA. Under his rule Mali adopted various laws and customs that are still followed by the people of the region.

Born in the west African city of Dakajala, Sundjata was the second son of the ruler of Manding, a kingdom of the Mandinka people. When Sundjata was only seven years old, his father died and his elder brother,

75

Dankaran-Tuma, took the throne. Persecuted by his brother, Sundjata went into exile with his mother, sisters, and younger brother.

The king of Manding owed allegiance to the emperor of GHANA. When Sundjata's brother became king, Ghana was being torn apart by civil war and was in a state of decline. Another powerful monarch in the region, King Sumanguru Kante of Susu, gained control over much of Ghana and dominated the kingdom of Manding. Unable to defend Manding, Dankaran-Tuma gave up his throne and fled.

The king of Susu brought a reign of terror to Manding and put down several revolts by the Mandinka and the nearby Malinke people. These groups sent a secret mission to Sundjata, asking him to return. The ruler of the kingdom where Sundjata was living gave him an army to lead back to Manding. Sundjata returned to his homeland, and the Malinke revolted against Susu. A fierce battle led to the defeat of Susu and the destruction of its capital.

Under Sundjata's leadership, the Malinke won victory after victory over other kingdoms and peoples in West Africa. They eventually built a vast nation—the empire of Mali—which extended from TIMBUKTU to the Atlantic Ocean. Sundjata, who ruled Mali from 1235 to 1255, created a fairly loose governmental structure. He gave the various kingdoms and peoples in the empire a great deal of autonomy* and allowed each community to follow its own traditions and customs.

* **autonomy**   independent self-government

* **clan**   group of people descended from a common ancestor

Sundjata kept the roads of the empire secure, established new laws and rules, and created alliances among Malinke clans* and between Malinke clans and others. Because of his grand accomplishments, Sundjata is known by many names and prestigious titles in the Malinke ORAL TRADITION. Among these are Sundjata the King, Lord Lion, and Master Hunter with the Venerable Bearing.

Sunni Ali

1464–1492
Ruler of Songhai

* **dynasty**   succession of rulers from the same family or group

* **Islam**   religion based on the teachings of the prophet Muhammad; religious faith of Muslims

Sunni Ali was a member of the Sunni Muslim dynasty* that ruled the Songhai Empire of western Africa in the 1300s and 1400s. Known for his immense energy and leadership skills, he expanded the borders of the empire.

By the time Sunni Ali came to power, the Songhai kingdom had lost much of its influence over the Middle NIGER RIVER region. Even the key trading center of TIMBUKTU had been taken over by nomadic TUAREG herders. Sunni Ali led a successful campaign to capture territory along both sides of the river, stretching from present-day NIGERIA into what is now central MALI. In 1468 his forces recaptured Timbuktu.

Many of the scholars and leaders of Timbuktu fled the city after its defeat, and some of those who stayed were mistreated and even killed. Muslim leaders looked upon Sunni Ali as a tyrant and a murderer and questioned his devotion to Islam*. Nevertheless, the state he founded later grew into one of the most powerful and important empires in the SAHEL. (*See also* **Islam in Africa, Sudanic Empires of Western Africa**.)

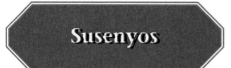

Susenyos

ca. 1580–ca. 1632
Emperor of Ethiopia

One of the most powerful emperors of ETHIOPIA, Susenyos attempted to change the Ethiopian Church. Soon after taking the throne in 1607, Susenyos decided that, for political and religious reasons, Ethiopia should accept the authority of the Catholic Church in Rome rather than the Coptic Church in ALEXANDRIA in Egypt. A Jesuit missionary, Pedro Páez, and Susenyos' brother Celakrestos encouraged the emperor in this matter, and he officially accepted the authority of Rome in 1622.

In 1625 Susenyos welcomed a Roman Catholic official named Alphonsus Mendes to his royal court. The official immediately began introducing Latin elements of Christianity into the Ethiopian church to make it more Roman Catholic in style. However, these efforts met with widespread public opposition and led to a series of revolts. Susenyos eventually gave the throne to his son FASILADAS, who expelled Mendes from Ethiopia and restored the authority of Alexandria. (*See also* **Christianity in Africa, Copts, Ethiopian Orthodox Church.**)

Swahili

The Swahili people live in towns and villages along a 1,000-mile stretch of the East African coastline, from SOMALIA to MOZAMBIQUE. Many also live on ZANZIBAR, Pemba, and the COMORO ISLANDS off the coast. The name Swahili, an Arabic term meaning "people of the coast," was given to them by Arabs who conquered the region in the early 1700s. However, the Swahili rarely use this name, preferring to identify themselves by names that refer to individual towns.

The Swahili are Muslims and use both the Arabic and the Roman alphabets for writing. Their language, Swahili, belongs to the Bantu family of African languages but includes many words borrowed from Arabic. It has become a common language of trade and communication throughout eastern Africa.

* **maritime** related to the sea or shipping

Swahili civilization, unlike that of neighboring African peoples, is urban, maritime*, and based on commerce. Since they first established towns along the coast before A.D. 1000, the Swahili have been agents in trade between Africa and Asia. Their economy suffered when Great Britain ended the SLAVE TRADE in the 1800s and more recently when long-distance shipping trade across the Indian Ocean declined. The Swahili are noted for their large, stone-built houses and towns, their elegant clothing and food, and for a high level of literary achievement, especially in poetry. (*See also* **Bantu Peoples.**)

Swaziland

Swaziland is a tiny landlocked kingdom located between SOUTH AFRICA and MOZAMBIQUE. Ruled by a hereditary king, Mswati III, Swaziland is the last absolute monarchy in Africa.

History and Government. Caught in the conflict between the British and Dutch in southern Africa during the late 1800s, Swaziland

77

Kingdom of Swaziland

POPULATION:
1,082,289 (2000 estimated population)

AREA:
6,704 sq. mi. (17,364 sq. km)

LANGUAGES:
siSwati and English (both official); Zulu, Afrikaans

NATIONAL CURRENCY:
Lilangeni (plural: Emalangeni)

PRINCIPAL RELIGIONS:
Christian 60%, Traditional 40%

CITIES:
Mbabane (administrative capital), 47,000 (1990 est.); Lobamba (legislative capital), 30,000 (1988); Manzini, Mhlambanyati, Tshaneni, Bunya, Goedgegun

ANNUAL RAINFALL:
35–90 in. (900–2,300 mm) throughout most of country

ECONOMY:
GDP per capita: $4,200 (1999 est.)

PRINCIPAL PRODUCTS AND EXPORTS:
Agricultural: corn, livestock, sugarcane, fruits, cotton, rice, sorghum, tobacco, peanuts, timber
Manufacturing: milled sugar, cotton, processed meat and wood, chemicals, machinery, beverages, consumer goods, paper milling
Mining: iron ore, coal

GOVERNMENT:
Independence from Britain, 1968. Hereditary monarchy with membership in the British Commonwealth. Governing bodies: Libandla (legislature) with Senate and House of Assembly; prime minister appointed by the monarch.

HEADS OF STATE SINCE INDEPENDENCE:
1968–1982 King Sobhuza II
1982–1983 Dzeliwe Shongwe (regent)
1983–1986 Ntombi Thawala (regent)
1986– King Mswati III

ARMED FORCES:
2,657 (1983 est.)

EDUCATION:
No information on education system; literacy rate 77% (1995 est.)

---

* **protectorate** weak state under the control and protection of a strong state

* **apartheid** policy of racial segregation enforced by the white government of South Africa to maintain political, economic, and social control over the country's blacks, Asians, and people of mixed ancestry

became a British protectorate* in 1903. In 1968 it achieved independence under King SOBHUZA II. A British-style parliament was created at that time, but Sobhuza dissolved it five years later, and in 1979 he established a new parliament with very little authority.

Sobhuza was a shrewd politician and capable ruler. He came to terms with his powerful neighbor South Africa, even though he opposed the racist apartheid* government there. He also founded a private fund called the Tibiyo Taka Ngwane that was free from both taxes and parliamentary control. The fund owned a major piece of every foreign investment in the country, forming a powerful base of capital to support the king's plans.

Sobhuza II's death in 1982 set off a power struggle within Swaziland. Mswati III, the king's second-youngest son, was named the successor. His mother ruled until 1986, when he reached his eighteenth birthday and assumed power. Mswati immediately fired the prime minister, dismissed his council of advisers, and appointed new people to his cabinet. He has been under great pressure to end the monarchy and transform Swaziland into a democracy. However, despite occasional pro-democracy protests and violence, the young king seems determined to retain his ancient title.

The king has control over the government at all levels. He appoints many members of parliament, which consists of a national assembly and senate. Traditional assemblies loyal to the king then choose candidates for a public parliamentary election. The king chooses his cabinet from the assembly, and appoints the prime minister as well.

See color plate 8, vol. 3.

Geography, Economy, and Culture. Covering less than 7,000 square miles, Swaziland has a very diverse geography. The western portion is mountainous, with a cool, moist climate. Central Swaziland is a gently rolling plateau that receives enough rainfall to permit commercial agriculture. This area is the country's most densely populated region and the source of most of its food. Eastern Swaziland consists of low-lying land with good soil but little rainfall. The Lebombo Plateau, which resembles central Swaziland, stretches along the nation's eastern border.

Swaziland's temperate climate and many rivers make it ideal for agricultural activity. Its main export crop is sugar, but it also produces pineapples and other citrus fruit. Timber from western Swaziland also plays an important role in the national economy. Although the country once had abundant coal and iron ore reserves, these resources have been largely exhausted. Manufacturing, especially the processing of timber and food items, contributes over one third of the country's gross domestic product (GDP)*. TOURISM is another important source of revenue.

Most of the people in Swaziland speak the siSwati language and share a common cultural heritage. Within this ethnic group, there are several different clans* arranged in a hierarchy*. The Nkosi Dlamini, the clan of the Swazi kings, dominates the other clans. The members of each clan traditionally assume specific roles in society. For example, women from certain clans, including the Simelane, Ndwandwe, and Nxumalo, are married into the royal clan to serve as queen mothers. People from some other clans, such as the Fakudze and Zwane, become national officials.

Although many Swazi practice CHRISTIANITY, first introduced by Western missionaries in the mid-1800s, they continue to hold traditional beliefs about the spirit world. Ancestors are revered and sacrifices are offered to them to ensure good luck and to prevent misfortune. In cases of illness or other trouble, many people seek help from diviners*, who explain how to solve problems caused by angered spirits. Others consult traditional healers, whose remedies often combine the use of modern medicines and ancient religious practices. (*See also* **Colonialism in Africa, Kings and Kingship.**)

* **gross domestic product (GDP)** total value of goods and services produced and consumed within a country

* **clan** group of people descended from a common ancestor

* **hierarchy** organization of a group into higher and lower levels

* **diviner** person who predicts the future or explains the causes of misfortune

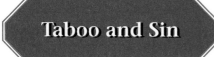

Taboo and Sin

* **deity** god or goddess

Sin and taboo are two ways of regulating behavior that are used by African religions and African social systems. A sin is a wicked act that breaks the laws of a deity* or deities. It is also a deliberate act—the sinner knows that he or she is committing a sin. Taboo is a type of social rule that must not be broken. If a person breaks a taboo, even unknowingly, serious misfortune is believed to result.

Sins. Sins are offenses against a god or goddess and are considered fundamentally wrong or evil. They are defined only by religious beliefs and teachings. Therefore, a sin is not necessarily illegal in terms of human law. A person may commit a sin that is not a crime or a crime that is not a sin.

African religions have various ideas about sin and how it is punished. Some faiths say that people are reborn from earlier lifetimes in order to pay for past sins. According to other religions, there is an afterlife during which the dead are punished for sin or rewarded for virtue. Some religions teach that people who commit sins but later repent, regretting their sinful acts and wishing to make up for them, may be purified by religious rituals. Concepts of sin, repentance, and purification are forms of social control. They encourage the specific moral behavior that all those who share a particular religion have agreed is desirable.

Taboo. The idea of taboo controls moral behavior as well. Most taboos involve certain prohibitions, entry into sacred places, or kinds of physical contact. Taboos in central Africa forbid pregnant women and small children to have anything to do with a person who has committed adultery*. A child's life is thought to be endangered if an adulterer eats food cooked on the same fire used to cook the child's food. The taboo breaker is not the adulterer, however, but the child's mother, who puts herself and her child at risk.

African taboos may involve such acts as walking on a dog's grave, touching a corpse, or failing to show the proper respect to certain beings, such as rulers or twins. In some parts of Africa the birth of twins is considered an extremely powerful event in which the deities interrupt the normal course of human birth. Twins are surrounded by taboos all their lives and must be treated correctly. Among the Lele of CONGO (KINSHASA), if a stranger who is a twin arrives at a village, the village must perform a ceremony of twin-entry or its hunting will not prosper.

Most Africans believe that if they break a taboo, punishment will follow swiftly and automatically—whether or not they intended to do wrong. The punishment may fall on the individual who broke the taboo, his or her relatives, or the whole community. Because any member of a group may suffer if someone breaks a taboo, community members often watch each other to make sure that taboos are observed. The effect of breaking a taboo can be undone if the taboo breaker performs the necessary acts of purification.

The concept of taboo reflects a view of the universe as having a natural world, a human social order, and a divine order. The divine order regulates the natural world through rules that humans must follow. The rules do not always have an obvious moral significance—in other words, they may not appear to be concerned with questions of good or evil. Generally, however, they are important for maintaining a community's customs. Respect taboos, such as taboos against insulting a leader, support the political system, and sexual taboos, such as those that punish incest or adultery, protect the institution of the family. When a society changes its ideas about the things that are important to it, old taboos fall out of favor, and new ones may arise. When this happens, it is almost as if a simple purification occurred, after which the old taboos no longer had any power. In a similar manner, strong community ties have become weaker in many parts of Africa, and the individual has gained importance at the expense of the group. In this situation, taboos are no longer enforced by the community, so it is up to each person to obey the taboos. In this way, taboos become more of a personal honor system than a community rule. (*See also* **Divination and Oracles, Religion and Ritual**.)

* **adultery** sexual relationship between a married person and someone other than his or her spouse

* **incest** sexual relations between relatives

Tafawa Balewa, Abubakar

1912–1966
Prime Minister of Nigeria

* **protectorate** weak state under the control and protection of a strong state

* **Islamic** relating to Islam, the religion based on the teachings of the prophet Muhammad

* **authoritarian** relating to strong leadership with unrestricted powers

The first prime minister of NIGERIA, Abubakar Tafawa Balewa helped keep a newly independent Nigeria united in the early 1960s despite serious ethnic and regional differences. A HAUSA born in northern Nigeria, Abubakar became a schoolmaster in 1933 and published a prizewinning novel the next year. However, politics was his true calling. In 1946 Abubakar became a member of the legislature of Northern Nigeria, a British protectorate* at that time. He called for the reform of the rule of emirs, the Islamic* princes of the region. Abubakar held other government positions during the 1950s, including vice president of the Northern People's Congress, minister of works, and minister of transport.

Elected prime minister of the Nigerian Federation in 1957, Abubakar held the same office after Nigeria gained independence in 1960. He soon gained a reputation for modesty and integrity and became widely respected both within the country and in other nations.

As leader of Nigeria, Abubakar faced many challenges. He had to deal with fierce political rivals, the authoritarian* rule of his party's leader, Ahmadu BELLO, and a nation divided by ethnic groups. Abubakar's greatest test came in 1964, when political crisis threatened to tear Nigeria apart. He boldly restructured the government and saved the nation from disintegration. However, Abubakar's success was short-lived, and in January 1966 a bloody mutiny erupted during which he was kidnapped and assassinated. He is remembered as one of Nigeria's finest politicians and leaders.

Tanzania

* **socialist** relating to an economic or political system based on the idea that the government or groups of workers should own and run the means of production and distribution of goods

See color plate 13, vol. 2.

The East African country of Tanzania was once one of the most prosperous places on the continent. For centuries, merchants traveled from Arabia and India to trade with the residents of towns along Tanzania's Indian Ocean coast. Today, however, the nation struggles because years of colonial neglect and socialist* reforms have made it one of the poorest and most debt-ridden countries in Africa.

GEOGRAPHY

Tanzania borders the Indian Ocean just below the equator. A narrow, fertile plain runs along its 500-mile coastline. From there the land gradually rises to a central plateau. A range of medium-size mountains extends through central Tanzania. Another, much higher, chain of mountains forms the country's western border with ZAMBIA, MALAWI, and CONGO (KINSHASA). Between the two mountain ranges lies the Rift Valley, which divides Tanzania roughly in half. At the northern end of the valley is a series of high peaks, including Mount Kilimanjaro, Africa's highest mountain.

Tanzania contains more surface water than any other African nation. Lake Victoria, Africa's largest lake, is located in the northwest, and Lakes Nyasa and Tanganyika lie along the western border. In addition, Tanzania has a number of smaller lakes and major rivers.

Tanzania

The nation's climate varies considerably from one region to another. The coastal plain and the northern inland areas receive ample rainfall, and most of the country's agriculture takes place in these regions. The central plateau is hotter and drier, and the mountainous uplands are cooler with heavy rainfall.

HISTORY AND GOVERNMENT

Evidence of coastal trading settlements in Tanzania dates to the A.D. 700s and possibly earlier. About this time traders from Arabia arrived and mixed with the indigenous* African population. Over the next several hundred years they formed a unique SWAHILI society. Their trading settlements flourished until shortly before the arrival of Portuguese traders in the 1500s.

Colonial Rule. European colonization of the region began with its occupation by the Germans in 1884. They created the colony of German East Africa, which included Tanganyika (now part of Tanzania), RWANDA, BURUNDI, and ZANZIBAR. After Germany's defeat in WORLD WAR I, the League of Nations* assigned Britain to administer Tanganyika.

* **indigenous**   native to a certain place

* **League of Nations** organization founded to promote international peace and security; it functioned from 1920 to 1946

82

* **exploit**   to take advantage of; to make productive use of

* **sisal**   plant whose leaves contain a stiff fiber used for making rope

* **nationalist**   devoted to the interests and culture of one's country

* **coup**   sudden, often violent, overthrow of a ruler or government

Jewels of Nature

Tanzania boasts several spectacular natural wonders that attract visitors from around the world. In the north is Mount Kilimanjaro, Africa's highest peak. Although just south of the equator, it is permanently capped with snow and ice. The precious blue stone tanzanite is found only on its southwestern slopes. Lake Victoria, on the border with Uganda, is Africa's largest lake and the second-largest freshwater lake in the world. Lake Tanganyika, in the western Rift Valley, is the world's longest freshwater lake, stretching over a distance of 410 miles. Its 4,700 foot depth also makes it the world's second deepest lake.

The British focused on exploiting* Tanganyika's natural resources. They established mines and raised crops for export, such as coffee, tea, sisal*, cotton, tobacco, and cashews. These are still the country's main agricultural products. The British appointed indigenous rulers as government agents to recruit labor, collect taxes, and monitor crop production. This association with colonial officials undermined the authority of the indigenous rulers. When a movement for independence emerged in the 1950s, conflicts developed between these traditional rulers and members of nationalist* groups, who saw them as allies of the British.

Independence Under Nyerere. In 1961 Tanganyika won its independence and Julius NYERERE, head of the Tanganyika African National Union (TANU), became the country's first president. Once in power, Nyerere moved to ensure that TANU would dominate the political and social life of the country. He banned opposition parties and placed the trade unions under TANU control. In 1965 a new constitution made the country a single-party state.

On the nearby island of Zanzibar, Nyerere's political allies staged a coup*, overthrowing the elected government in 1964. At their request, Tanganyika and Zanzibar were joined to form the United Republic of Tanzania the following year.

Nyerere launched a series of socialist reforms that involved state control of industries and reorganizing agricultural production. In 1967 he announced the Arusha Declaration, a program designed to move rural people to planned villages to increase crop production and improve delivery of public services. Specifically, the plan was supposed to create communities that worked closely together, which in turn would encourage more advanced production methods, promote group production of crops, and provide more efficient access to education, health services, and drinking water. Instead, the plan turned out to be a disaster. People were forced to abandon their farms and relocate. Within a few years agricultural production dropped dramatically, forcing Tanzania to import large quantities of food. The country fell deeply into debt.

Restructuring. In the early 1980s, in return for assistance from the World Bank and the International Monetary Fund, Tanzania agreed to sell its state industries, reduce the size of the government, and lift restrictions on imports and foreign investment. However, this program failed to stabilize the economy. In 1985 Nyerere resigned his presidency, and Ali Hassan Mwinyi took over. Mwinyi, too, was unable to turn the economy around. As the situation worsened, people began to press for political change.

In 1991 Tanzania passed the Political Parties Act, allowing multiparty elections. Four years later Ben Mkapa of the Chama Cha Mapinduzi party won the presidency, but his opponents received over 40 percent of the vote. Although the nation is now a republic, the assembly and the courts are weak and the president still determines government policy.

The city of Dodoma, in central Tanzania, has been selected as the site of the nation's new capital and the government has been gradually moving there. Meanwhile, many administrative offices remain in the old capital of DAR ES SALAAM.

ECONOMY AND CULTURE

Tanzania is one of Africa's least developed countries. Agriculture, which employs over 90 percent of the population, dominates the economy. But in recent years declining prices and periodic droughts have severely hurt farmers' incomes. In other areas of the economy, mining and TOURISM show some promise. Gemstone mining has grown and new gold deposits have been discovered. Tourism is rebounding after years of decline, as game reserves along the border with KENYA attract foreign visitors. However, Tanzania's other industries remain underdeveloped, partly because of the poor condition of the nation's infrastructure*.

One of Tanzania's strengths is its social unity. Unlike many African nations, Tanzania did not adopt the official language of its European colonial rulers. Although the country has over 120 language groups, most Tanzanians speak Swahili, which is also the main language used by the media. The presence of a common language, combined with the long-term rule of a single leader (Nyerere), have helped spare Tanzania the ethnic strife that has troubled many other nations.

Most of Tanzania's population is divided among Christians, Muslims, and those who practice traditional religions. However, Zanzibar is pri-

* **infrastructure**   basic framework of a society and its economy, which includes roads, bridges, port facilities, airports, and other public works

Mount Kilimanjaro, in northeastern Tanzania, looms high over the surrounding plateau. Rising to 19,341 feet, Kilimanjaro is the highest peak in Africa.

United Republic of Tanzania

POPULATION:
35,306,126 (2000 estimated population)

AREA:
364,928 sq. mi. (945,166 sq. km)

LANGUAGES:
Swahili and English (both official); Chagga, Gogo, Ha, Haya, Luo, Maasai, others

NATIONAL CURRENCY:
Tanzanian shilling

PRINCIPAL RELIGIONS:
Christian 45%, Muslim 35%, Traditional 20%

CITIES:
Dar es Salaam (capital), 2,347,000 (2001 est.); Dodoma (to be new capital) 1,238,000 (1999 est.); Zanzibar City, Tanga, Mwanza, Arusha, Morogoro

ANNUAL RAINFALL:
30–100 in. (770–2,570 mm), varying by region

ECONOMY:
GDP per capita: $550 (1999 est.)

PRINCIPAL PRODUCTS AND EXPORTS:
Agricultural: coffee, sisal, tea, cotton, cashews, tobacco, cloves, wheat, fruits, vegetables, livestock
Manufacturing: agricultural processing, oil refining, footwear, cement, textiles, wood products, fertilizer
Mining: diamonds, petroleum.

GOVERNMENT:
Tanganyika gained independence from UN trusteeship administered by Britain in 1961; Zanzibar became independent from Britain in 1963; Tanganyika and Zanzibar united under the name United Republic of Tanzania in 1964. Republic with president elected by universal suffrage. Zanzibar elects own president for domestic matters. Governing body: 274-seat Bunge (National Assembly).

HEADS OF STATE SINCE INDEPENDENCE:
1961–1985 President Julius Nyerere
1985–1995 President Ali Hassan Mwinyi
1995– President Benjamin William Mkapa

ARMED FORCES:
34,000 (2001 est.)

EDUCATION:
Compulsory for ages 7–14; literacy rate 68%

* **secular** nonreligious; connected with everyday life

* **fundamentalist** member of a group that emphasizes a strict interpretation of religious beliefs

marily Muslim, while northeastern Tanzania is largely Christian. The country is officially a secular* state, but in recent years Christian and Muslim fundamentalists* have sought to gain greater political influence. (*See also* **Arabs in Africa, Colonialism in Africa, Independence Movements, Languages, Minerals and Mining, Wildlife and Game Parks**.)

Téwodros

ca. 1820–1868
Emperor of Ethiopia

* **feudal** relating to an economic and political system in which individuals gave services to a landlord in return for protection and the use of land

* **vernacular** native language or dialect of a region or country

Considered the first modern ruler of Ethiopia, Téwodros set out to reunite his country, then a cluster of warring states. Born to noble parents and originally named Kasa, he was educated at Christian monasteries. He became a bandit in the early 1840s, and in 1852 he launched a military campaign against feudal* chiefs throughout Ethiopia. Three years later, he was crowned emperor and took the name Téwodros, meaning "King of Kings."

Téwodros had mixed success during his years as emperor. He pioneered the use of Ethiopia's modern vernacular* language, Amharic, over the classical literary language, Ge'ez, which had dominated for centuries. His attempts to reorganize local government angered local leaders and left him struggling to hold Ethiopia together. He made efforts to modernize his military but was unable to convince the British to give him the advanced equipment he desired. In 1862 Téwodros imprisoned a British official and other foreigners after the British failed to acknowledge a letter of friendship. The British responded by sending a military expedition to the emperor's fortress in 1868. Surrounded by British troops, Téwodros chose to commit suicide rather than submit to them.

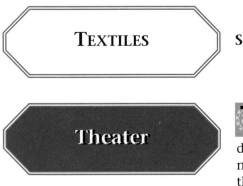

TEXTILES

See *Crafts.*

Theater

* **indigenous**   native to a certain place

* **ritual**   ceremony that follows a set pattern

* **Islamic**   relating to Islam, the religion based on the teachings of the prophet Muhammad

Theater in Africa takes many different forms and comes from diverse roots. Indigenous* customs, such as storytelling, ritual*, dance, and masquerades, are the oldest types of theater on the continent. In North Africa and other areas dominated by Islamic* culture, theater often includes reciting popular tales and acting out religious stories, such as the deaths of the grandsons of the prophet Muhammad. Since the arrival of Europeans, Africans have also staged plays in the style of Western theater—dramas and comedies based on scripts.

Today, African artists often combine various forms to create new styles of theater. For example, many modern African plays are Western in structure but include traditional elements. In many cases, African plays deal with controversial political and social issues.

Traditional Theater. The types of performance that existed in Africa before the arrival of Europeans are generally referred to as traditional theater. Some traditional theater is performed for entertainment, such as the storytelling of the Akan people of GHANA. Other traditional theater has important religious and social meaning. Examples of such performances include the ancient ritual dramas and dances of the KHOISAN people of southern Africa; the spectacular masquerades performed in SIERRA LEONE, NIGERIA, and Ghana; and the songs and ritual stories acted out by the XHOSA and ZULU people in southern Africa.

Traditional theater in all African cultures shares certain features. It does not have a script or a "correct" version that performers must follow. Characters are not portrayed as individuals but as general types, such as the dishonest merchant, the prostitute, or the foreigner. Performances often criticize or make fun of political and social targets, such as corrupt chiefs or greedy prophets of foreign religions. Song, music, and dance are highly important elements of the performance.

African traditional theater is a group activity, often without boundaries between creators, performers, and audience. Unlike modern plays, traditional rituals and tales are not written by individual playwrights. They have been molded from the culture and customs of an entire community and are passed on by memory from generation to generation. Rather than taking place on a stage at a planned time and date, performances are part of the social and cultural activities associated with daily life and with major events such as birth, INITIATION RITES, hunting, marriage, SPIRIT POSSESSION, and death.

The People's Theater

Popular theater is aimed at ordinary people, such as students and rural villagers. In Africa this type of theater combines traditional and Western elements and uses live music and dance in addition to acting. Performed in local languages, it often has timely or local themes.

Most popular theater companies are independent groups operating without the sup-port or control of universities and government agencies. The groups travel frequently, and sometimes their performances carry powerful messages. In South Africa during the 1980s, plays put on by black trade unions increased workers' political awareness and strengthened opposition to racist laws.

A good example of African traditional theater is the Koteba of MALI. This light-hearted performance has two parts. The first consists of music, chanting, and dancing, with the audience participating. The second part is a series of short plays and skits made up by performers. These comic presentations make fun of character types such as the blind man, the miser, the leper, and others. The official theater company of Mali, the National Koteba, works to preserve the techniques of traditional performance.

The Colonial Era. During the colonial era European authorities discouraged or even banned some forms of traditional theater. Most colonists had little respect for non-Western culture. In addition, Europeans believed that most traditional theater was linked to African religious practices, which they wanted to eliminate and replace with Christianity.

Europeans introduced new styles of theater, as well as new subject matter, to Africa. Missionaries taught elements of Christianity by having people act out scenes from the Bible. Students performed short plays in school. Europeans in major colonial cities established theater companies that presented white audiences with familiar plays in European-style settings. In EGYPT in the late 1800s, a movement to translate European literature into Arabic led to Arabic versions of French plays. They were performed with Egyptian slang and settings to make them more understandable to local audiences.

Colonial administrators also used theater as a means of communicating with and educating Africans. In the 1930s in Nyasaland (now MALAWI), plays were staged for African audiences to promote health care. In the 1950s a play called *The False Friend* encouraged farmers to adopt new agricultural techniques.

Despite colonial domination, Africans continued to perform traditional theater whenever possible, and their performances reflected the changes that were taking place in African life. During rituals of spirit possession in southern MOZAMBIQUE, performers began to impersonate foreigners. Elsewhere, Africans created dances, masks, and songs that imitated and also mocked the culture of the white colonists. Traditional theater sometimes took on political significance, such as in KENYA, where Africans performed indigenous rituals during the MAU MAU rebellion against colonial authorities.

As young Africans studied Western literature in colonial schools, some of them began writing new plays in the Western style, using both African and European languages and themes. The Egyptian dramatist Tawfiq al-Hakim wrote plays based on legends and myths from both European and Arabic culture. In southern Africa, Herbert Dhlomo wrote a play in English about a Xhosa legend.

Modern Theater. By the 1930s modern African theater was emerging, with new styles and wider recognition. Egypt became a major theatrical center not just of North Africa but of the entire Arab Middle East. Visits by Egyptian theater companies inspired the growth of theater in

Theater

African theater productions often include music, dancing, and storytelling. In this picture, members of the Somali National Theater Company perform in Mogadishu, Somalia.

* **apartheid** policy of racial segregation enforced by the white government of South Africa to maintain political, economic, and social control over the country's blacks, Asians, and people of mixed ancestry

MOROCCO and TUNISIA. Throughout Africa, playwrights began experimenting with new subject matter.

For many African playwrights, theater offered a way to express views on important issues and perhaps even to bring about social or political change. Beginning in the late 1950s, South African playwrights such as Athol FUGARD wrote about people living in the shadow of apartheid*. In the 1970s the Black Consciousness movement in South Africa argued that before Africans could achieve political freedom, they must liberate their traditional culture from the restrictions imposed by white authorities. Theater groups such as the Peoples' Experimental Theatre stood trial under South Africa's Terrorism Act for presenting plays that the government considered dangerous or possibly revolutionary.

As other African nations were freed from colonial rule in the 1960s, independence brought new energy to theater. Many writers rejected colonial influences and began to use traditional elements in creative ways. West African playwright Ola Rotimi wrote in English but added African PROVERBS and expressions to his plays. Focusing on episodes from African history, his works included *Kurunmi* (1969), a play about wars among the YORUBA people.

While some playwrights explored the effects of colonialism on Africa, others emphasized African social problems. In her play *The Dilemma of a Ghost* (1964), Ghanaian writer Ama Ata Aidoo addresses the subject of conflicting cultures by showing the turmoil in a village when a young man introduces his African-American wife. Marriage and family relationships form the material of many plays with social messages. Daudo Kano and Adamu dan Gogo of Nigeria criticized the practice of polygamy* in *Tabarmar Kunya* (*A Matter of Shame,* 1969).

Important modern playwrights have come from all parts of Africa. Many of these artists continue to play a role in changing the social and political directions of their countries. Izz al-Din of Morocco is known for his works on the subject of revolution. In his play *Thawrat Sahib al-Himar* (*The Donkey-Owner's Revolt,* 1971), the heroine confronts her male-dominated society and questions its practices. Nigerian writer Wole SOYINKA, the first African to win the Nobel Prize for Literature, has written plays criticizing aspects of modern Nigerian society and politics. Kabwe Kasoma of ZAMBIA and Tse-gaye Gabre-Medhim of ETHIOPIA have attempted to shape the development of their countries by writing plays that expose the truth behind historical events and cultural tensions. In some African nations, such playwrights—like other writers—have been jailed, exiled, or even killed for expressing their views. Kenyan playwright Ngugi wa THIONG'O was arrested for criticizing the government in his plays, and he eventually left Kenya so that he could work safely.

In recent decades, African theater has been expanding both within the continent and worldwide. Many African nations, including BENÍN and IVORY COAST, host local theater festivals, and an international association of performers is based in CONGO (BRAZZAVILLE). The International Theater for Development Festival, held every two years in Ouagadougou, BURKINA FASO, promotes theater that is used to encourage social change or to debate important issues in African life. Some African plays and musicals, such as *Sarafina!* (1990) have become popular hits in the United States and other countries, and many African performing groups now bring African theater of all varieties to audiences around the world. (*See also* **Dance, Masks and Masquerades, Music and Song, Oral Tradition.**)

* **polygamy** marriage in which a man has more than one wife or a woman has more than one husband

Thuku, Harry

1895–1970
Kenyan political leader

* **nationalist** devoted to the interests and culture of one's country

H arry Thuku led a nationalist* group in KENYA that opposed the land and labor policies of the British colonial government. Born into a poor family in northern Kenya, he attended a missionary school. At the age of 16, he traveled to NAIROBI, where he worked as a messenger before being jailed on minor charges. After his release from prison in 1913, he worked for a newspaper, the *Leader of British East Africa,* and began to learn about political issues. He was especially angered by agricultural issues and by the system of forced labor, in which colonial leaders forced laborers to work for low wages.

Under British colonial rule some of Kenya's best farmland had been given to European settlers. Africans, forced off their land and desperate for work, had to take jobs with low wages and poor working conditions. In the early 1920s the colonial government raised the taxes paid by African workers. The move angered many Kenyans, who formed political groups such as the East African Association (EAA) to fight the colonial land distribution and labor systems. Thuku became the first president of the EAA.

In 1922 Thuku was arrested, and the EAA staged demonstrations throughout Kenya in protest. During the uprising colonial troops killed 20 people in Nairobi. Thuku spent about nine years in detention, using his time to study agriculture. When he returned home in 1930, he worked on his own farm, which became one of the most successful in Kenya. (*See also* **Colonialism in Africa, Labor, Land Ownership.**)

Timbuktu

* **Islamic** relating to Islam, the religion based on the teaching of the prophet Muhammad

* **mosque** Muslim place of worship

* **sub-Saharan** referring to Africa south of the Sahara desert

Located near the NIGER RIVER in northern MALI, the town of Timbuktu rose to greatness as a center of trade in the 1300s. It was a stop on the caravan routes that crossed the SAHARA DESERT, and river traffic linked it with regions to the southeast and southwest. Culturally, Timbuktu was a point of connection between Islamic* North Africa and the civilizations of western Africa. The city attracted merchants, scholars, and students from every direction.

Timbuktu may have originated as a seasonal camp for the BERBERS, Saharan nomads who brought their livestock to water and pasture along the banks of the Niger. By the late 1200s it had become part of the empire of Mali. In 1325 the Malian ruler MANSA MUSA visited the city and ordered that a mosque* be constructed there. Known as Djinguereber, or "The Great Mosque," it has been enlarged and repaired many times and still stands. In the 1350s the great Arab traveler IBN BATTUTA stopped in Timbuktu during an African journey that included the leading cities of Mali.

Timbuktu reached its peak in the 1500s, when it was part of the Songhai Empire. Traders passed through the city carrying gold from sub-Saharan* Africa to the Mediterranean coast. The Sankore Mosque, the city's second large mosque, was a center of advanced study in Islamic law and religion. Distinguished scholars taught students who spread their teachings widely in western Africa. The city's glory was shattered in 1591, when an invading force from MOROCCO defeated the Songhai and took over much of their empire. The Moroccans made Timbuktu the capital of Songhai and set up local rulers called pashas. The pashas soon shook off the reins of Moroccan control and ruled Timbuktu as an independent state until the early 1800s. However, weakened by rivalries among the pashas, Timbuktu's power and trade gradually declined.

From the 1770s until 1893, Timbuktu was repeatedly invaded by desert-dwelling TUAREGS and by neighboring states. During those years European explorers competed for the prize of being the first to travel to Timbuktu and back safely. The honor went to Frenchman René Caillié, who managed to visit the city and return to Europe with an account of it in 1828. Timbuktu came under French rule in 1893 and remained part of French colonial Africa until Mali gained its independence in 1960. Today Timbuktu is a popular tourist destination. (*See also* **Sudanic Empires of Western Africa, Travel and Exploration.**)

Tinubu, Madame

1805–1887
Nigerian merchant

Madame Tinubu was a Nigerian woman who flourished as both a trader and a politician. Her people rewarded her services with the title *iyalode,* the highest honor a woman could receive, and she has become a legend.

Tinubu spent her life in towns on the southwestern Nigerian coast that traded with Europeans. Born in Abeokuta, she was married in about 1832 to a prince who later became king of the city-state of LAGOS. As a merchant in Lagos, Tinubu traded local products for a variety of European imports. As a politician, she became deeply involved in rivalries within the ruling class of Lagos. She grew wealthy and powerful but gained enemies who resented her success.

In the 1850s the British began intervening in the political situation in Lagos. They regarded Madame Tinubu as a "terror" who promoted the SLAVE TRADE and caused trouble. In 1856 she was forced to leave Lagos. Returning to Abeokuta, she rebuilt her business and again became active in politics. Today a plaza in Abeokuta is named after her, and her tomb is a tourist attraction. In Lagos a major street and square bear her name. (*See also* **Nigeria, Trade, Women in Africa.**)

Tippu Tip

ca. 1837–1905
Arab trader and ruler

* **sultanate** territory ruled by a Muslim leader called a sultan

Hamed bin Muhammed el-Murjebi, known as Tippu Tip, was an Arab trader on the CONGO RIVER who established a powerful empire during the late 1800s. Working as an ivory merchant between the east coast and Lake Tanganyika, Tippu Tip gradually built up a military force and gained control of the Upper Congo region.

During the 1800s the sultanate* of ZANZIBAR had taken over the SWAHILI trade routes dealing in ivory and slaves. Zanzibar's Sultan BARGHASH IBN SA'ID gave sections of one of these trade routes between the coast and the interior to Tippu Tip and to Mirambo, a Nywamwezi chief.

Both Tippu Tip and Mirambo became powerful independent rulers in the region. However, when Mirambo lost the sultan's trust, Tippu Tip gained control over the trade route. The sultan hoped that Tippu Tip could prevent the Belgians, led by Henry Morton STANLEY, from sending ivory down the Congo River to the western coast of Africa. The sultan wanted to keep his monopoly* on the supply of ivory for trade in Zanzibar.

* **monopoly** exclusive control or domination of a particular type of business

Named governor of the Upper Congo region, Tippu Tip had authority over a large territory. He appointed his own officials, including many Arab traders, and administered justice. He also negotiated an arrangement between Zanzibar and the Belgians and kept peace among the competing local chiefs. Tippu Tip is a perfect example of a trader who, in an effort to make more money, actually turned into a strong political leader. Because he temporarily owned the only firearms in the area, he was able to maintain political domination over a large area. In 1891 Tippu Tip returned to Zanzibar, where he died. Soon afterward his empire was conquered by European forces. (*See also* **Arabs in Africa, Colonialism in Africa, Ivory Trade.**)

Togo

small, narrow country on the Gulf of Guinea, Togo got its name from the Ewe words *to,* meaning "water", and *go,* meaning "coast" or "bank". During the colonial period it was controlled by a succession of European powers—Germany, Britain and France, and then France alone. For most of the time since its independence in 1960, the country has been ruled by one-party government and military dictatorship.

GEOGRAPHY

Togo lies on the southern coast of the West African bulge, between BÉNIN and GHANA. BURKINO FASO borders the country to the north. Only about 30 miles wide, Togo's coast is usually hot and humid and experiences two rainy seasons per year. Farther north, the climate becomes cooler and drier, and the country widens to its maximum breadth of about 100 miles. Overall, Togo's climate is considerably drier than that of its neighbors in the region.

Four major rivers flow though the narrow land of Togo. Most of the country is flat, but a range of low mountains runs along the western border with Ghana. The country's highest point is Mount Agou, rising to 3,225 feet. Swamp and rainforest dominate the south, while grassland covers most of the north.

HISTORY AND GOVERNMENT

People first settled in northern Togo between A.D. 600 and 1100. The southern region was populated around the 1100s and 1200s, when Ewe groups moved into the area from NIGERIA. Over the next several centuries, many different ethnic groups migrated into what is now Togo.

Colonial Rule. Although Portuguese navigators were the first Europeans to visit the region around 1471, it was Germany that eventually colonized Togo. In 1884 the Germans, who were looking for access to the NIGER RIVER, signed a protectorate* agreement with Chief Mlapa III in the coastal town of Togo. Thirteen years later the Treaty of Paris confirmed the borders of the German colony known as Togoland. At that time the colony included part of the Gold Coast, the area that is now Ghana.

To ship cash crops from the colony's interior to Europe, Germany built roads, railroads, and a broadcasting system. Most of the development took place in the south, while the north was largely neglected. Southern Togolese generally fared better under German rule than the country's northern peoples. Many even obtained posts in the colonial government.

Shortly after World War I broke out in 1914, English and French troops occupied Togoland. After the war it was divided between the occupying powers. France received the larger, eastern portion of the territory, while England took control over the western portion. The southern portion of the country continued to benefit most under British and French rule.

* **protectorate** weak state under the control and protection of a strong state

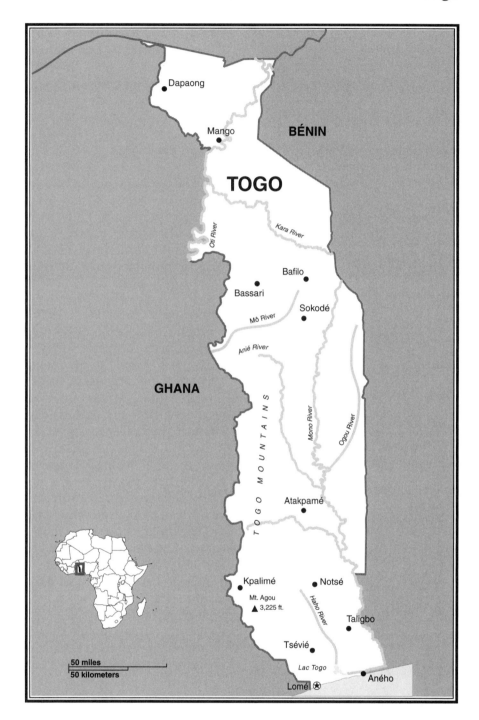

The breakup of Togoland divided members of its main ethnic groups, the Ewe in the south and the Konkomba in the north, between the two new colonies. Each of the colonies experienced ethnic tensions between these rival groups as well as calls to unify British and French Togoland. However, in 1956 the majority of the inhabitants of British Togoland voted to become part of the British colony of Gold Coast. That same year, French Togoland voted to become a self-governing republic within the French Community and changed its name to the Republic of Togo.

Togo

Nana Benz

Textiles are not only a growing source of export revenue for Togo, but also a means of communication and social commentary. A popular form of textile is cloth that is waxprinted with intricate designs. The designs have names such as "divorce" and "dynasty" that reflect popular culture or tensions between the sexes.

Women from the Ewe and Mina ethnic groups control most of this cloth industry. Such women are commonly referred to as Nana Benz. This term combines nana, a title of respect, with Mercedes Benz, the most popular form of transportation among these wealthy women.

Early Years of Independence. The 1956 election installed Nicolas Grunitzky as Togo's first prime minister. Two years later his brother-in-law, Sylvanus OLYMPIO, succeeded him. When Togo gained its independence from France in 1960, Olympio became Togo's first president. Hoping to free Togo from economic dependence on France, he championed a program of high taxes and trade restrictions. Although his plan balanced the budget, it was not popular—nor was the president's authoritarian* rule.

In 1963 a military coup* led by Sergeant Étienne Eyadema assassinated Olympio and replaced him with Grunitzky. However, after four years of little progress Eyadema overthrew Grunitzky and declared himself president. Hoping to unify Togo and to give the military a key role in politics, Eyadema created a party called the Rassemblement du Peuple Togolais (RPT). He proclaimed the RPT the nation's only legal political party and planned to use it to bring development to the long-neglected north, his homeland.

Eyadema's Rule. From 1970 to 1992 Eyadema ruled Togo without opposition. However, as corruption within his government weakened the country's economy, unrest grew. In 1985 a series of bomb attacks rocked the capital city of Lomé. Eyadema began a campaign of killing and torturing anyone suspected of being against him, conduct that brought criticism from international human rights groups. When he accused Ghana and Burkina Faso of harboring political opponents, he strained Togo's relations with its neighbors as well.

In 1991 Eyadema responded to public pressure for multiparty democracy by establishing a one-year transition government. Talks were scheduled to discuss how a new political system would be put into place. However, one month after the conference began Eyadema cancelled it because it proposed taking away most of his powers.

Over the next two years, political violence tore the country apart and organized strikes brought the economy to a standstill. Between 200,000 and 300,000 Togolese fled the country. Opposition parties refused to participate in elections scheduled for 1993, which foreign observers claimed were tainted by voting irregularities. Eyadema won with over 95 percent of the vote.

The 1998 presidential elections were also unfair. Eyadema created new government bodies, filled with his supporters, to oversee preparations for the election. At the last minute, the election date was moved up two months to give opponents less time to prepare, and Eyadema again won the presidency. The following year the RPT swept legislative elections, although opponents claim that only about 10 percent of registered voters bothered to participate.

By 1999 the Eyadema regime had come under increasing fire from outside the country. Amnesty International, a leading human rights group, called Togo a "state of terror," listing hundreds of political executions. Economic sanctions* begun by the European Union (EU) in 1993 were hurting the economy.

In July 1999 Eyadema finally seemed willing to compromise, agreeing to discuss "national reconciliation" with his opponents in talks

A woman sells brooms on a street in Lomé, the bustling capital of Togo.

* **gross domestic product (GDP)** total value of goods and services produced and consumed within a country

overseen by representatives from various European and African countries. Eyadema promised to call new legislative elections in 2000 and create an independent electoral commission to oversee voting. However, Eyadema's opponents did not trust him and were unwilling to take part in political discussions. Doubts about Eyadema's sincerity about reforming the government were reinforced when the legislative elections planned for March did not occur.

ECONOMY

Like many of its West African neighbors, Togo's economy depends heavily upon agriculture. The vast majority of the workforce is employed in farming, which accounts for much of the country's gross domestic product (GDP)*. The main export crops are cotton, cocoa, and coffee.

Phosphates, used to make fertilizers, are the country's leading export. Although a rise in the price of phosphates during the 1970s promised to transform the economy, prices leveled off in the 1980s. Togo also manufactures a number of items for export including cement, refined sugar, beverages, footwear, and textiles. However, development of both new and existing industries is limited by the country's reliance on imported electricity. TOURISM, once an important industry for Togo, has declined since the mid-1980s because of the nation's political unrest.

95

The Republic of Togo

POPULATION:
5,018,502 (2000 estimated population)

AREA:
21,930 sq. mi. (56,790 sq. km)

LANGUAGES:
French (official), Ewe, Mina, Kabye, Dagomba, Komkomba

NATIONAL CURRENCY:
CFA franc

PRINCIPAL RELIGIONS:
Traditional 70%, Christian 20%, Muslim 10%

CITIES:
Lomé (capital), 513,000 (1990 est.); Sokodé Palimé, Atakpamé, Bassari, Tsévié, Anécho

ANNUAL RAINFALL:
Ranges from 40 in. (1,020 mm) in the north to 70 in. (1,780 mm) in the south.

ECONOMY:
GDP per capita: $1,700 (1999 est.)

PRINCIPAL PRODUCTS AND EXPORTS:
Agricultural: cocoa, coffee, cotton, yams, cassava, corn, beans, rice, millet, sorghum, livestock, fish
Manufacturing: food processing, cement, textiles, beverages
Mining: phosphates

GOVERNMENT:
Independence from French-ruled UN trusteeship. Republic under transition to multi-party democratic rule; president elected by universal suffrage. Governing bodies: National Assembly (legislative body) elected by popular vote; Council of Ministers and prime minister appointed by the president.

HEADS OF STATE SINCE INDEPENDENCE:
1960–1963 President Sylvanus Epiphanio Olympio
1963–1967 President Nicolas Grunitzky
1967– President General Gnassingbe Eyadema

ARMED FORCES:
7,000 (2001 est.)

EDUCATION:
Compulsory for ages 6–12; literacy rate 52%

PEOPLES AND CULTURES

Togo contains dozens of different ethnic groups. The Ewe and the Mina dominate the south. During colonial times, both of these groups profited from trade with Europeans and took advantage of commercial and educational opportunities. As a result they became the privileged classes after independence and still maintain that role, despite Eyadema's efforts to improve the position of northern peoples.

A great variety of ethnic groups live in northern Togo, including the Kabye, Komkomba Basari, Kotokoli, Tamberma, Tchokossi, Moba, and Gourma peoples. Many of these groups trace their language and cultural traditions to Burkina Faso. Northerners are mostly small-scale farmers, although some now work in the government. Some government workers are employed by the national government, while some are part of local authorities. At the local level, political figures often share power with a council of elders, who advise political and religious leaders to aid in decision-making. In addition, in some northern areas, there is a figure known as an "earth priest" who holds a position of authority and, at times, conducts rituals that ensure the fertility of the land and good crop harvests. The most prominent northern people are the Kabye, largely due to the fact that Eyadema claims Kabye descent.

About 70 percent of all Togolese practice traditional African religions. Some 20 percent are Christian, mostly Roman Catholic. Togo has relatively few Muslims, but Islam* is growing in popularity. As in many African countries, those who practice Christianity and Islam also mix in elements of traditional worship. (*See also* **Colonialism in Africa, West African Trading Settlements.**)

* **Islam** religion based on the teachings of the prophet Muhammad; religious faith of Muslims

Tombalbaye, François-Ngarta

1918–1975
President of Chad

The first president of CHAD, François-Ngarta Tombalbaye promoted the interests of Christian groups in southern Chad at the expense of Muslims in the north. Born in southern Chad and educated by Protestant missionaries, Tombalbaye became a school teacher. However, his interests eventually turned to politics, and in 1946 he helped create the Chad Progressive Party. He later became president of the first Chadian trade union. After being elected to the French National Assembly in 1952, Tombalbaye rose in importance, serving as vice president of the Grand Council of French Equatorial Africa and as Chad's prime minister.

When Chad became independent in 1960, Tombalbaye won the presidency. He began supporting Christian interests—particularly those of his own ethnic group, the Sara—over those of the nation's Muslims and ruthlessly eliminated his Muslim political opponents from northern Chad. At the same time, he launched a cultural revolution aimed at restoring national unity. However, his revolution failed when he revived a traditional, but long abandoned, INITIATION RITE. The ceremony, which involved deep facial scarring, caused many of Tombalbaye's supporters to leave his political party.

By the mid-1970s Tombalbaye faced strong opposition in the north, growing political unrest in the south, and dissatisfaction among the military. On April 13, 1975, a group of army officers and police surrounded Tombalbaye's residence and asked him to surrender. Resisting arrest, he was shot dead in his home.

Touré, Samori

ca. 1830–1900
Ruler in Guinea

* **savanna** tropical or subtropical grassland with scattered trees and drought-resistant undergrowth

* **Islam** religion based on the teachings of the prophet Muhammad; religious faith of Muslims

Samori Touré built a state that stretched far across the savannas* of what is now the Republic of GUINEA and defended his kingdom for many years against French colonization. Touré was born along the upper Milo River in the highlands of Guinea. The valley of the Milo was an important long-distance trade route that linked the Guinea coast to the interior. Merchants from different areas settled at key points along the route. Many were originally Muslims, although some abandoned Islam* to adopt the beliefs of the local people. Samori Touré belonged to such a family.

In the 1850s Touré learned the arts of war in conflicts among the small states that competed for control in the Milo River valley. He then became a military leader among his mother's kinfolk. Organizing the local warriors into disciplined units of foot soldiers and mounted troops, he taught them to use imported horses and firearms. Around 1874 Touré declared himself king. He extended his military power over commercially valuable areas such as gold fields. As his state expanded to cover an immense territory, he fought to defend it from the French, who were colonizing the SAHARA and parts of western Africa.

To bind his subjects together with more than military might, Touré embraced the Muslim faith in the mid-1880s and ordered his people to do the same. Around the same time he reluctantly signed a treaty of peace and trade with the French. Some of his subjects rebelled against him, partly because he had forced them to become Muslims and partly because he had suffered military setbacks and could not give them the loot and spoils of war.

Starting in 1888 Touré reorganized his army. He acquired repeating rifles and recruited African soldiers who had fought for the French or British to teach his troops the techniques of European warfare. A few years later he decided to move eastward. To discourage the French from settling on his land, he ordered all the inhabitants of his kingdom to destroy their villages, take their food, and follow his army.

During the 1890s Touré conquered vast new territories, including much of modern-day IVORY COAST. Although he hoped to find a region that neither the French nor the British were colonizing, he instead found himself trapped between French and British armies. In addition, he suffered uprisings by Africans who resented the abuses inflicted by his army and his practice of enslaving the people he defeated. Touré was returning with his followers to Guinea in 1898, when the French captured him. They sent him to GABON, where he soon died of pneumonia. Touré had resisted the French for more than 17 years, and his capture was the final step in the French military conquest of West Africa.

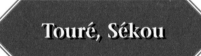

Touré, Sékou

ca. 1922–1984
First president of Guinea

A leader of the INDEPENDENCE MOVEMENT in GUINEA, Sékou Touré became the first president of the newly independent Republic of Guinea in 1958. Born to a modest Muslim family in upper Guinea, Touré had little education. However, he had natural talent as a speaker and leader and he acquired some Islamic learning. After practicing a variety of trades, Touré took a job with the colonial postal administration. He soon also became a trade union leader and politician. In 1947 he helped found the Democratic Assembly of Africa, and he later served as the secretary-general of the local branch of that political party. He was a strong supporter of pan-Africanism—a movement that encouraged the development of black identity and sought to unify blacks in Africa and around the world.

In his role as a union leader and politician during the 1940s and 1950s Touré organized many labor strikes and spoke out often against colonialism. He denounced African chiefs who served as colonial administrators and appealed to people on the margins of society, such as slaves, youth, and women. Touré also established the General Union of North African Workers. His political influence increased throughout the 1950s as he was elected to the territorial assembly of Guinea, became mayor of the capital city of CONAKRY, and served as a representative to the French National Assembly.

When France allowed its African colonies to vote on the issue of independence in 1958, Touré spoke out in favor of immediate independence for Guinea, making the famous statment, "We prefer poverty in freedom to [riches] in slavery." The people of Guinea voted overwhelmingly for that idea, and Guinea became the first French colony in sub-Saharan* Africa to achieve independence. Touré became the first president of the new republic.

* **sub-Saharan** referring to Africa south of the Sahara desert

* **Soviet Union** nation that existed from 1922 to 1991, made up of Russia and 14 other republics

* **communist** relating to communism, a system in which land, goods, and the means of production are owned by the state or community rather than by individuals

* **nationalize** to bring land, industries or public works under state control or ownership

After Guinea's independence France withdrew much of its support. Facing an economic crisis and finding little help from Western nations, Touré turned to the Soviet Union* and other communist* countries for help. Under communist influence, he formed a one-party state, abolished civil rights, and nationalized* industry. As Guineans grew more and more opposed to his radical policies, Touré tightened police security and killed or imprisoned tens of thousands of people. More than one million Guineans fled the country. Beginning in the late 1970s, Touré began to reform the nation's economy and undo various communist policies, a trend that continued after his death in 1984.

Traveling to experience places and people other than their own, tourists spend money on hotels, restaurants, tours, transportation, entertainment, visits to museums and historic sites, and souvenirs. The business of providing those goods and services, the tourism industry, accounts for a significant part of the incomes of some African countries.

History. Tourism in Africa began in the 1800s, when Europeans making what was called the "grand tour" of Europe began extending their travels to include more exotic destinations. MOROCCO, ALGERIA, SOUTH AFRICA, and especially EGYPT and the NILE RIVER valley attracted many European visitors. Tourists favored these areas largely because they were located on the Mediterranean Sea, or because they had been colonized by Europeans and were regarded as linked to Europe culturally.

A different type of African tourism was popular from about 1918 to 1939, the years between WORLD WARS I and II. Wealthy Europeans and North Americans traveled to Africa for safaris, excursions on which they hunted big game such as elephants and lions. Many returned to their homes with trophies in the form of animal heads or skins and with photographs of their hunting adventures.

Tourism Today. Since the end of World War II in 1945, Africa's tourism industry has boomed. As commercial airlines made travel faster and less expensive, many more people could afford to make overseas visits. Tour companies developed and advertised package tours, or preplanned vacations, of a week or two in Africa.

Tourists come to Africa to enjoy a wide variety of experiences—from natural wonders to cultural landmarks. Ski resorts in the mountains of Morocco and Algeria attract tourists from the Middle East. Archaeological and historical marvels, such as Egypt's PYRAMIDS and the stone ruins of Great Zimbabwe, also draw crowds. The most popular countries for mass tourism have been South Africa, KENYA, ZIMBABWE, Morocco, TUNISIA, and Egypt. However, the operators of package tours now offer visits to more remote parts of Africa.

Ecotourism, or tourism in natural settings, is the fastest growing trend in African tourism. Visitors on safari tours in eastern and southern Africa aim cameras instead of rifles at local wildlife. Tourists to Africa's Indian

See color plate 10, vol. 2.

Ocean islands, such as the COMOROS and the SEYCHELLES, scuba dive along spectacular coral reefs. Others seek a glimpse of mountain gorillas in UGANDA, lemurs in MADAGASCAR, or rare birds in BOTSWANA. In Ghana's Kakum National Park, tourists can explore the rain forest canopy on a walkway that is suspended more than 90 feet above the ground.

Impact on African Life. Tourism has negative as well as positive effects. One is that the local people usually receive only a small part of the income from tourism. Most of it goes to foreign tour operators and African governments. Another is that tourists ignorant of local values and customs sometimes behave or dress in ways that offend Africans. In some nations, such as Egypt in the 1990s, radical political and religious groups have attacked popular tourist sites to make trouble for national governments.

See color plate 12, vol. 2.

Even ecotourism poses problems. Just by passing through an area tourists may damage wildlife habitats, such as delicate reefs and rain forests. The pollution and development associated with a growing tourism industry may harm the environment for both animals and people. In some nations local peoples have been displaced from their homelands in order to preserve wilderness for ecotourism. In Tanzania, the Maasai people have been banned from the Ngorongoro Crater and Serengeti National Park, forcing them to give up their traditional cattle-herding lifestyle.

Despite such problems, however, tourism has become a key contributor to the income of many African countries. Recognizing the economic benefits of tourism, African governments have promoted it within their countries in a variety of ways. Some have established WILDLIFE AND GAME PARKS and protected marine areas; others have created new tourism policies to ensure that more tourism earnings directly benefit local communities. In some areas with few economic possibilities, tourism has provided jobs and economic development. For example, Algeria has constructed several successful resort hotels in oases of the SAHARA DESERT.

Trade

* **precolonial** referring to the time before European powers colonized Africa

Trade has always been the engine of economic growth. Individuals and communities that trade successfully with their neighbors gain wealth and power. In precolonial* times, Africa's natural riches gave it an important place in international trading networks. However, the SLAVE TRADE and European colonization profoundly disrupted the development of African economies, and the impact of these events is still felt today.

PRECOLONIAL TRADE

In Africa, as elsewhere around the world, trade arose shortly after humans formed permanent farming communities. Before this development people had spent much of their time securing food to ensure the group's survival. These settled communities produced enough food and other goods to support themselves, but no surplus to trade with other groups.

Origins of Trade. The spread of AGRICULTURE led to two significant changes in the pattern of economic activity. First, it created extra food that could serve as a commodity* for trade with other groups. Second, it allowed fewer people to produce more food, thus freeing individuals to pursue skilled craftwork such as weaving or iron working.

The creation of food surpluses and specialized crafts provided a basis for trade between communities. Groups that produced certain foods or goods could trade them with other groups who lacked those items. In exchange, they could obtain things from their trading partners that they could not produce themselves. By the first century A.D., Africans had developed a diverse economy in which people traded and went to markets regularly.

The Growth of Market Systems. Several types of market systems grew up to handle trade in precolonial Africa, and not all of them were marketplaces. Food sellers often visited individual households to find buyers for their goods. Herders learned the times of year when farming villages would have surplus produce and would travel to those villages to exchange meat, milk, hides, and other animal products for vegetables and grain.

As the volume of trade in an area increased, people created marketplaces and more sophisticated market systems. One of the most common systems, still popular today, is the periodic market system. In such a system, several villages in the same general area hold markets on different days of the week. Often the system forms a ring around a centrally located village. This central village might hold a market one day, followed by a village to the south the following day and one to the north the next.

Such a periodic system has several advantages over a single market. Rotating market days between villages reduces the average travel time to market and the cost of transporting goods. Moving the market from one village to another also expands the circle of people who come into contact regularly. Thus, the market turns into a vital and valuable social space, especially in isolated rural areas. Studies have shown that African women often visit the market where they can see people they want to see and fulfill their social obligations, even if that market is not the closest one.

Long-Distance Trade. While local trade flourished throughout Africa, regional and long-distance trade developed more fully in western Africa than elsewhere on the continent. The region contained valuable commodities such as gold and salt that merchants could transport easily—ideal goods for long-distance trade. The revenue brought by these goods covered the cost of transporting them and still provided a handsome profit.

* **commodity** article of trade

See color plate 8, vol. 1.

See color plate 6, vol. 2.

Trade

The city of Cape Town, South Africa, is an important manufacturing center. Goods produced there are shipped all over the world.

Trade in western Africa also benefited from the growth of strong, centralized states such as those of the ASANTE and MOSSI. In these kingdoms a separate merchant class arose to sell goods that other members of the society produced. Revenue from trade enabled the kingdoms to build strong armies and maintain control over their subjects. Because these armies also protected traveling merchants, many trade routes ran through these kingdoms.

Western Africa had more people living close together than did other parts of Africa. The region's many towns and cities were natural locations for markets. In some cases urban areas emerged because of the trade: towns grew up along trade routes to serve the needs of traveling merchants and earn money from the commercial traffic. Some town-based markets appeared along the East African coast as well.

European Contacts and the Slave Trade. African trade grew quickly after the development of agriculture around the late 1000s B.C., and by the A.D. 100s merchants from India and southern Asia were traveling to the East African coast. Sometime after the 500s camel caravans from Arabia and the Mediterranean were making their way across the SAHARA DESERT to the gold fields of western Africa. By this time people in western coastal communities had developed trade networks linking them to the interior of the continent. They exchanged fish and sea salt for gold, agricultural goods, and CRAFTS.

These coastal communities had their first direct contact with European traders in the late 1400s. The Portuguese built a series of trading posts and forts along the western African coast, between present-day SENEGAL and GHANA. Other European powers, including Spain, France, England, and Denmark soon followed. Although these countries came in search of gold at first, their outposts eventually turned into major centers of the Atlantic slave trade.

Until the 1500s Africa was the main supplier of gold to South Asia and the Mediterranean region. But by the 1500s, African gold supplies began to drop off just as Spaniards in the Americas found new sources. Europeans established plantations in the "New World" that relied on large numbers of low-cost indigenous* workers to produce high profits for their owners. Because Europeans had largely destroyed some Native American societies through disease, hard labor, and battle, they looked for other sources of workers. They decided to bring in enslaved Africans.

A limited trade in slaves already existed within Africa, and slavers from Arabia also took some captives from East Africa to the Middle East. But the demands of plantation agriculture in the Americas gave rise to a slave trade of enormous scale, far greater than anything that had occurred up to that point. Between 1500 and 1850, the transatlantic slave trade forced more than 13 million Africans to leave their homelands. Many died on the slave ships crossing the ocean.

Limits on African Trade. Although trade played a key role in the culture and economy of precolonial Africa, its growth was hindered by the continent's challenging landscape. Geographic features such as deserts and jungles made transporting goods across the land extremely difficult. However, most items had to be taken overland because few rivers allowed long-distance travel by boat.

In most cases merchants hired or enslaved people to walk and haul goods on their heads or backs, a form of transport called porterage. Because humans cannot carry great weights, porterage limited the distance a merchant could go to market and the amount of goods he could take. Africa did have pack animals, but many areas also had the tsetse fly

* **indigenous** native to a certain place

103

that carries a deadly disease called sleeping sickness. Animals cannot survive long in the tsetse zones, so traders did not use animals or wheeled carts and wagons widely in precolonial Africa.

Because of these difficulties, long-distance trade was only profitable for goods, such as gold, that had great worth relative to their size. Food, tools, and other everyday items did not have enough value to justify the expense of transporting them to distant lands. People traded them only at local markets.

TRADE IN COLONIAL AFRICA

In 1807 Great Britain outlawed the slave trade and began to police the slave trading activities of other countries. As a result, European interest in Africa shifted from the export of slaves to the exploitation* of natural resources. European nations began to explore ways of profiting from Africa's agricultural and mineral wealth.

* **exploitation** relationship in which one side benefits at the other's expense

Colonial Trade Practices. To tap Africa's natural riches, Europeans first had to gain control over them by conquering the indigenous peoples and seizing their land. Colonial authorities then gave the property to companies or individual settlers. Colonial plantations soon produced coffee, tea, spices, and even vegetable oils for lubricating the new industrial equipment produced in Europe. Other companies opened large and dangerous mines to extract copper, gold, and other valuable minerals for export to Europe.

To speed the transportation of raw materials, colonial powers built roads and railroads to connect interior areas to the coast. These projects dramatically reduced the cost of bringing goods to ports for shipment to Europe. Ports with rail connections swelled into large cities that dominated the commercial activity of the colonies. Meanwhile, settlements at a distance from rail lines suffered economically.

Effects of Colonial Trade Policy. The colonial economy had devastating effects on Africans. Deprived of their land, many were forced to work on the plantations and in the mines for little pay under brutal conditions. Workers often had to travel great distances to work because a colony's economic activity was usually concentrated in a few areas of intensive production and one or two large cities. Families were frequently split up as men found work on plantations, in mining camps, or in towns while other family members remained in the countryside.

Colonial trade policy also undermined the African economy. The raw materials so cheaply produced did not go to make goods for local use. Instead the materials were sold to Europe, where the new industrial cities turned them into manufactured goods that were shipped back to Africa for sale. Colonial companies made enormous profits with this system. By contrast, colonial governments neglected African industry to prevent local competition for European goods. By the time most African countries won independence, their economies were almost totally dependent on raw materials. This situation led to serious problems in the following years.

Shopping Without Money?

Until the 1900s cash currencies were rarely used for buying and selling in Africa. Most people employed the barter system—exchanging goods and services without paying money. Under colonial rule, however, people had to pay taxes in cash, and some communities used cloth, metal rods, or cowrie shells as currency. Yet barter remains an important form of trade in some parts of Africa. In countries such as Rwanda, where war has ravaged the local economy, barter has again emerged as the preferred means of exchange.

POSTCOLONIAL TRADE

At independence, most African economies had little industrial development. The selling prices of their raw materials could swing up or down unpredictably, and these price changes could create an economic boom or bust with unsettling speed. In addition, the transportation infrastructure* served few areas within each country. Although they achieved political freedom, African nations continued to struggle under economic burdens caused by the policies of their former colonial masters.

* **infrastructure** basic framework of a society and its economy, which includes roads, bridges, port facilities, airports, and other public works

Postcolonial Developments. Throughout the 1960s, high prices for minerals and agricultural products led to economic growth in Africa. However, a fall in commodity prices and a sharp increase in the cost of fuel oil crippled many African economies in the early 1970s. Earning little from exports and forced to pay high prices for imports, African economies went downhill rapidly, and local currencies lost much of their value. Many countries borrowed money from the World Bank and the International Monetary Fund, but few could repay even the interest on these loans.

Meanwhile, African leaders tried to develop industry in their countries. Many leaders hoped to limit the role of foreign corporations, but few local companies had the funds to launch major projects. Many governments formed state-owned corporations to handle utilities, infrastructure*, and other needs. Unfortunately, most state companies proved highly inefficient or corrupt. African industries are still struggling to make inroads in international markets, and multinational corporations continue to dominate trade within Africa.

In the 1980s and 1990s, the World Bank and International Monetary Fund demanded that African nations restructure their economies to earn money to repay their loans. Many African leaders continued to push agriculture and industry toward exports, while removing barriers to imports. They also cut spending on social programs such as health care and education and cut the value of their currencies. As a result, Africans lost services and purchasing power and services, and unrest in urban areas grew.

To lessen the demand for increased wages, governments artificially lowered the price of food. However, this hurt local farmers, who began to withhold food from the regular market and sell it in illegal markets where they could get higher prices.

Current Bases of African Trade. Despite efforts to diversify their trade economies, most African nations still depend heavily on the export of raw materials. Agricultural products make up the bulk of these exports, accounting for more than 80 percent of foreign revenues in some countries. For most of these countries, exports are a trap from which they seem unable to escape.

Mineral resources are the other mainstay of African overseas trade. In NORTH AFRICA, the nations of LIBYA, ALGERIA, and TUNISIA rely on revenues from petroleum and natural gas. MOROCCO and Tunisia export large amounts of phosphates, a major ingredient of fertilizers. NIGERIA man-

See map in Minerals and Mining (vol. 3).

105

aged to produce and export oil in the 1970s, but corruption has drained much of that wealth from the public treasury. In southern Africa, BOTSWANA has developed diamond, copper, and coal industries. SOUTH AFRICA is also a world leader in gold and diamond production.

The outlook for a recovery in African trade is certainly dim. Most countries still shoulder heavy debt payments that crush their ability to spend money on domestic needs. Foreign companies continue to control many vital national resources, but many investors are cautious about placing money in countries with unstable political environments. Local investors often prefer to put their limited funds into established companies overseas. Finding a solution to the problem will require the cooperative efforts of Western nations and international organizations to forgive African debts, provide economic aid, and diversify trade between Africa and the rest of the world. (*See also* **Colonialism in Africa; Development, Economic and Social; Economic History; Global Politics and Africa; Ivory Trade; Markets; Minerals and Mining; Money and Banking; Plantation Systems; Slave Trade; Transportation; West African Trading Settlements.**)

Transportation

* **infrastructure** basic framework of a society and its economy, which includes roads, bridges, port facilities, airports, and other public works

Africa suffers from an overall lack of transportation facilities, and many of those that do exist are inefficient, inconvenient, unreliable, and poorly maintained. Moreover, the quality and availability of transportation varies greatly from one place to another. Methods of getting around in Africa range from jet aircraft to camels. Upgrading and expanding the transportation infrastructure* is a major challenge facing most African nations.

HISTORY OF TRANSPORTATION

Most of Africa's transportation systems were developed during the colonial era. Designed to serve the interests of the European colonial powers, these systems largely ignored the needs of local populations. Colonial policies have had a profound effect on transportation facilities in Africa today.

Colonial Transportation. European colonization and settlement altered the nature of transportation in Africa dramatically. The most obvious change was technological. Mechanized transport, such as steamships and railroads, replaced canoes and animals as cargo carriers. This allowed the movement of greater quantities of goods, more quickly and reliably, over longer distances. Modern transportation also overcame various problems associated with Africa's difficult terrain and climate, such as seasonal flooding.

Although colonial authorities greatly expanded the ways of moving people and goods, the networks they created were focused on bringing raw materials from interior regions to coastal ports. This approach benefited European mining companies and white settler plantations, but it did little to help ordinary Africans get around more easily or to improve their access to markets, schools, and shops. In many cases, modern transportation actually reduced people's mobility as new and more expensive forms of transport replaced affordable indigenous* ones.

After the Colonial Period. As African nations won their independence, they sought to restructure transportation systems to suit the needs of their people. A major goal of many states was to link rural districts to each other and to the growing urban areas. Most focused on constructing new roads rather than railroads because they were cheaper to build and maintain and could be more easily completed in difficult terrain.

At the end of the colonial era there were few overland links between African nations. The colonial powers had seen no reason for building highways or railroads to the colonies of rival nations. After independence many new African states wanted to construct highways connecting them with their neighbors. Unfortunately, this goal was only partly realized.

* **indigenous**   native to a certain place

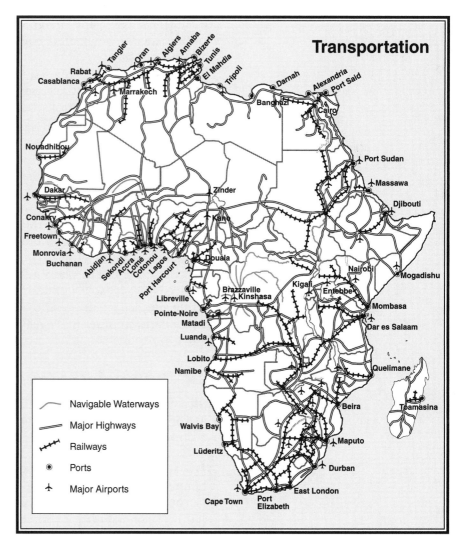

Transportation

Legend:
- Navigable Waterways
- Major Highways
- Railways
- Ports
- Major Airports

* Soviet Union   nation that existed from 1922 to 1991, made up of Russia and 14 other republics

See color plate 12, vol. 4.

Many of the same European countries that had colonized Africa took part in the modernization of African transportation after independence. Some African nations also received help from the Soviet Union* and their allies. Despite these efforts, transportation networks grew slowly and had much less economic impact than expected. Local organizations lacked the money and expertise to develop a transportation infrastructure, so the job fell to the governments of each country. However, the financial condition of most African nations severely limited the amount of money available for such projects. Moreover, the roads, railways, and ports that were built often deteriorated due to a lack of funds for maintenance. An economic downturn in the 1970s and 1980s aggravated the problem by further reducing the money available to spend on transportation.

Technological changes also had a negative effect on African transportation. As oceangoing ships became larger and more sophisticated, few African ports could handle them. Nor were the ports equipped to deal with containerization—a system in which specially designed ships carry goods in large metal boxes called containers. Aircraft got bigger as well, making it less profitable for airlines to serve Africa's small market for air passengers and freight. In addition, new ships and planes required special navigation equipment that African seaports and airports did not have.

All these factors contributed to a crisis that has caused many African nations to reconsider their transportation plans. Instead of building new facilities, many nations have devoted more money and effort to improving and maintaining existing ones. National airlines and railroads, for example, have tried to increase efficiency by standardizing their vehicles. This reduces maintenance costs because the vehicles all use the same parts. Having fewer types of vehicles also makes it easier to train pilots and drivers.

One of the greatest challenges facing African nations is providing adequate transportation for their poorest people, both those in urban areas and remote rural communities. In the past African nations focused their transportation programs on the needs of corporations and government. Some recent plans attempt to offer solutions for people who lack access to reliable public transportation. Such plans include promoting simpler and more affordable technologies, such as bicycles and donkey carts, in order to decrease reliance on expensive forms of mechanized transport.

AIR TRANSPORTATION

Africa's air transportation lags far behind networks in other regions of the world. The continent commands a very small share of global air traffic, and its airlines are, for the most part, extremely uncompetitive.

African Airlines.   Africa possesses very few large air carriers, and only a handful of the world's leading airlines are based on the continent. This lack can be explained in part by colonial history. The European powers in Africa operated only a couple of airlines from a few major cities. Air connections to the outside world were limited; connections between African destinations were even rarer.

At the time of independence, most African countries with air service nationalized* their airlines. These carriers then had to compete with other government programs for funding. Many had to borrow money to keep operating and are now heavily in debt and lack funds for maintenance and modernization. In addition, deregulation* in the airline industry in the 1970s led to greater competition and lower fares, making it extremely difficult for African airlines to compete effectively.

A major trend in recent years has been the formation of global alliances between airlines in order to reduce costs and share passengers. However, only a few African airlines have joined such alliances. In some cases, major international airlines have bought a stake in local carriers. For example, KLM Royal Dutch Airways acquired part of Kenya Airways when that carrier was partially privatized*. Unfortunately, most African airlines are so heavily indebted that they are unattractive to foreign investors.

Air Traffic. Africa is a very minor player in the area of international air traffic. The continent's airlines account for less than 2 percent of international air passengers and airfreight. The vast majority of this traffic is between Africa and Europe. In addition, the number and frequency of scheduled international flights to and from Africa is extremely limited, and Africa's largest airports handle far fewer passengers each year than the largest American and European airports.

Flights between African countries are also limited, with few and infrequent connections between cities. This is primarily a result of the continent's poverty, because the majority of Africans cannot afford to travel by plane. It also reflects the small market for business travel within Africa. Business travelers contribute a significant share of airline revenues in the United States, but a very small percentage in Africa.

SEAPORTS

Several factors influence the establishment and growth of seaports. These include the presence of a good natural harbor and links to areas of economic activity in the interior. Both of these factors have played a significant role in the development of Africa's ports.

Despite its large size Africa contains few major seaports, and these few are unevenly distributed around the continent. In part, the lack of ports can be explained by the fact that Africa has few good natural harbors. It also stems from colonial history. The European colonial powers typically built only one or two major roads and railroads to connect mining and agricultural areas with a single seaport on the coast. As a result, most coastal African nations have only one port that dominates seaborne traffic.

Africa has several different types of seaports. The largest are designed solely for the export of minerals or crude oil and have no other significant role. The most important general-purpose cargo ports—including Abidjan, Cape Town, Dakar, and Lagos—are also major urban centers.

* **nationalize** to bring land, industries or public works under state control or ownership

* **deregulate** to remove restrictions on a particular activity, particularly those imposed by government

* **privatize** to transfer from government control to private ownership

Carrying the Mail

The earliest air routes in Africa were created to carry the mail. In West Africa, the French airmail service led to regular air routes in the late 1920s and early 1930s. In East Africa, a Cape (South Africa) to Cairo (Egypt) route was opened and operated by Britain's Imperial Airways. These pioneering mail services established the basis of air transport in sub-Saharan Africa and created air routes that remain relatively unchanged to the present day.

In the early 1900s, the Portuguese rulers of Mozambique used the forced labor of Africans to build roads and lay rail lines. The elegant train station of Maputo in Mozambique offers a reminder of the country's colonial past.

Even these ports suffer from inadequate and outdated facilities, though, a result of tight-fisted colonial policies and the weak economies of modern African states. Finally, various medium-sized ports—such as FREETOWN in Sierra Leone and DAR ES SALAAM in Tanzania—serve as commercial hubs for particular regions.

Not all African countries have access to the sea. Landlocked countries such as NIGER and UGANDA must depend on neighboring coastal states for access to ocean ports. This presents difficulties for those nations but also forces ocean ports to be competitive and offer better services to attract business. Some landlocked countries have ports on lakes and rivers that play an important role in regional transport between African nations.

RAILROADS

The coming of railroads to Africa in the late 1800s had a significant impact on the continent's economic and political development. Railroads served as avenues for the export of raw materials and the import of finished goods. They also allowed European powers to exert political control over territory and thus justify their colonial claims over the land.

Rail Networks. Colonial rail-building policies left most African nations with only one or two major lines running from a seaport to the interior. As a result, only a handful of African nations have more than 500–600 miles of track. SOUTH AFRICA, with about 13,000 miles of track, boasts the largest rail network on the continent. Many landlocked countries, such as CHAD and RWANDA, have no railroads at all.

The colonial powers also made no effort to link together the various parts of their colonies with rail networks. For this reason, even nations with fairly large rail systems contain many areas with little or no access to railroads. In recent years African governments have proposed plans to join existing national railways to form a system linking the continent. This would greatly benefit landlocked countries with no rail access, but the cost of such a project makes its completion unlikely.

Rail Technology and Traffic. African railroads are burdened with outdated equipment and inefficient routes. Colonial railroads were built cheaply and quickly, often using lightweight track. To help speed construction and keep costs down, engineers avoided building tunnels or embankments, so many lines have sharp curves, steep inclines, and roundabout routes. These factors limit both the speed at which trains can travel and the loads that they can carry. Aside from South Africa, which has modern and efficient railways, most African rail systems are inefficient, poorly run, and technologically backward.

The main activity of most African railroads is carrying freight, particularly raw material for export. However, the volume of freight varies considerably from year to year because of the changing demand for the raw materials. In recent years railroads have lost a large amount of traffic to highways. Most railroads also offer passenger service, but slow travel make this an unattractive option. Only in South Africa do railroads serve as a main element of urban mass transit.

The same financial problems that affect other forms of African transportation hamper the development of better rail service as well. International lending agencies have recommended closing inefficient rail lines in some nations as a way to reduce government spending. As a result, Africa's rail network is likely to shrink even further in the near future. (*See also* **Colonialism in Africa; Development, Economic and Social; Economic History.**)

TRANSVAAL

See *South Africa.*

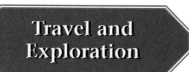

Early in recorded history, people from outside Africa visited—or at least knew about—the lands on Africa's northern coast. In ancient times kingdoms of the Middle East and southern Europe had dealings with EGYPT. Phoenicians from what is now Lebanon founded the colony of CARTHAGE (in present-day TUNISIA), the Greeks established settlements

Travel and Exploration

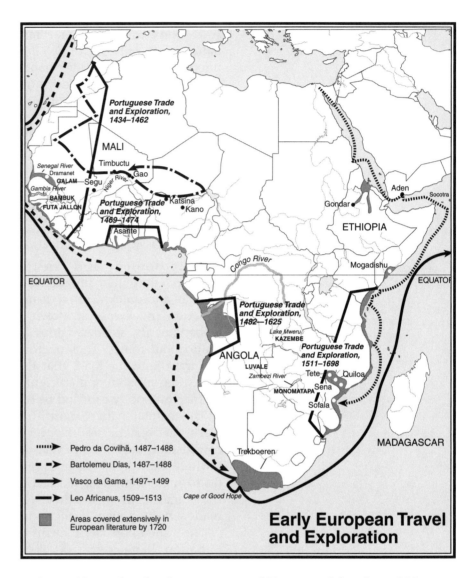

Early European Travel and Exploration

Legend:
- ⋯⋯▶ Pedro da Covilhã, 1487–1488
- --▶ Bartolemeu Dias, 1487–1488
- ⟶ Vasco da Gama, 1497–1499
- ▶ Leo Africanus, 1509–1513
- ▢ Areas covered extensively in European literature by 1720

* **medieval** referring to the Middle Ages in western Europe, generally considered to be from the A.D. 500s to the 1500s

* **Islam** religion based on the teachings of the prophet Muhammad; religious faith of Muslims

in LIBYA, Alexander the Great conquered Egypt, and for about 300 years the Romans included the coastal region of North Africa in their empire.

The rest of Africa, however, remained a mystery to the outside world until medieval* travelers began exploring the continent. Arabs crossed the northern and western parts of Africa. The Chinese learned much about eastern Africa's coast along the Indian Ocean. Europeans spent hundreds of years charting the shores of Africa and then probing all of the continent's interior. Driven by trade, conquest, religion, science, or curiosity, generations of explorers gradually revealed Africa to the rest of the world.

Arab Travelers. Beginning in the A.D. 600s, invaders from the Arabian peninsula colonized Egypt and North Africa. They introduced Arabic language and culture and the religion of Islam* to the region. Eventually some Arabs began venturing south into the SAHARA DESERT and beyond it to the Africa they called the *bilad al-sudan*, "the land of the blacks." Reports of their journeys appear in books from as early as

112

the 900s. Most of these accounts were written by scholars who stayed comfortably north of the desert and collected tales from returning travelers. The early Muslim travelers took particular interest in two African kingdoms: Kanem, located north of Lake Chad, and Ghana, on the border of present-day MAURITANIA and MALI (not part of modern Ghana).

Trade motivated many Arab merchants to travel. They bought slaves, gold, and other goods from the lands on the southern edge of the desert. One Arab account compares the experiences of two traders, one with gold and the other with slaves, returning north across the desert. The first trader had a fairly easy trip, but the second had constant trouble with slaves who were hungry, sick, or trying to escape.

* **sub-Saharan**   referring to Africa south of the Sahara desert

The spread of Islam was closely related to travel into sub-Saharan* Africa. Some early references describe Arab travelers as holy men who performed religious services for local rulers. Such functions as fortune telling, praying for rain, and interpreting dreams gave Arab travelers a chance to plant the seeds of Islam and gain converts. One notable holy man, Abdullah bin Ya Sin, may have brought Islam to ancient Ghana in 1076.

The first extensive eyewitness account of travels in sub-Saharan Africa comes from the Arab IBN BATTUTA. In 1330 he sailed along the eastern coast, visiting Mombasa and Kilwa (now in TANZANIA). A second expedition 20 years later took him from MOROCCO across the Sahara to the empire of Mali. Another traveler from Morocco, Muhammad al-Maghili, visited Mali's Songhai Empire in the 1490s and left a detailed description of the empire's Islamic life and customs.

Chinese in Africa. Information about Africa filtered into China for centuries before the first recorded visit to the continent by Chinese explorers. The Chinese traveled mainly along the eastern coast of Africa, and reports of their journeys turn up in a variety of places. For example, the memoirs of a man named Tu Huan, held captive by Muslims in central Asia in the mid-700s, include accounts of the city of MEROË in what is now SUDAN that he heard from his captors.

* **dynasty**   succession of rulers from the same family or group

China's overseas trade increased during the Sung dynasty* (960–1279), and contacts with foreign merchants brought the Chinese information about eastern Africa. The earliest known Chinese map of Africa, dating from the early 1300s, accurately shows the shape of the southeastern part of the continent. At the time Europeans believed that southern Africa stretched far to the east and that the Indian Ocean was a landlocked sea.

Yet the Chinese did not gain firsthand experience of Africa until the early 1400s, when the rulers of the Ming dynasty sent a series of naval fleets to the Indian Ocean. Two of these missions reached the Horn of Africa, the peninsula that extends eastward below the Gulf of Aden. As a result, information about this region of Africa appeared in official Ming histories and in unofficial accounts. Descriptions of giraffes aroused special interest because the giraffe seemed to resemble a Chinese mythical animal called the *ch'i-lin,* believed to bring good fortune. When an African ruler sent a giraffe to the Chinese emperor, the event was celebrated as a sign of "endless bliss." Through these contacts the

113

Chinese knew far more about eastern Africa than Europeans did. But Europeans soon began a vigorous program of exploration and conquest that greatly expanded their knowledge of African geography.

European Exploration before 1500. Little is known about European travelers in Africa before 1500. European rulers and merchants maintained a policy of secrecy about African travel, commerce, and politics to prevent rivals from taking advantage of their knowledge. Although medieval Europeans did visit the Christian kingdom of ETHIOPIA, no reports of this contact have survived. In the 1400s the Portuguese made some daring explorations of the coastal areas of Africa, but most of Portugal's historical documents perished in an earthquake in 1755.

Ethiopia and Europe developed relations through their shared religion, Christianity. Ethiopians visited Rome in 1302, and for several centuries afterward Europeans tried to visit Ethiopia. Some travelers were blocked from their goal by the Muslim rulers of Egypt. Others reached Ethiopia but were prevented from returning home by Ethiopian officials. One such traveler, Pedro da Covilhã, left Portugal in 1487 and went as far east as India before venturing south from Egypt into Ethiopia. Covilhã arrived in Ethiopia but never left—a later traveler named Francisco Alvarez met him there in 1525.

The major European effort to explore Africa before 1500 took place at sea, not on land, and focused on Africa's western coast. In 1419 Prince Enrique of Portugal, known to later historians as Henry the Navigator, set up a research center on Portugal's south coast to gather information about Africa and to sponsor expeditions southward into waters unknown to European sailors. After the prince died in 1460, Portugal continued to send these explorers out to sea.

By the 1480s the Portuguese had charted most of Africa's western shores. Bartolomeu Dias reached the southern tip of the continent in 1487–1488. A decade later Vasco da GAMA led the first expedition to sail around southern Africa and enter the Indian Ocean. Gama and other Europeans of the time were chiefly concerned with commerce and conquest in Asia, not Africa, but Portugal's voyages also opened the way for Portuguese trade and exploration in Africa. A region around the mouth of the CONGO RIVER later became the Portuguese colony of ANGOLA, and another area on the Indian Ocean coast became the colony of MOZAMBIQUE.

European Exploration from 1500 to 1800. Europeans completed the exploration and mapping of the African coastline in the early 1500s. For the next 300 years, their knowledge of sub-Saharan Africa grew slowly and was limited mostly to coastal trading areas for gold, ivory, and slaves. But a few travelers did explore parts of the African interior and left records of their journeys.

One such traveler, LEO AFRICANUS, an African who lived in Europe and converted to Christianity, made two visits to western Sudan between 1509 and 1513, and Europeans relied on his writings for nearly 300 years. Around the same time, António Fernandes of Portugal explored

Remember: Words in small capital letters have separate entries, and the index at the end of this volume will guide you to more information on many topics.

Mozambique and visited gold mines in Mutapa, a kingdom of the south-eastern interior. Eventually the Portuguese established control over the valley of the ZAMBEZI RIVER in that part of Africa. Meanwhile, in western Africa, English traders probed inland along the Gambia River, while the French used the Senegal River as a highway into the interior.

As a Christian kingdom in Africa, Ethiopia continued to hold a powerful fascination for Europeans. A number of travelers managed to visit Ethiopia in the 1500s and 1600s—and to return to Europe with tales of their experiences. António Fernandes was one of them. James Bruce of Scotland traveled in Ethiopia between 1769 and 1772, and his vivid accounts of the country's warfare and court life caused a sensation in Europe. His book *Travels to Discover the Source of the Nile* (1790) became a classic of adventure and travel writing.

The popularity of books such as Bruce's, especially in London and Paris, showed Europeans' growing interest in African exploration at this time. In 1788 the Association for Promoting the Discovery of the Interior Parts of Africa (usually called the African Association) was formed to sponsor expeditions. A few years later, the Association sent Scottish explorer Mungo Park to chart the course of the NIGER RIVER. Park's adventures included imprisonment by an Arab chief, a long ill-

This drawing re-creates the famous meeting of journalist Henry Morton Stanley and explorer David Livingstone in central Africa in 1871. Through their travels and writings, Stanley, Livingstone, and other Europeans brought some knowledge of African geography and cultures to the rest of the world.

Travel and Exploration

Quest for Timbuktu

Arab descriptions fired European curiosity about Timbuktu, the fabled city in the interior of western Africa. Beginning in the late 1700s, British and French explorers vied to be first to visit Timbuktu. The French Geographical Society fueled the competition by offering a cash prize. In 1826 Alexander Gordon Laing, a British officer, reached Timbuktu but died before returning with the news. Two years later the young Frenchman René Caillié made his way to Timbuktu disguised as a Muslim pilgrim. Caillié did not find an exotic city of gold, only "badly built houses of clay." Nonetheless, on his return to France he received a hero's welcome.

ness, and a difficult journey alone, but he failed to map the Niger. Ten years later the British government sent him to try again, this time with 40 men. Park and his companions traveled down the river by boat for hundreds of miles before drowning while under attack by local people.

European Exploration after 1800. At the beginning of the 1800s, European maps of Africa's interior had large blank areas. For the next 100 years, European travelers, explorers, missionaries, diplomats, and soldiers fanned out across the continent.

Explorers in western Africa continued Mungo Park's quest. Dixon Denham, a British army officer, set out to trace the Niger after crossing the Sahara and finding Lake Chad. Like Park, however, Denham died on the Niger. His servant, Richard Lander, later explored the lower Niger but died in an ambush in 1834. Despite resistance by local people, other British travelers soon completed the journey on the Niger by boat.

Besides mapping major geographic features, many travelers gathered information about the peoples, cultures, languages, and natural history of Africa. Perhaps the most scholarly explorer of western Africa was Heinrich BARTH of Germany, who traveled in LIBYA, NIGER, and the region south of Lake Chad. Some travelers, however, were simply big-game hunters. South Africa especially appealed to British hunters, and some of them made trips into unknown territory in search of game trophies.

David LIVINGSTONE, a Scottish missionary doctor, achieved great fame as the key figure in African exploration during the mid-1800s. Driven by hatred of the slave trade and the belief that his course was directed by God, Livingstone made several very long journeys. During a three-year crossing of the African continent he became the first European to see the great waterfalls of the Zambezi River and named them for Britain's Queen Victoria.

The search for the source of the Nile River grew into an obsession for many Europeans. In 1856 Britain's Royal Geographical Society sent Richard Francis BURTON and John Hanning Speke to solve the mystery, considered one of the great geographic puzzles of the age. In the course of their exploration Speke sighted Lake Victoria. He identified it as the river's source, confirming this fact with a second expedition. Speke had found the source of the White Nile River, the longer of the two main branches of the Nile.

However, some doubt remained, and in the 1860s Livingstone undertook another expedition to settle the matter. While searching for the "fountains of the Nile," Livingstone lost contact with the outside world. In 1871 the American journalist Henry Morton STANLEY made a famous journey to find the explorer. Stanley's book about his meeting with Livingstone made him an international hero, and he went on to lead several long and grueling expeditions across central Africa.

Women also played a role in the exploration of Africa during the late 1800s. The century's last important European traveler was Mary KINGSLEY of Great Britain. Her book *Travels in West Africa* (1895) describes two journeys and criticizes the policies of colonial governments and missionaries toward the African people. Kingsley's book was widely read, and like other popular works of travel and exploration did much to shape the images of Africa held by most Europeans and Americans.

Yet these images did not provide the full story of European involvement in Africa. By the second half of the 1800s, exploration in Africa had cleared the way for full-scale conquest and colonization. European nations hired explorers such as Stanley and Pierre Savorgnan de Brazza to help establish colonial governments. Britain, France, Portugal, Germany, and Italy all competed furiously to gain control over the continent and divide it among themselves. European exploration led to colonization, which left deep wounds in the politics and cultures of Africa. (*See also* **Arabs in Africa, Islam in Africa, Maps and Mapmaking, Roman Africa, Sudanic Empires of Western Africa.**)

Tribalism

ribalism is identification with a particular ethnic group or "tribe." In discussions of African politics and culture, tribalism usually appears as the opposite of NATIONALISM, devotion to the interests and culture of one's entire country. African leaders seeking to build new nations sometimes regard tribalism as primitive, an obstacle to developing a modern national identity. Another view of tribalism, however, is that it shows pride in one's cultural and historical roots and builds unity among people who share a common heritage.

Defining Tribalism. Africans themselves and people outside Africa generally agree that the basic social and cultural units of the continent are tribes (often called ethnic groups, peoples, societies, or communities). Nations are made up of combinations of these groups. A major difficulty in discussing tribalism, however, is deciding how to identify a "tribe." Foreigners and Africans have used different approaches.

European missionaries and scholars were the first to classify Africans into tribes. In various situations they used language, location, or political organization as the basis for classification. Africans who shared a language were considered to be part of the same group. However, because most African languages include many dialects, identifying people by language could be complicated. Some Europeans used location as the method of classification, regarding a group occupying a single area of land as a tribe. Unfortunately, for the most part the territorial boundaries of groups were not precisely marked or matched to those of language use. As to political organization, some Europeans thought that a single political unit could be considered a tribe. The problem with this view was that an African king might rule over many different linguistic or geographic "tribes," perhaps brought under his rule by conquest.

Africans use other methods of classifying themselves, related to systems of exchange—including trade and marriage—and shared beliefs and traditions. People who share a group identity handle trade issues, such as prices and credit, one way among themselves and another way with outsiders. When it comes to marriage, people have almost always preferred to find a spouse within their own group. Therefore, a group in which intermarriage occurs can be regarded as a tribe. Africans also rec-

117

Tribalism

Among the Samburu people of Kenya, elders take a leading role in making decisions for the group.

ognize identity groups based on a shared cosmology, or view of the universe. A common set of religious beliefs and ceremonies and a sense of obligation to help members of the community may define a tribe as well.

Colonialism and "Tribes."   When Europeans began to colonize Africa they soon discovered that the local social and political systems were very different from those of the nations of Europe. One of the Europeans' first steps was to map their African territories, drawing boundaries around groups that they regarded as distinct tribes and defining them as political units.

Some of the groups identified by the Europeans had chiefs, recognized leaders with whom the colonial rulers could deal in matters of administration and taxation. If a group did not have a political leader, the colonial authorities appointed a chief. Some communities refused to accept these "invented chiefs," leading to prolonged conflict with the authorities. In many cases, however, multiple small groups were placed under the rule of one appointed chief. These larger groups came to be treated as a single people, an "invented tribe." Just as the borders of many modern African nations reflect territorial lines drawn by European powers, some of the tribal groupings now found in Africa were created by colonial administrators.

The Europeans built new towns and cities in the colonies, and Africans came to these urban centers to work. In the cities tribal identity became less important than social or economic class. However, when urban workers returned to their rural homes when they were old or sick, they generally returned to their ethnic or tribal identities as well, a pattern that continues today.

Tribalism Today. In modern Africa tribalism can mean several things. It may refer to the desire to preserve traditions, such as group names, values, and customs. Sometimes, however, the word *tribalism* is raised as an accusation. African nationalists—and those outside Africa who support them—may view those who disagree with them as "tribalists." For example, rural Africans who do not share the ambitions of the governing class or who disapprove of government programs may be dismissed as "tribalists" without a sense of civic responsibility toward the nation.

Ethnic identity is a central issue in Africa, where on more than one occasion ethnic rivalries have led to civil war. Yet in searching for a solution, some observers have suggested that tribalism and nationalism need not be regarded as opposites. Instead, both approaches perform the same function—-establishing a group's identity—-in different ways, and can contribute to strengthening African societies. (*See also* **Boundaries in Africa, Colonialism in Africa, Ethnic Groups and Identity**.)

Tshombe, Moïse Kapenda

1917–1969
Prime Minister of Democratic Republic of Congo

* **autonomy** independent self-government

* **coup** sudden, often violent, overthrow of a ruler or government

Moïse Kapenda Tshombe was one of the first leaders of CONGO (KINSHASA). Born in Katanga province in what was then the colony of Belgian Congo, he was trained as a Methodist preacher and a teacher and later became a merchant. In 1958 he helped found the Confederation of Tribal Associations of Katanga, an organization aimed at protecting the interests of ethnic groups in Katanga province.

Tshombe took a leading role in his country's INDEPENDENCE MOVEMENT. In meetings with colonial authorities in 1960, he recommended a system of government in which each province would have almost total autonomy*. When the colony gained independence as the Democratic Republic of Congo in June 1960, Tshombe was elected president of the provincial government of Katanga. Soon afterward he proclaimed Katanga's withdrawal from the central government headed by Patrice LUMUMBA. Lumumba was assassinated the following year.

When UNITED NATIONS troops were sent to control the growing political unrest in Congo in 1963, Tshombe fled to Spain. One year later the Congolese government asked him to return, made him prime minister, and ordered him to put down rebellions in the eastern part of the country. He succeeded but was then fired by president Joseph Kasavubu. The political struggle that followed led to a military coup* by MOBUTU SESE SEKO, and Tshombe again fled to Europe. While attempting to regain power in a coup in the late 1960s, he was arrested and taken to a prison in Algeria, where he died.

119

Tuareg

* **Islamic** relating to Islam, the religion based on the teachings of the prophet Muhammad

* **nomadic** referring to people who travel from place to place to find food and pasture

* **ritual** ceremony that follows a set pattern

The Tuareg are an Islamic* people who dwell in and around the SAHARA DESERT. They speak Tamacheq, one of North Africa's Berber languages. Numbering about one million people altogether, Tuareg can be found mainly in MALI and NIGER but also in BURKINA FASO, ALGERIA, and LIBYA.

Descendants of the nomadic* BERBERS, North Africa's original inhabitants, the Tuareg appeared first in Libya and spread into regions bordering the Sahara. They incorporated local farming peoples into their society, sometimes trading with their neighbors, sometimes raiding them for slaves. Tuareg culture has several distintive features, including a custom that requires men to veil their faces and a religion that blends traditional beliefs and rituals* with Islam.

In the past Tuareg peoples earned a living by breeding livestock, gardening in desert oases, operating trading caravans, running Islamic schools, and practicing metalwork. Agriculture is not easy for the Tuareg for several reasons. In the parts of Mali and Niger where most Tuareg live, the land is primarily made up of flat desert plains, rugged grasslands, and desert borderland. In these areas, some crops can be raised, but only if daily irrigation is used, and repeated droughts have made even basic irrigation a difficult prospect. Livestock and salt, two other staples, have declined in value and further hurt the Tuareg's economic stability. More recently some Tuareg have become migrant laborers, while others have begun making art and craft items for North Africa's tourist trade. Fleeing drought and political unrest in their home countries, many Tuareg have moved south to cities and rural areas in western Africa. In the early 1990s some Tuareg joined an armed revolt against the governments of Mali and Niger. Since rebel and government forces signed an agreement to end the fighting in 1995, movements to revive Tuareg culture have flourished. (*See also* **Islam in Africa**.)

Tubman, William Vacanarat Shadrach

1895–1971
President of Liberia

Considered the man who modernized LIBERIA, William Vacanarat Shadrach Tubman served as president of that nation for 27 years. Born in southeastern Liberia, Tubman was a descendant of freed American slaves who had moved to Liberia from Georgia in the 1800s. A member of Liberia's ruling class, he received a college education and became a lawyer in 1917. Because he often took legal cases without receiving payment, Tubman became known as a "poor man's lawyer."

Ambitious and well liked, Tubman joined the True Whig Party in 1923 and became the youngest senator in Liberia's history. He became a member of the Supreme Court in 1937 and was elected president of Liberia in 1944. Although he imposed one-man rule, Tubman remained a popular leader. He organized economic development programs, established a national public school system, extended full rights of citizenship to Africans in remote areas of the country, and gave all Liberians the right to vote. In addition, in 1963 Tubman helped draw up plans for the ORGANIZATION OF AFRICAN UNITY (OAU), an organization founded to promote harmony and cooperation among African governments.

* **Islamic** relating to Islam, the religion based on the teaching of the prophet Muhammad

* **nomadic** referring to people who travel from place to place to find food and pasture

See map in Archaeology and Prehistory (vol. 1).

* **sub-Saharan** referring to Africa south of the Sahara desert

* **autonomy** independent self-government

* **dynasty** succession of rulers from the same family or group

The small North African nation of Tunisia lies in the center of the continent's Mediterranean coast. Its two neighbors—ALGERIA and LIBYA—are both many times larger. Mostly Islamic* with a rich Arab culture, Tunisia came under French rule in the 1880s and gained independence in 1956.

Most of the country's main cities, including Tunis—the capital—Bizerte, Sousse, Sfax, and Gabes are located along the coast. Northern Tunisia, the most mountainous part of the country, includes the Northern Tell and High Tell chains of the ATLAS MOUNTAIN system. The north is also the wettest region, with average annual rainfall of about 60 inches, and it has the country's only river, the Mejerda. Central Tunisia, flatter and drier, is made up of plateaus and plains. It contains seasonal salt lakes, the largest of which is Shatt al-Jarid. The southern part of the country lies in the SAHARA DESERT.

HISTORY AND GOVERNMENT

In ancient times Tunisia was settled and conquered by various powers drawn to the rich agricultural areas along the coast. Meanwhile, various BERBER-speaking nomadic* groups lived in the drier interior.

Carthage and Rome. In the 800s B.C., settlers from Phoenicia in the eastern Mediterranean founded the city of CARTHAGE on Tunisia's northern shore. Carthage dominated Mediterranean commerce until the 200s B.C., when it fought a series of wars with Rome. In 146 B.C. the Romans sacked Carthage and incorporated it in the province of Africa, which included Tunisia and parts of eastern Algeria. Although Carthage never fully regained its glory, the Romans made it the capital of Africa and a major center in their empire.

In the A.D. 400s the Vandals, a people of northern Europe, attacked Rome and its possessions. They seized the province of Africa and held it until 533, when the region was taken over by the Byzantine Empire, the eastern portion of the Roman Empire.

Arab Rule. Muslims from the Arabian Peninsula invaded Byzantine Tunisia in the 640s. By the end of the century they had conquered the province of Africa—which they called Ifriqiya—and established permanent settlements there. Under Arab rule Tunisia continued to trade with its Mediterranean neighbors. It also developed commercial connections with sub-Saharan* Africa, a major source of gold and slaves. Yet Tunisia's most significant political links were now with Muslim powers to the east and west. Over the next 1,200 years, Tunisia was conquered by a series of Muslim states but always managed to maintain its autonomy*.

Tunisia's first Muslim rulers were the Umayyads from Damascus, in present-day Syria. After taking control of Carthage in 698, they moved the provincial government to Kairouan, an inland town. Tunis, a small town near Carthage, became the main port. The Aghlabids, another Muslim dynasty*, governed Ifriqiya from 800 to 910. The next rulers, the Fatimids, used Ifriqiya as a base to conquer EGYPT. In 973 they moved their capital to CAIRO, and placed the Zirid family in charge of Ifriqiya.

Tunisia

In 1159 the Almohads of Morocco conquered the region, but Ifriqiya did not have an effective government until the Hafsid family came to power in the 1220s. The Hafsids transferred the capital to Tunis, which led to the replacement of the name Ifriqiya with Tunisia.

During the 1500s Spain and the Ottoman Empire competed for control of the lands bordering the Mediterranean. In 1574 the Ottomans took control in Tunisia and appointed local army officers, known as

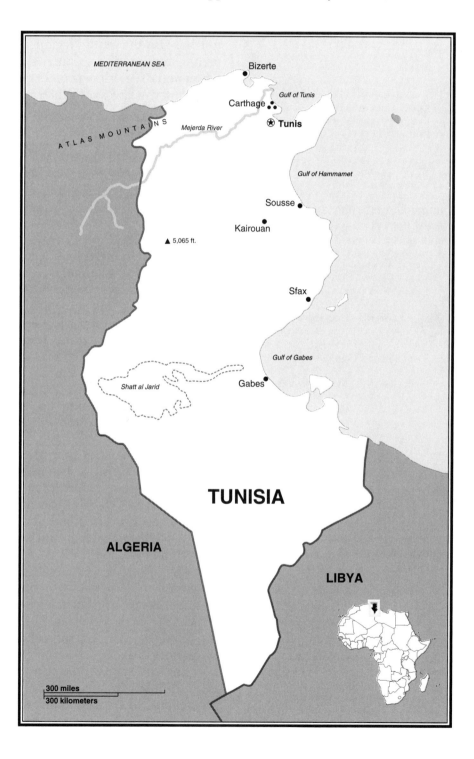

122

Military Mastermind

Hannibal, one of the greatest generals of all time, led the army of the ancient city of Carthage in the 200s B.C. As a boy he vowed never to be an ally of Rome—Carthage's great rival. Hannibal became a military officer. He took command of the Carthaginian army when he was only 25 and led it across Spain in a series of conquests. In 218 B.C. Hannibal's forces crossed the snow-swept Alps, with horses and elephants in tow and hostile tribes hurling stones from above. Arriving in Italy, he won a series of major battles. However, after returning to North Africa in 203 B.C., Hannibal suffered defeat by the Romans.

* **protectorate** weak state under the control and protection of a strong state

* **nationalism** devotion to the interests and culture of one's country

* **polygamy** marriage in which a man has more than one wife or a woman has more than one husband

* **discrimination** unfair treatment of a group

* **dowry** money or property that a woman brings to the man she marries

deys, to run the country. The deys gained considerable power, and eventually the Ottoman rulers in Istanbul had only symbolic authority in Tunisia. In the 1600s the deys were replaced by another group of officers, the Muradid beys. The Muradids were followed in 1705 by the Husaynid beys, who ruled Tunisia until the arrival of the French.

French Rule. The French invaded Tunisia in 1881 and two years they later made it a protectorate*. Soon many Europeans, mostly French but also some Italians, migrated to Tunisia and settled on the best land. In response, educated Tunisians formed a variety of organizations to protect their rights and to seek autonomy and independence. The Young Tunisians, founded in the late 1800s, was followed by the Destour Party in the 1920s and the Neo-Destour Party—led by Habib BOURGUIBA—in the 1930s. As the independence movement gathered force in the early 1950s, it met with fierce resistance from the European settlers and led to occasional violence.

On March 20, 1956, France granted independence to Tunisia. The following year Tunisia became a republic with Habib Bourguiba as its first president, a position he held for 30 years. Bourguiba was reelected in 1964 and 1969 and was named president for life in 1974. His Neo-Destour Party, known after 1964 as the Socialist Destour Party, was the only legal political party in the country. Various opposition leaders and government ministers who fell into disfavor were jailed, forced into exile, or even killed.

President Bourguiba maintained close ties with France. Although he supported Arab nationalism*, his relations with other Arab leaders were often strained. In 1974 he agreed to unite Tunisia with Libya, but then withdrew from the plan.

When Bourguiba became too ill to govern in 1987, Prime Minister Zine el-Abidine Ben Ali assumed the presidency. Ben Ali has released political prisoners, abolished the post of president for life, and legalized some opposition parties. However, he has dealt severely with members of the Islamic opposition. Although the government's election practices have been questioned, Ben Ali was reelected in 1989, 1994, and 1999, and his party has maintained a large majority in the National Assembly. The president has formed strong relationships the United States and organizations such as the International Monetary Fund and the World Bank. At the same time he has worked toward closer ties with Arab neighbors, founding the Arab Maghreb Union with Algeria, Libya, MAURITANIA, and MOROCCO in 1989.

Women's rights have been an important issue in the Bourguiba and Ben Ali governments. Starting with his 1956 Personal Status Code, Bourguiba introduced dramatic marriage reforms, outlawing polygamy* and forced marriage. He also granted women the right to vote. Ben Ali has passed laws against workplace discrimination* and has changed a law requiring women's obedience to their husbands. Men remain the legal heads of families and payment of dowry*, opposed by some Tunisian feminists, is still legal and widely practiced.

Tunisia

The women of a Bedouin family in Matmata, Tunisia, prepare to have tea. In the past Bedouins were nomadic Arabs who lived in desert or semidesert areas.

* **socialist** relating to an economic or political system based on the idea that the government or groups of workers should own and run the means of production and distribution of goods

* **inflation** increase in prices

See map in Minerals and Mining (vol. 3).

124

ECONOMY

In the 1960s Tunisia adopted various socialist* economic policies. Since the 1980s it has introduced some reforms that have helped to control inflation* and encourage the growth of manufacturing and tourism. Exports and imports have both increased, but progress has been uneven and unemployment remains high. In 1995 Tunisia signed a free trade agreement with the European Union, its principal trading partner. It also has commercial relations with Algeria, Libya, and the United States.

About one-fifth of the Tunisian labor force works in agriculture. Crop yields vary considerably according to conditions such as drought and rainfall. Wheat, barley, grapes, olives, and citrus fruits are the most important crops. Farmers also raise sheep, goats, and cattle.

Tunisia exports large quantities of oil. It also produces phosphates—used in making fertilizer—natural gas, iron ore, and lead. Manufacturing industries include textiles, leather goods, food processing, and chemicals. Tourism, particularly along the country's Mediterranean beaches, is another major source of jobs and foreign currency.

Some Tunisians still follow a nomadic lifestyle—though their numbers are declining—and others farm small plots of land. However, more than 60 percent of the population now lives in cities and towns near the coast. Many urban dwellers are unable to find steady jobs, forcing them to take casual work with lower wages. Large numbers of Tunisians have migrated abroad, primarily to Europe. Money sent home by those working abroad makes up a significant part of the economy.

PEOPLES AND CULTURES

The vast majority of Tunisians identify themselves as Arab. Most of the rest are Berbers. Many centuries of Arab domination helped to spread Arab culture in Tunisia and allowed it to become firmly rooted there.

Tunisia's Arab heritage has influenced the way the people dress. Some women cover their entire bodies, including the head, with a single white rectangular cloth known as a *safsari*. Others have adopted the *hijab*, a simpler head covering. Men often wear a plain calf-length robe and a *shashiya*—a brimless, red felt cap. Other Tunisians dress in European clothes. Elaborate, richly embroidered garments are worn for weddings.

Influences. Tunisian music, art, literature, and education reveal the influence of Arab and European cultures. For example, refugees from Spain brought *maaluf*, an urban, classical music, to the region. Written for violin, lute, and drum, *maaluf* performances often last several hours. Tunisia has a centuries-old literary tradition. Before the colonial era authors from the region wrote secular* poetry and philosophy as well as influential religious texts. Ibn Khaldun, a historian born in Tunis in the 1300s, wrote *Muqaddama*, a complex work of social theory. Since the 1900s Arabic-language novels have become increasingly popular.

Before the period of French rule, Tunisian education emphasized religious subjects such as study of the Qur'an—the Islamic sacred text—and religious law. Grammar, logic, and medicine were also offered. The most

* **secular** nonreligious; connected with everyday life

 The Republic of Tunisia

POPULATION:
9,593,402 (2000 estimated population)

AREA:
63,170 sq. mi. (163,610 sq. km)

LANGUAGES:
Arabic (official); French; some Berber dialects

NATIONAL CURRENCY:
Tunisian dinar

PRINCIPAL RELIGIONS:
Muslim 98%, Christian 1%, Jewish and other 1%

CITIES:
Tunis (capital), 1,897,000 (2001 est.); Bizerte, Sousse, Sfax, Gabes

ANNUAL RAINFALL:
Varies from 60 in. (1,524 mm) in the north to 8 in. (203 mm) in the Sahara region.

ECONOMY:
GDP per capita: $5,500 (1999 est.)

PRINCIPAL PRODUCTS AND EXPORTS:
Agricultural: olives, grain, dairy products, tomatoes, citrus fruits, beef, sugar dates, almonds
Manufacturing: textiles, footwear, food processing, beverages
Mining: petroleum, phosphates, iron ore
Services: tourism

GOVERNMENT:
Independence from France, 1956. Republic with president elected by universal suffrage. Governing body: 163-seat Majlis al-Nuwaab (Chamber of Deputies), members elected by universal suffrage.

HEADS OF STATE SINCE INDEPENDENCE:
1957–1987 President Habib Bourguiba
1984– President Zine al-Abidine Ben Ali

ARMED FORCES:
35,000 (2001 est.)

EDUCATION:
Compulsory for ages 6–16; literacy rate 67% (2001 est.)

notable centers of learning were in Kairouan and at Tunis's Zaituna Mosque-University. In the 1800s European models of education became increasingly influential. Sadiqi College, a prestigious secondary school founded in Tunis in 1875, focused on science, math, and European languages. Since independence, strong government support for education has helped to reduce adult illiteracy rates. Most classes are taught in Arabic, except in the universities, where French is widely used. A small group of educated French-speaking Tunisians controls government administration and much of the country's wealth.

Religion. Most modern Tunisians are Sunni Muslims. A small number of Jews—remnants of a community founded more than 2,000 years ago—still live in the country. A once-vibrant Christian community, which produced the religious scholar Augustine, disappeared by the 1100s. During the colonial era many European Christians settled in Tunisia, but most of their descendants left after independence.

Recently, a movement to base the government on Islam has gathered force. The movement is supported by Nahda, an illegal political party. President Ben Ali's government opposes the movement and has tried to suppress it. The role of Islam in Tunisian society is perhaps the most serious question facing the nation. (*See also* **Arabs in Africa, Colonialism in Africa, Islam in Africa, North Africa: Geography and Population, North Africa: History and Cultures.**)

Tutu, Desmond Mpilo

1931–
South African religious leader and activist

* **theology**   study of religious faith

* **apartheid**   policy of racial segregation enforced by the white government of South Africa to maintain political, economic, and social control over the country's blacks, Asians, and people of mixed ancestry

A leader of the Anglican Church, Desmond Mpilo Tutu is best known for his tireless efforts for peace, unity, and human rights in SOUTH AFRICA. Born in Klerksdorp, he hoped to become a doctor but could not afford medical training. Instead, he became a schoolteacher and attended the University of South Africa. After graduating in 1958 he suffered a serious illness and decided to become a priest of the Anglican Church. He studied for three years in England, then taught theology* at various universities throughout southern Africa. In 1972 he returned to England to work for the World Council of Churches.

When Tutu came back to South Africa three years later, he quickly became an important figure in both the religious and the political world. In the church he rose to positions never before held by a black person, including dean of St. Mary's Cathedral in Johannesburg and bishop of LESOTHO. While serving as the general secretary of the South African Council of Churches in the late 1970s, Tutu spoke out strongly against apartheid*. He encouraged South Africans to stage nonviolent protests and urged foreign nations to apply economic pressure to South Africa's racist government. He won the Nobel Peace Prize for those efforts in 1984. In 1986 Tutu became archbishop of Cape Town, the head of South Africa's Anglican church—a role he held for ten years.

As apartheid came to an end in the early 1990s, Tutu played a major role in bringing peace and unity to the long-divided nation. He worked together with Nelson MANDELA, the nation's first black president, who in

1996 named Tutu chairperson of the Commission on Truth and Reconciliation.

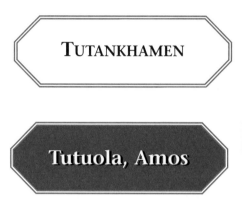

TUTANKHAMEN

See *Pharaohs.*

Tutuola, Amos

1920–1997
Nigerian writer

N igerian novelist Amos Tutuola gained fame for his retelling of traditional YORUBA myths, legends, and fables. The son of a poor farmer, Tutuola struggled to obtain an education. He gathered and sold firewood to help his father pay for his schooling. When his father died in 1939, however, the family could no longer afford Tutuola's tuition, and he had to leave school. Over the next several years, he held jobs in a variety of trades, including farming, metalworking, and photography. Finally, he took a job as a messenger at the Department of Labor.

It was while waiting for messages to deliver that Tutuola wrote his first novel, *The Palm-Wine Drinkard and his Dead Palm-Wine Tapster in the Deads' Town* (1952). The novel tells of a "drinkard," or alcoholic, who embarks on a journey to the land of the dead to find his deceased tapster, a person who serves liquor. During the journey, the "drinkard" encounters wicked creatures and magical places and eventually gains wisdom. Tutuola's story borrows from Yoruba mythology, and its structure is based on both modern novels and traditional oral stories. Although the novel received praise in England, some Nigerians criticized it, saying that Tutuola's use of poor grammar and Yoruba folklore were unsophisticated.

Despite the criticism, Tutuola continued to write. His second novel, *My Life in the Bush of Ghosts* (1954), received more praise abroad than in Nigeria. He did not become popular in his own country until 1962, when he wrote a stage version of *The Palm-Wine Drinkard.* Tutuola's other works include *Simbi and the Satyr of the Dark Jungle* (1955), *Yoruba Folktales* (1986), and *The Village Witch Doctor and Other Stories* (1990). (*See also* **Literature.**)

TUTSI

See *Rwanda.*

Uganda

T he East African nation of Uganda once served as a symbol of everything that could go wrong in post-independence Africa. Ruled by corrupt dictators and torn by ethnic violence, Uganda was a land of poverty and despair despite its rich natural resources. Since the late 1980s, however, Uganda has made a remarkable turnaround, and many people have looked to it as a model for progress in modern Africa.

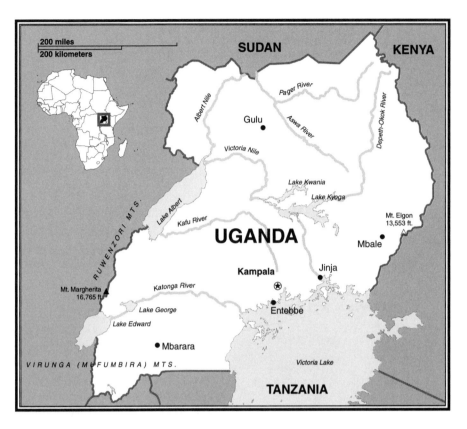

GEOGRAPHY

Uganda lies in the Great Lakes region of east-central Africa and shares borders with five other countries: SUDAN to the north, KENYA to the east, TANZANIA and RWANDA to the south, and the CONGO (KINSHASA) to the west.

Located on the equator, the country rests on a high plateau that makes the climate fairly moderate. Much of the country is mountainous, with high peaks rising in the east, west, and southwest. The western end of the Rift Valley, an enormous trench, also passes through Uganda.

Water—rivers, streams, lakes, and swamps—covers about 15 percent of the surface area of Uganda. Among the most prominent bodies of water are Lake Victoria, the world's second-largest freshwater lake, and the NILE RIVER. The Nile begins in Lake Victoria and flows into Lake Albert before traveling more than 3,000 miles north to the Mediterranean Sea.

Uganda enjoys abundant rainfall and very fertile soil, excellent conditions for agriculture. The south and west receive an average of about 90 inches of rain per year. The extreme northeast is much drier, and many people there raise animals rather than plant crops.

HISTORY AND GOVERNMENT

Before the arrival of Europeans in the mid-1800s, Uganda was made up of many autonomous* societies. In the north, most people lived in

* **autonomous**   self-governing

small communities without a strong central authority. In the south, many groups were ruled by chiefs or kings. The largest kingdom was Buganda, on the shores of Lake Victoria in the southern part of Uganda. Muslim traders from the Indian Ocean coast established businesses in Buganda and won influence at the court of the Ganda king.

European Involvement. The first Europeans to visit Uganda were explorers such as John Hanning Speke, who came in 1862 in search of the source of the Nile River. Missionaries arrived about ten years later, and merchants such as Frederick LUGARD of the Imperial British East Africa Company were in the area by 1890. Four years later the British declared a protectorate* over the area.

* **protectorate** weak state under the control and protection of a strong state

This was a time of turmoil in which Africans fought each other and the British. Christians and Muslims went to war in 1888–1889, and Catholics and Protestants clashed three years later. The kingdom of Bunyoro in the north fought with the British and their allies from the powerful kingdom of Buganda. But the Ganda ruler later rebelled against British authority and took up arms against some of his chiefs, who had converted to Christianity.

The Uganda Agreement. In 1900 the British and representatives of the region's major chiefdoms and kingdoms signed the Uganda Agreement. This document recognized the existence of four separate kingdoms—Buganda, Bunyoro, Toro, and Ankole—within the British colony of Uganda and allowed each state to govern itself. However, Buganda received more autonomy and a larger share of the benefits of colonial development, such as education by Christian missionaries, than the other kingdoms.

A main goal of British rule in Uganda was to exploit the land's fertility. The British put people to work growing crops such as cotton, coffee, and tea to sell as exports. Much of this farming took place in Buganda, as did other economic activity. The British also established their government in this kingdom in a new town called Entebbe, and many Ganda received civil service jobs and helped the British rule the colony.

Development in the south proceeded rapidly, but the British did not establish firm control over the northeast until the late 1920s. Many northerners then moved south to find work, often in the colonial police forces. Some Ganda in the south felt that their privileged position was threatened.

Another source of ethnic tension was the large number of Asian merchants. Asians owned the majority of the sugar plantations, dominated the cotton industry, controlled the manufacturing and importing of most goods, and ran most of the shops in Kampala, the major city that became the capital in 1958. Many indigenous Africans resented the Asians' wealth and power.

The division of Uganda into separate kingdoms produced lasting rivalries. Bunyoro repeatedly pressed to regain the land it lost in its war with Buganda. Meanwhile, the Ganda king demanded independence from the rest of Uganda in an effort to protect Buganda's autonomy.

Raid on Entebbe

Uganda's dictator Idi Amin Dada made world headlines in the summer of 1976 when he allowed a hijacked airliner to land at the Entebbe airport. The plane, with many Israeli citizens aboard, had been seized by Palestinian terrorists demanding freedom for a group of imprisoned Palestinians. The world watched breathlessly as a week of suspense ended with a daring raid by Israeli commandos. They stormed into the airport terminal and freed the hostages. Seven hijackers, three hostages, and one commando died in the raid.

As political parties formed during the 1950s, religious rivalries reappeared. The Democratic Party was a Catholic stronghold, while the Uganda People's Party had Protestant roots. Local and regional power struggles seemed more important than national unity and independence from Britain. The one thing many Ugandans shared was resentment of the Asian community. A nationwide boycott of non-African businesses in 1954 resulted in many Asians leaving the country when it became independent.

A Difficult New Beginning. In October 1960, Uganda gained independence from Britain and held its first elections the following year. The new constitution called for a single state with little autonomy for individual kingdoms. Buganda rejected this arrangement and refused to participate in the elections. As a result, the Democratic Party won.

The following year a member of the Lango ethnic group named Milton OBOTE joined forces with a Ganda political party. The coalition won the election, with the Ganda king MUTESA II as president and Obote as prime minister. Obote then consolidated his power and pushed aside his Ganda allies. When they tried to stage a coup* in 1966, the national army, led by General Idi AMIN DADA, crushed the Ganda and forced Mutesa to flee the country.

* **coup** sudden, often violent, overthrow of a ruler or government

During the early years of Obote's reign, Uganda made progress in education, the economy, and other areas. However, Obote abolished all political parties except his own and put many Lango into high government, army, and judicial posts. He turned the country towards socialism* and steadily lost support. In 1971 the army revolted, bringing Amin to power.

* **socialism** economic or political system based on the idea that the government or groups of workers should own and run the means of production and distribution of goods

Uganda Under Idi Amin. At first Idi Amin enjoyed wide popular support. A former national heavyweight boxing champion, he seemed friendly and confident. But beneath his smiles was a cold-blooded and brutal tyrant. Over the next eight years, he plunged Uganda into a world of terror and corruption that claimed perhaps as many as a million lives.

Amin quickly turned against anyone he thought might threaten his control over Uganda and its wealth. In 1972 he expelled all Asians from the country. Most black Ugandans approved of this action, but the country's economy suffered from the loss of these experienced businesspeople. Amin also drove out clergy and missionaries and outlawed some Christian groups. In addition he targeted the Lango and other rival ethnic groups. He did not hesitate to use violence, torture, and murder to advance his goals.

In the end, however, it was Amin's military adventures in other countries, not his reign of terror at home, which led to his downfall. In 1979 he invaded Tanzania to punish its president, Julius NYERERE, for supporting Ugandan rebels. The invasion failed badly, and Tanzanian troops stormed into Kampala and forced Amin to flee to Saudi Arabia.

The Movement. Uganda's government was restored with elections. Obote manipulated the process and regained his position as president.

But he could not control ethnic violence in the country, and Ugandans lost patience with his corruption. A rebellion in 1985 pushed him out of office, followed by more than a year of chaos. Finally Yoweri M USEVENI, the leader of the main rebel group, captured Kampala and proclaimed himself president.

Museveni set about trying to rebuild and unify Uganda. He hoped to overcome the ethnic divisions that had plagued the country for so long, and he argued that political parties increased these rivalries. He therefore outlawed political parties and set up the National Revolutionary Movement, a system of government that claimed to include all Ugandans. Though many feared he would rule as a dictator, Museveni formed a commission to draw up a constitution that would provide fundamental freedoms and protection of HUMAN RIGHTS. The commission spent years consulting people in all parts of Ugandan society, hoping to create a constitution by consensus.

The constitution, adopted in 1995, established a parliament with members elected by the people but forbidden to run as members of a party. The president, also elected, was limited to two terms of five years. The constitution also provided for a vice president, a cabinet of ministers, and independent system of courts.

In 1996 Museveni won Uganda's first free and open presidential election in over 30 years. But the country still faced major problems. Rebel

Since the mid-1980s, Uganda's president Yoweri Museveni has sought to overcome ethnic tension in his country and build a stable government.

Uganda

forces in northern and western Uganda, supported by Sudan, fought Museveni's government. Museveni had also involved his country deeply in the civil wars raging in Rwanda and Congo (Kinshasa). His political opponents continued to call for a democracy with political parties. Despite these difficulties, Uganda seemed to recover steadily from the devastating years of Obote and Amin.

In 2001 Museveni won reelection, but his main political opponents refused to participate in the elections and questioned the legitimacy of his victory. Many Ugandans, as well as foreign diplomats, have grown uneasy with Museveni's interventions in Congo and elsewhere. Although the glow of Museveni's early days has faded, many people still hope that he can bring peace and prosperity to Uganda.

ECONOMY

Agriculture is Uganda's main economic activity, employing more than 90 percent of the population and accounting for nearly all of the country's exports. Coffee ranks as the country's most important export. Manufacturing, mining, and the rest of the economy contribute little income. However, tourism has made a strong comeback during the relative calm of the Museveni years. Visitors have long admired Uganda's abundant and varied wildlife and spectacular scenery, including several major national parks.

Museveni's government has improved economic performance by trying to encourage producers to rely less on traditional exports and by selling unprofitable state-owned companies to private investors. New

Daily Life

Plate 1: The manufacture of textiles made of homegrown cotton is an important industry in Ivory Coast. Some of the brightly patterned fabric is sold in markets, such as the one shown here in Abidjan.

Plate 2: Many of the people of the Kalahari live by keeping cattle or goats. A herder in Botswana drives along his goats, which are raised for their meat, milk, and hide.

Plate 3: Sugarcane, an important crop in Madagascar, is grown on plantations in the northwestern part of the island and on the east coast. Here workers harvest sugarcane.

Plate 4: Soccer is the most popular sport in Africa. Teams compete at the local, national, and international level. In Mombasa, Kenya, soccer players take the field near the ruins of Fort Jesus, built by the Portuguese in 1593.

Plate 5: In 1997 Uganda adopted a policy known as Universal Primary Education to increase school attendance and the level of literacy. These children attend a primary school in Kampala, the country's capital.

Plate 6: In rural areas of Zambia, women make flour the hard way—by pounding millet, a kind of grain, in a mortar. They cook the flour with water to create a thick porridge, a basic part of their diet.

Plate 7: Religion plays a significant role in the daily life of Africans. For Muslims that means stopping whatever they are doing five times a day, turning toward the holy city of Mecca, and praying. This Muslim man observes the call to prayer in war-torn Somalia.

Plate 8: The Venda, a cultural group with a shared language, live in the northeastern corner of South Africa. Venda women have something of an artistic tradition, especially in wall painting and sculpture. Here a Venda woman makes pottery.

Plate 9: Dogon children stand in front of a great house in a village in Mali. Such houses serve as the home of the senior man in an extended family or of the village headman. Grouped around the great house are the small dwellings of the rest of the villagers.

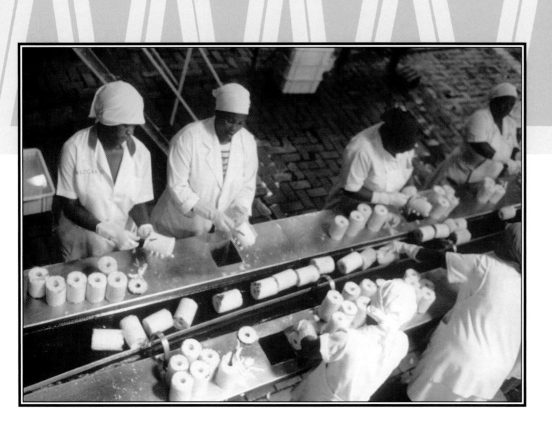

Plate 10: Sugar is the main export crop of Swaziland, but the country also produces citrus fruit and pineapple. Here Swazi women core and prepare pineapples for canning at a food-processing plant.

Plate 11: In the Sahara desert, salt is the most important trade good. Men cut slabs of salt from the earth at the mining settlement of Taoudenni in northern Mali. Arranged in rows, the slabs will be carried south across the desert on an old trade route.

Plate 12: One way to get around the town of Antsirabe on Madagascar is to rent a *pousse-pousse,* the local version of a rickshaw. *Taxi-brousses* (minibuses or limousines) are popular for travel between towns.

Plate 13: The development of oil and natural gas resources has brought new revenue to some countries in Africa. Tunisia has built refineries, such as the one shown here, and oil is now one of its main exports.

Plate 14: In Cairo, Egyptian men go to tearooms to drink coffee or tea, chat with friends, and read the paper.

Plate 15: Cape Town, the oldest city in southern Africa, was founded in 1652 as a supply base for the Dutch East India Company. Now a major port and manufacturing center, Cape Town is known for its historical buildings and parks. Visitors come to enjoy the nearby beaches, mountains, and vineyards.

government policies have brought inflation under control, and improved tax collection has increased revenues. The country borrowed heavily from the World Bank and International Monetary Fund, which called for many of these changes. In 1998 these institutions recognized Uganda's improving economy and announced a program to forgive some of the country's debt.

PEOPLES AND CULTURES

Several different language families exist in Uganda, providing a foundation for the country's political and ethnic divisions. BANTU speakers dominate the southern portion of the country, where good conditions for agriculture led to the formation of centralized societies that developed into kingdoms. People in the north speak languages of the Eastern Nilotic, Western Nilotic, and Sudanic families. Many northerners raised herds of livestock because the region's climate was too dry for large-scale farming.

All of Uganda's ethnic groups—both northern and southern—are dominated by men. Property and political power pass through the male side of the family, and women are generally treated as socially inferior. The constitution acknowledges this problem by guaranteeing seats in Parliament to women representatives.

About two-thirds of Uganda's people are Christian, while the rest are divided about evenly between ISLAM and traditional African religions. However, most of those who follow Islam or Christianity include traditional beliefs and customs in their worship. In recent years many new religious groups have arisen in Uganda. One of these, the Movement for the Restoration of the Ten Commandments, gained notoriety in 2000 when many of its members committed mass suicide. (*See also* **Colonialism in Africa; Kagwa, Apolo; Tribalism; Wildlife and Game Parks; Women in Africa.**)

Umar ibn Sa'id Tal

ca. 1794–1864
Muslim leader in West Africa

* **Islam** religion based on the teachings of the prophet Muhammad; religious faith of Muslims

* **theology** study of religious faith

* **pilgrimage** journey to a shrine or sacred place

A Muslim cleric, or religious leader, Umar ibn Sa'id Tal played an important role in spreading Islam* across a broad area of West Africa. Through his writing, military achievements, and his role in the religious brotherhood of the Tijaniyya, he remains a prominent figure for Muslims in West Africa.

Born in the valley of the Senegal River, Umar was the son of a local cleric and teacher in a Muslim society dominated by the FULANI people. A gifted student, Umar trained as a Muslim cleric, studying Islamic law, theology*, and literature. He was also initiated into the Tijaniyya.

Between 1828 and 1830 Umar made three pilgrimages* to the holy cities of Mecca and Medina in Arabia, earning the honorary title al-Hajj ("the pilgrim"). Soon after, he began spreading the Tijaniyya brotherhood in West Africa. Umar spent time in many of the Muslim centers of West Africa and by the 1840s he had developed a very loyal group of followers. During this period he also wrote his major work, *Al-Rimah*, which remains an important resource for the Tijaniyya today.

133

Between 1852 and his death in 1864, Umar led his followers and other Muslims in a jihad, or holy war, against non-Muslim kingdoms in the upper Senegal and Niger River valleys. In 1862 he conquered the Fulani state of Segu on the NIGER RIVER. However, the inhabitants of Segu soon joined forces with a powerful leader in TIMBUKTU. Umar's army was defeated by the armies of Timbuktu and its allies, and Umar was killed. (*See also* Islam in Africa.)

Unions and Trade Associations

nformal worker's unions and trade associations first appeared in Africa during the 1890s. However, organized union activity did not get underway until after World War I in the British colonies and after World War II in French colonies. Few unions arose in Portuguese territories such as ANGOLA and MOZAMBIQUE. In SOUTH AFRICA, years of rule by racist white governments led to unions for each race.

Development of Unions. In English-speaking Africa, white-collar professionals organized separately from unskilled or semiskilled blue-collar workers. The issue of wages was important for both groups, but blue-collar workers had much greater need to protect their incomes and jobs. During the Great Depression of the 1930s, many people lost their jobs, producing a surplus of available workers. This drove down wages for those who did find jobs.

As the situation worsened in the late 1930s, colonial authorities worried that unhappy workers would blame their troubles on the government and give their support to nationalist* politicians seeking to end colonial rule. To appeal to workers, Britain decided to allow unions in its African colonies to register with the government. This made the unions legally recognized organizations. However, ties between unions and INDEPENDENCE MOVEMENTS remained strong. Many early African political leaders emerged from the union movement.

In many North African nations, the union movement was linked to nationalist efforts as well. In the late 1940s in TUNISIA, the General Union of Tunisian Workers, led by Ferhat Hached, worked closely with nationalist politicians. Because of his association with the independence movement, Hached was later assassinated by the Red Hand, a French organization opposed to independence. In 1955 a nationalist party in MOROCCO helped form the Union Marocaine du Travail (UMT), which is now one of the nation's largest unions. Today the UMT is no longer affiliated with any political party, although it works to maintain good relations with the government.

In most colonies unions were made up of people of different races and ethnic backgrounds. However, this was not the case in South Africa, where two separate union movements developed—one for whites and one for blacks. In 1919 an African named Clement KADALIE founded the most important black union in South Africa, the Industrial and Commercial Worker's Union. Around the same time, South African socialists* and communists* organized white workers into unions. One

* **nationalist** devoted to the interests and culture of one's country

* **socialist** relating to an economic or political system based on the idea that the government or groups of workers should own and run the means of production and distribution

* **communist** relating to communism, a system in which land, goods, and the means of production are owned by the state or community rather than by individuals

such union had the slogan, "Workers of the World Unite for a White South Africa." The division between white and black union movements became even wider in 1922, when several white unions violently forced the government to agree to protect their members from black competition. In the late 1900s black unions grew more powerful, ultimately playing a major role in ending South Africa's apartheid* regime.

Post-Independence Africa. Since gaining independence in the mid-1900s, only a few African nations have produced strong union movements. In Morocco and Tunisia union members have struggled for democracy and human rights as well as for better wages, occasionally suffering imprisonment and violence from government authorities. In South Africa unions which are allied with the African National Congress (ANC), have become more active since the ANC took power in 1994. In NIGERIA, oil workers struck in 1994 to protest election results. Some scholars suggest that countries such as these have strong and active unions because these nations are more involved in the world economy than many poorer African states. To help increase union activity and effectiveness throughout the continent, an association called *the Organisation de L'Unité Africaine* (OATUU) works to coordinate the action of African unions. Based in GHANA, its members include about 50 different national unions. (*See also* **Colonialism in Africa, Economic History.**).)

* **apartheid** policy of racial segregation enforced by the white government of South Africa to maintain political, economic, and social control over the country's blacks, Asians, and people of mixed ancestry

United Nations in Africa

* **humanitarian** referring to a concern for human welfare

C reated after World War II, the United Nations (UN) is an international organization that promotes peace and security among member states and cooperation on economic, social, cultural, and humanitarian* issues. When the UN was founded in 1945, only four African countries were independent states and members of the organization: EGYPT, ETHIOPIA, LIBERIA, and SOUTH AFRICA. By 2000 more than 50 African countries had joined the United Nations.

As members of the United Nations, African states have a voice in international affairs, debating issues affecting member states and providing support for various UN programs. African nations have perhaps their most important role in the General Assembly, the branch of the United Nations consisting of all member states. The General Assembly discusses and makes recommendations on issues under consideration by the organization.

Role in Africa. The United Nations has a significant impact on African countries through its policies and the activities of its agencies. In its role in promoting world peace and security, the UN has been active in many of Africa's trouble spots. It has intervened or acted as a negotiator in numerous wars resulting from the struggle for independence and in internal conflicts. In 2000 it had three major peacekeeping operations in Africa: in CONGO (KINSHASA), SIERRA LEONE, and WESTERN SAHARA.

The United Nations is also involved in economic development activities in Africa—the least developed region in the world. Economic devel-

135

opment involves increasing the efficiency and productivity of a country's economy and improving the living conditions of its people. Nearly all UN development agencies play an active role on the continent. A special agency, the United Nations Economic Commission for Africa (ECA), was created in 1958 to assist African states in their efforts to improve and expand their economies.

UN Agencies. UN agencies provide a variety of different services in Africa, from food and economic assistance to education and financial advice. The ECA works to promote economic cooperation among African nations, raise the level of economic activity in each country, and increase the standard of living of African peoples. Each of the agency's divisions focuses on particular issues, such as agriculture, industry, trade, natural resources, transportation, and communications. The ECA has also played a key role in bringing the plight of African countries to international attention.

Created in 1965, the United Nations Development Programme (UNDP) works to help UN member nations around the world with their development efforts. The agency is the largest source of technical support for developing countries worldwide. Assistance usually consists of providing experts, equipment, and training. One of the agency's programs, the United Nations Capital Development Fund, focuses on small-scale development projects such as building irrigation systems, roads, and housing in poor communities.

The United Nations High Commissioner for Refugees (UNHCR), established in 1951, assists REFUGEES displaced as a result of war, social unrest, or persecution. The agency offers protection for refugees, ensuring that they are treated according to international guidelines. It also provides refugees with emergency food, shelter, medical care, education, and counseling, as well as assistance with resettlement in their homelands or in other countries. UNHCR was particularly active in Africa in the 1990s, when millions of refugees were forced to leave their homes in SOMALIA, ERITREA, RWANDA, and other countries because of famine, ethnic violence, and internal strife.

Established in 1945, the Food and Agriculture Organization (FAO) is dedicated to raising levels of nutrition and standards of living by improving the production and distribution of food and other agricultural goods. In Africa the FAO has worked to change agricultural policies, conserve the environment, and develop institutions and infrastructure* to support increased production. The agency provides both technical assistance——such as distributing seed samples and fighting soil erosion—and training.

The World Bank, also known as the International Bank for Reconstruction and Development, is a specialized UN financial agency. In the 1990s it was Africa's largest source of loans. The bank also provides research grants and technical advice and training related to its loan projects.

Other UN agencies that play an active role in Africa include the United Nations Environment Programme (UNEP), the United Nations

* **infrastructure** basic framework of a society and its economy, which includes roads, bridges, port facilities, airports, and other public works

Population Fund (UNPF), the United Nations Children's Fund (UNICEF), the World Health Organization (WHO), and the United Nations Educational, Scientific, and Cultural Organization (UNESCO). (*See also* **Annan, Kofi; Development, Economic and Social; Global Politics and Africa; Human Rights.**)

UNIVERSITIES AND COLLEGES

See *Education.*

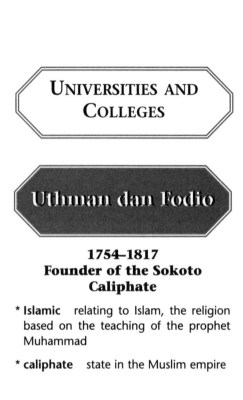

Uthman dan Fodio

1754–1817
Founder of the Sokoto Caliphate

* **Islamic** relating to Islam, the religion based on the teaching of the prophet Muhammad

* **caliphate** state in the Muslim empire

U thman dan Fodio was an Islamic* scholar and preacher who founded the Sokoto caliphate* in what is now northern NIGERIA. In the 1800s Sokoto became one of the largest independent states in Africa.

Born in the town of Gobir, Uthman belonged to a family of Islamic scholars. He grew up speaking Fulfulde, the language of the FULANI people, but he was educated in Arabic. At the age of 20 Uthman began preaching Islam in rural areas, later moving to the court of the sultan of Gobir. Unlike many preachers at the time, he used simple language to teach the basics of Islam to herders, farmers, and women.

By the time he was 50, Uthman had become so popular that the rulers of Gobir feared his influence. Threatened with attack, he fled Gobir for the town of Gudu where he was elected imam, or spiritual leader. He announced a jihad, or holy war, against various Muslim states that did not recognize his leadership. Over the next several years his supporters fought their way across Hausaland in northern Nigeria. By 1808 the last HAUSA city had fallen and an area of more than 200,000 square miles had been united under Uthman's leadership. Four years later Uthman divided the empire between his son, Muhammad Bello, and his brother, Abdullah dan Fodio.

In addition to his political and spiritual leadership, Uthman wrote over 100 Arabic works and some 50 poems, mostly in Fulfulde. He had 37 children, many of whom became religious leaders and scholars. His daughter Nana ASMA'U was a noted poet and a pioneer in educating women. (*See also* **Islam in Africa.**)

Van Riebeeck, Jan

1619–1677
Dutch colonial administrator

J an Van Riebeeck was a Dutch merchant who founded Cape Colony, the first European settlement in what would later become SOUTH AFRICA. Born in the Netherlands, Van Riebeeck began traveling at an early age with his father, who worked for the Dutch East India Company. In time he, too, worked for the company, and he became wealthy through his trading activities in Asia. However, the company discovered that he was trading on his own, and banished him from Asia.

As punishment Van Riebeeck was sent to lead an expedition to the Cape of Good Hope at the southern tip of Africa in 1652. The plan was to create a supply station for Dutch ships headed for Asia. However, Van

Riebeeck decided to build a fort to protect his people from both the Africans and from other Europeans.

Eventually Van Riebeeck decided to found a colony, establishing a settlement that later became CAPE TOWN. He imported slave labor to work the land and began to buy cattle from the local KHOISAN people. After a time he had bought all the cattle from nearby groups and had to trade with others much farther away to obtain new animals. The settlers eventually owned so many cattle that they had to seize land from the Khoisan to graze their herds.

The land seizures led to war in 1659, but the settlers retreated to their fort and held out against the Khoisan. Afterwards, Van Riebeeck ordered thorn bushes to be set up on the borders of the colony to keep out the indigenous* population. This was the beginning of racial separation in the colony that would lead in time to the South African policy of apartheid* in the 1900s. Although Van Riebeeck continued to trade with the Khoisan, he would have preferred to conquer them. However, his superiors in Holland would not allow him to pursue such a policy.

Van Riebeeck led the settlement until 1662, when he was named governor of Malacca, in what is now Malaysia. Three years later he retired to the Dutch colony of Batavia (modern-day Indonesia) where he died a wealthy man. (*See also* **Colonialism in Africa, Southern Africa, History of.**)

* **indigenous**   native to a certain place

* **apartheid**   policy of racial segregation enforced by the white government of South Africa to maintain political, economic, and social control over the country's blacks, Asians, and people of mixed ancestry

VEGETATION

See *Climate; Ecosystems; Plants: Varieties and Uses.*

Verwoerd, Hendrik Frensch

1901–1966
South African politician

* **apartheid**   policy of racial segregation enforced by the white government of South Africa to maintain political, economic, and social control over the country's blacks, Asians, and people of mixed ancestry

Hendrik Verwoerd created South Africa's policy of racial segregation known as apartheid*. As prime minister in the early 1960s, he followed racist policies that deepened the divide between whites and blacks.

Born in the Netherlands, Verwoerd moved with his family to SOUTH AFRICA when he was two years old. His father, a grocer, was a missionary for the Dutch Reformed Church. After completing high school, Verwoerd went to Germany to study at universities in Hamburg, Leipzig, and Berlin.

Returning to South Africa in 1927, Verwoerd became a professor of psychology at the University of Stellenbosch. Later he held professorships in sociology and social work. He and others at the university opposed South Africa's plan to take in Jewish refugees from Nazi Germany. In 1937 Verwoerd became editor of the Afrikaans-language newspaper *Die Transvaaler,* which he used to express his anti-British, anti-Jewish, and pro-Nazi views.

Verwoerd joined the racist National Party and, in 1948, became a member of the Senate. He was the party's leader in the Senate for eight years and served as minister of "native affairs." During this time he devised the policy of apartheid, calling for total segregation of all races in the country and restricting the black population to reservations known as Bantustans. In 1958 Verwoerd became prime minister.

Apartheid increased tensions between blacks and whites, which led to various organized protests. In 1960 police fired on 5,000 peaceful protesters in Sharpeville, a black township south of JOHANNESBURG, killing 69 and wounding over 300. Shortly afterward a white farmer tried to assassinate Verwoerd at an agricultural show in Johannesburg. Verwoerd was wounded, but survived and made a full recovery.

During a 1961 conference of prime ministers of the British Commonwealth, Verwoerd pressed Britain to recognize South Africa as a fully independent republic. Although he was turned down at the time, two months later the Republic of South Africa was created. Over the next few years apartheid increasingly isolated the country from the rest of the world, but Verwoerd refused to modify the policy. In 1966 he was stabbed to death by a white man who entered the parliament disguised as a messenger. (*See also* **Apartheid**.)

Vodun

* **deity**   god or goddess

* **taboo**   religious prohibition against doing something that is believed to cause harm

* **diviner**   person who predicts the future or explains the causes of misfortune

* **cult**   group bound together by devotion to a particular person, belief, or god

* **ritual**   religious ceremony that follows a set pattern

Vodun is a traditional religious practice of southern BÉNIN. Also known as Orisha to the YORUBA people of the region, Vodun was brought to the Americas by slaves. There, especially in Haiti, it developed into a form called voodoo.

People who practice Vodun believe that their ancestors entered into agreements with several deities* called the Vodun, which represent forces of nature. The ancestors promised the Vodun that people would offer them food and service and would obey certain taboos*. Followers claim that misfortunes—such as natural disasters, illness, or the death of a child—occur when someone breaks the contract that the ancestors made with a particular Vodun. When trouble arises, a diviner* identifies the exact cause of the problem. Then the offending person may soothe the angry Vodun by giving offerings and performing ceremonies.

Cults and Rituals. Among the many people who practice Vodun, only a few are members of cults* dedicated to its deities. Male priests lead these cults, often inheriting their positions from their fathers. The cults' many female members are expected to obey the priests without question. However, women play a prominent role in public ceremonies, where some called *vodunsi*—said to be the Vodun's "slaves" or "wives"—perform dances and rituals*. Sometimes these women enter a trance, in which a Vodun is believed to inhabit their bodies. The practice of such Vodun rituals is usually considered more important than the underlying beliefs.

Perhaps the most important role of Vodun is as a social and political force. Through rituals such as divination and INITIATION RITES that last for several years, Vodun priests exercise great authority over their followers and others in the community. In many cases they compete with other social and political institutions for local control. From 1975 through the 1980s, the government of Bénin banned Vodun, believing that its powerful influence might lead people to oppose the revolutionary policies the government wanted to promote. When a new government was established in 1991, authorities encouraged a massive revival of Vodun, hoping to gain favor with the rural population.

Vodun Today. In the cities Vodun has lost some of its power to explain misfortune. The idea of age-old contracts between village elders and gods of nature seems unconvincing in an urban setting where events appear to depend largely upon human actions. City dwellers frequently blame their troubles not on the Vodun but on WITCHCRAFT, actions by human witches or sorcerers* that can be fought through magic. Diviners who once claimed that troubles were caused by the Vodun now explain them as the result of witchcraft or a combination of Vodun and witchcraft.

* **sorcerer**   magician or wizard

Not everyone in Bénin practices Vodun. Nonetheless, most people believe that the Vodun deities exist and many people who are not members of a Vodun cult turn to the practice in times of stress. Only Bénin's Islamic* groups and a few Protestant Christian groups, including the Methodists and the Jehovah's Witnesses, do not share the belief in a universe of Vodun. Both followers and opponents have criticized Vodun for allowing occasional corruption or excessive control by priests and for charging extremely high fees to perform initiation rites. Many people also feel threatened by the secrecy that surrounds Vodun practices. (*See also* **Religion and Ritual, Spirit Possession.**)

* **Islamic**   relating to Islam, the religion based on the teachings of the prophet Muhammad

Warfare

arfare has played a role in almost every society in human history. As societies grow larger and more complex, the nature of conflict and the motivation behind it tend to change. In Africa, where warfare once consisted of quick raids made by small bands of people, these changes are evident. Modern African nations have permanent professional armies backed by powerful weapons, and conflicts between different ethnic or political groups and between countries have developed into long-term fighting on many parts of the continent.

THE NATURE OF WARFARE

Some scholars who study warfare place conflicts in one of two main categories: proto-war and war. The distinction lies in the type of society involved, the reasons for conflict, and the weapons used.

Proto-War. Proto-war often involves small societies without a hierarchical* structure, such as small groups that function with little or no central authority. In HUNTING AND GATHERING bands, for example, no single person commands the group at all times. Instead, informal or temporary leaders assume authority in certain situations. Other groups have leaders such as chiefs or elders, whose role may be more permanent, but the power relationships between leaders in the group are less defined than those among officials in modern states.

* **hierarchical**   referring to a society or institution divided into groups with higher or lower levels

In Africa, nonhierarchical groups usually wage war by creating kin militia. The members of the militia are related by descent or marriage and may all be about the same age. Usually consisting of no more than 30 soldiers, kin militias are organized on a temporary basis from people who have other roles in society. They use simple weapons, from farming tools to small firearms, and lack the command structures and supply lines of modern armies.

Small and temporary, with few arms or supplies, kin militias generally suffer few casualties* in their conflicts. Campaigns last a few days or weeks at most, and the losers often leave the area. The victors rarely have the ability to pursue their enemies or impose their will on the defeated group. Militia members then return to their normal lives.

Proto-wars often stem from personal grievances and disputes over property. Conflict may arise, for example, if one group takes livestock or kidnaps women from another. Because both animals and women have important roles in the economy, their loss poses a threat to the community. Each group must define how severe such losses are and how much violence it should use to deal with the situation.

* **casualty** person killed or injured in an accident or military action

War. As states grow more complex, leadership becomes centralized and the powers of rulers are more clearly defined. Before the modern era African states such as chiefdoms featured strong rulers supported by lower officials with limited authority. Although more structured than that of a band or tribe, the leadership of these pre-modern states lacked the complex organization typical of the government of a modern state.

The size and power of modern governments allow them to control the resources produced by their people. These resources can be used to support a professional army, created for the sole purpose of making war. Such armies have many members, specialized roles for different soldiers, and weapons designed specifically for war.

Full-scale military campaigns between armies can last for years and result in thousands or even millions of casualties. The winning state gains power over the one that loses, and the outcome of war can lead to long-term changes in power relations between the warring societies. Such conflicts are classified as war.

In African states before colonial times, personal disputes often caused conflicts. But the states also went to war to gain control of sources of income such as property, money, food, or labor, and the losers were forced to give these up to the victors.

In modern African states, wars are often fought to determine who will be part of the ruling class. Most ordinary Africans live in poverty, but state officials enjoy comfortable lives. As a result, members of the ruling class struggle to stay within it, while challengers strive to enter it. In some cases, officials who have fallen out of power have organized movements and armies in the name of national liberation. These movements sometimes disguise the personal ambitions of their leaders. To attract supporters they frequently make use of existing ethnic rivalries or invent new ones.

Morals or Money?

Around 1800 in the area that is now Chad, a personal dispute between two rulers led to full-scale war. Sabun, the ruler of Wadai, charged that the king of Bagirmi had married his own sister. Sabun proclaimed that this incest was a moral outrage that demanded punishment. Wadaian forces invaded and conquered Bagirmi, giving Wadai access to riches and revenue once controlled by Bagirmi. The centralized power of the Wadaian state allowed it to mobilize a real army, and the conflict permanently affected power relations between Wadai and Bagirmi.

Warfare

Children fought on both sides of the civil war in Angola. Former UNITA rebel leader General Zacarias Mundombe thanks one of these child soldiers for his efforts.

SOURCES OF CONFLICT IN MODERN AFRICA

Since African nations gained their independence, they have fought most of their wars over three main issues: the struggle for internal control, disputes over borders, and rivalries for dominance of a region.

Internal Power Struggles. Once they overthrew European colonial rulers, most African nations went through periods of conflict as different groups sought to control power and define the nature of the state. In many cases African groups that had been allies during the struggle for independence turned against each other. They had set their ethnic and political differences aside during the fight for freedom, but these tensions resurfaced after the foreign rulers left.

NIGERIA and ANGOLA provide examples of conflicts caused by ethnic and political differences. In the Biafran War in Nigeria (1967–1970), the IGBO people tried to secede* from the nation because the government and economy were dominated by the HAUSA, YORUBA, and FULANI ethnic groups. This war represented a common situation in postcolonial Africa, as the Nigerian federal government was uncertain what role the nation's different regions should play on the national level. Political differences played the major role in the civil war in Angola that began in 1975. When Portuguese rule collapsed, two rival rebel groups fought for control over the state: the MPLA, backed by the

* **secede** to withdraw formally from an organization or country

142

* **Soviet Union**   nation that existed from 1922 to 1991, made up of Russia and 14 other republics

Soviet Union* and Cuba, and UNITA, supported by South Africa and the United States.

Border Disputes. At independence African nations generally agreed to accept the boundaries drawn during the colonial era, but some lines had never been well defined. Morocco and Algeria fought a war over their border in 1963. They did not draw up a preliminary agreement until 1972 and did not sign the agreement until 1989.

Ethiopia has had several disputes concerning boundary lines with neighbors. It fought with Somalia over borders in 1964 and again in both 1977 and 1988, winning the third conflict. But the tables turned for Ethiopia in 1993, when Eritrea won its fight to secede from the nation and form an independent state.

Regional Rivalries. A number of wars have erupted in Africa because of rivalries between nations in a region. In the 1970s and 1980s, for instance, Libya engaged in a series of conflicts with Niger, Tunisia, Chad, and Sudan as part of an effort to dominate Arab states in the Sahara region. More recently, several African nations have sent troops and arms to fight on both sides of the civil war in Congo (Kinshasa).

Nations in Southern Africa have also competed for regional power. The civil war in Angola served as a major site of this competition during the 1970s and 1980s. The white government of South Africa intervened on the side of Angola's UNITA forces, while the black leaders of Zambia, Zimbabwe, Botswana, Tanzania, and Mozambique supported the nation's MPLA. This conflict, like others during the Cold War*, also attracted outside powers such as the United States and the Soviet Union, which hoped to gain global advantages from local fighting.

* **Cold War**   period of tense relations between the United States and the Soviet Union following World War II

Controlling Conflicts. Few of the wars fought in the years since African nations gained independence have had a permanent impact. In most cases the conflicts have ended in stalemates and ceasefires. These agreements have often depended on the diplomatic efforts of others.

The charter of the Organization of African Unity (OAU) called for a commission to settle disputes between African nations, but the commission never formed. Instead, many conflicts have been settled through the personal efforts of African leaders. Foreign powers such as the United States and former colonial nations such as France have also helped resolve disputes. Global organizations, including the United Nations and the International Court of Justice, have played a peacekeeping role as well. However, many of these efforts have been poorly handled or taken on mainly to serve the interests of the mediators.

In the 1990s African states have borne more of the burden of peacekeeping, with both negotiations and armed forces. Neighboring countries have sometimes acted collectively to deal with conflicts that affect their region. This trend seems likely to continue in the coming years. (*See also* **Boundaries in Africa, Colonialism in Africa, Global Politics and Africa, Government and Political Systems, Independence Movements, Refugees.**)

West African Trading Settlements

West African
Trading Settlements

Europeans began setting up trading posts on the coast of western Africa in the mid-1400s. The result was a string of European settlements from present day SENEGAL to the coast of modern NIGERIA. Centuries later these trading posts became the bases for European colonial claims in western Africa.

European traders referred to sections of the coast by the main goods traded there: grain, ivory, gold, and slaves. The Grain Coast (in modern LIBERIA) and the Ivory Coast (in the country of the same name) had relatively few trading posts. The greatest number of settlements appeared on the Gold Coast (now part of GHANA).

The Portuguese, the first Europeans to visit the western coast of Africa, established trading posts on the CAPE VERDE Islands in the 1460s and began building forts on the Gold Coast in 1482. For more than a century they were the only Europeans in the region. After 1621 however, a Dutch trading firm called the West India Company captured some of Portugal's African bases. Similar trading companies formed in England, France, and Denmark and became active on the African coast. In addition, the German realm of Brandenburg-Prussia founded several trading settlements that were operated by Dutch merchants.

The trading companies and the nations they represented tended to concentrate on particular regions. The French established their influence in Senegambia, the region around the Senegal and Gambia rivers. The English gained the dominant position in SIERRA LEONE. By 1700 the Gold Coast was crowded with 23 forts and some smaller trading posts, mostly built by the English, Dutch, Danish, and Brandenburgers. As the demand for slaves in the Americas grew, European interest shifted eastward to the Slave Coast, the area that is now BÉNIN and NIGERIA. The English, French, Portuguese, and Dutch were active there, and the first three erected permanent forts. All along the coast, however, much commerce took place outside the settlements as African traders dealt directly with European ships or even individual Europeans who were not attached to trading companies.

European trading settlements ranged from mud-and-thatch buildings staffed by one or two people to great stone forts that housed 80 Europeans and an even larger number of African servants. Towns grew up around some of the major trading settlements—for example, Elmina developed around the Portuguese fort of São Jorge da Mina on the Gold Coast. Europeans in the settlements frequently formed relationships with African women. By the 1700s their Creole* descendants had created powerful families that played an increasingly important role in local trade and politics.

* **Creole** person of mixed European and African ancestry

Europeans had no political control over their African neighbors, though they sometimes formed alliances with one party in a local dispute. The Europeans also had little influence on local religious practice. The efforts of Western missionaries in Africa did not really get underway until the 1800s.

Some European settlements were fortified and armed to protect against attack by rival Europeans. Maintaining such forts became too expensive for the companies, however, and after the mid-1700s the

European governments took responsibility for them. After the Atlantic SLAVE TRADE ended in the 1800s, the trading settlements lost their original purpose. Instead, they became the starting points for imperialist* expansion as the European nations carved out colonial claims in Africa. (*See also* **Colonialism in Africa, Ivory Trade, Trade, Travel and Exploration**.)

* **imperialist** relating to the political, economic, and cultural domination of one country or region by another

Western Sahara is a former colony on the northwestern coast of Africa whose status remains unresolved. Once an overseas province of Spain, it was called Spanish Sahara until 1976. Since that time, Western Sahara has been the subject of competing claims by various African nations. Furthermore, Polisario, a political party in Western Sahara, wants to make the region an independent state.

Land and People. With an area of about 102,000 square miles, Western Sahara borders the Atlantic Ocean, MOROCCO, ALGERIA, and MAURITANIA. Located in the SAHARA DESERT, it is barren and dry, with an average yearly rainfall of less than two inches. Western Sahara has two main areas: Río de Oro in the south and Saguia el Hamra in the north.

The indigenous* people of Western Sahara are the Sahrawi—a mixture of BERBERS, who have lived in the region for about 2,000 years, and Arabs, who migrated there in the 1200s. Traditionally the Sahrawi were nomadic* herders and traders but during the colonial era they established some permanent settlements. El Aaiún, near the coast, was the colonial capital and is still the major town. Smara, located inland at an oasis, contains historic Muslim monuments.

* **indigenous** native to a certain place

* **nomadic** relating to people who travel from place to place to find food and pasture

History and Government. In the past the region that is now Western Sahara has been linked to various Muslim states that rose and fell in Morocco. However, it was never formally part of Morocco. In 1884 Spain claimed the region. The Spanish planned to use it as a base for further colonization in North Africa, but were prevented from expanding by the French in Mauritania.

In the 1930s an independence movement emerged in Morocco, and its supporters viewed Spanish Sahara as part of Morocco. After Morocco became independent in 1956, it claimed Spanish Sahara and sent troops to occupy the region. Spanish forces drove the Moroccans back. In the 1960s Mauritania also claimed Spanish Sahara, and valuable deposits of phosphates—minerals used in making fertilizer—were discovered in the region.

Competition over Spanish Sahara increased in the early 1970s, when Sahrawi seeking self-government formed Polisario (Popular Front for the Liberation of Saguia el Hamra and Río de Oro). In an effort to curb Morocco's power and influence in the region, Algeria supported Polisario. Outbreaks of guerrilla* fighting by Polisario members led Spain to withdraw its claim to the colony in 1976. After the departure of the Spanish forces, Mauritania and Morocco divided Western Sahara. However, Polisario began attacking the outposts of the two powers.

See map in Minerals and Mining (vol. 3).

* **guerrilla** type of warfare involving sudden raids by small groups of warriors

145

Western Sahara

POPULATION:
244,943 (2000 estimated population)

AREA:
97,000 sq. mi. (252,000 sq. km)

LANGUAGES:
Arabic (official); Berber dialects

NATIONAL CURRENCY:
Moroccan dirham

PRINCIPAL RELIGION:
Muslim

CITIES:
El-Aaiún (Laayoune), Cabo Bojador, Bu Craa, Smara (Semara), Ad Dakhla

ANNUAL RAINFALL:
Less than 2 in. (50 mm)

ECONOMY:
GDP per capita: N/A

PRINCIPAL PRODUCTS AND EXPORTS:
Agricultural: fish
Manufacturing: handicrafts
Mining: phosphates

GOVERNMENT:
Claimed and administered by Morocco since 1979, but independence movements and guerrilla warfare have left the sovereignty of the land unresolved. The UN administered a cease fire in 1991, and the government remains in transition.

EDUCATION:
N/A

In 1979 Mauritania made a peace agreement with Polisario and left the territory, but Morocco has continued to claim Western Sahara and to mine its phosphates. The UNITED NATIONS has proposed holding an election in which the Sahrawi could decide whether to join Morocco or to establish an independent state. However, plans for the election have been delayed several times. During the late 1980s and 1990s, relations between Morocco and Algeria improved, and Algeria's support of Polisario declined. At the same time Morocco established tens of thousands of settlers in Western Sahara. (*See also* **Independence Movements, Minerals and Mining, North Africa: Geography and Population, North Africa: History and Cultures.**)

Wildlife and Game Parks

Elephants passing in slow, stately groups, lions lazing under a tree in the noonday heat, shaggy mountain gorillas feeding in a clearing in the rain forest—these images instantly suggest Africa, which is famous around the world for the amount and variety of its wildlife. Yet the rapid growth of Africa's human population, accompanied by the use of ever more land for farming and other human activities, threatens many individual species and the future of Africa's wildlife in general.

African nations are working to protect their natural heritage by developing wildlife management plans and by setting land aside as national parks and game preserves. The most successful conservation efforts will probably be those that recognize the needs and desires of the African people as well as the need to protect animals.

African Mammals. Africa is home to an astonishing variety of mammals. The continent's herbivores, or plant-eating animals, range from elephants, rhinoceroses, and hippopotamuses to hoofed mammals, such as the giraffe and the African buffalo. Vast herds of grazing

* savanna tropical or subtropical grassland with scattered trees and drought-resistant undergrowth

* species narrowest classification of organisms; subgroup of genus

See color plate 11, vol. 2.

animals, such as zebras and wildebeests, roam the open plains and savannas*. Africa's many varieties of antelope include the hartebeest, gnu or wildebeest, dik-dik, gazelle, impala, springbok, oryx, reedbuck, and eland, the largest antelope.

More than 60 species* of carnivores, or flesh-eating mammals, prey on the herbivores and sometimes on smaller and weaker carnivores. In addition to hunting live animals, the carnivores devour carcasses. Africa is home to three kinds of large cats—lions, leopards, and cheetahs—and smaller felines such as the serval and wildcat. Wild dogs, jackals, foxes, hyenas, civets, and weasels are also predators.

Forty-five species of monkeys and two species of great apes, the chimpanzee and the gorilla, live in Africa. The continent also has many species of lemurs, small animals that belong to the primate family, like monkeys and apes. Most lemurs live in trees and are nocturnal, or active at night, although a few are active by day. The island of MADAGASCAR has the largest variety of lemurs in the world.

Some of the mammals that live in Africa are found nowhere else in the world. These include giraffes, hippopotamuses, jumping hares, and the long-snouted, insect-eating tenrecs of Madagascar. Another animal

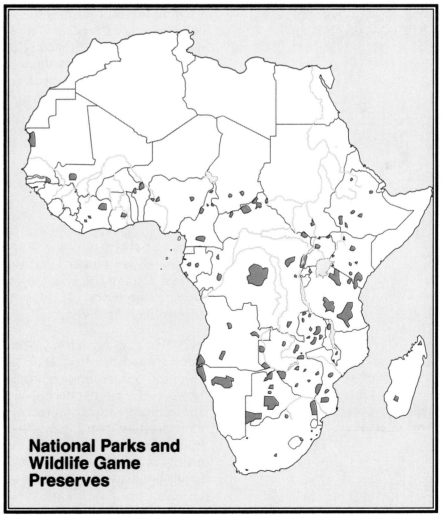

National Parks and Wildlife Game Preserves

Wildlife and Game Parks

unique to Africa is the aardvark, a large nocturnal animal with a piglike body, long tail, rabbitlike ears, and a long snout. The aardvark rips open termite nests with its sharp claws, then uses its sticky almost one-foot-long tongue to lap up the insects inside.

Bird, Reptile, and Marine Life. Nearly 2,000 species of birds spend at least part of each year in Africa. In addition to varieties of hawks, eagles, owls, larks, kingfishers, and other birds found elsewhere in the world, several bird species are native only to Africa. These include the ostrich, Africa's largest bird; the hammerkop, which resembles a heron; and touracos, birds with brightly colored feathers. Several species of small, drab birds are called honey guides because people follow them to honeybee nests.

A great many reptiles and amphibians creep, slither, or hop along Africa's varied terrain. Reptiles include lizards, tortoises, crocodiles, and many types of snakes. Some snakes, such as the mamba and the Egyptian cobra, are venomous enough to be dangerous to humans. Boa constrictors and iguanas live only on Madagascar. Among Africa's amphibians are various salamanders and frogs, including the bizarre hairy frog of CAMEROON.

Of the almost countless species of insects in Africa, several are regarded as pests. Locusts devour crops and other vegetation; mosquitoes carry malaria; and tsetse flies carry trypanosomiasis, or sleeping sickness, a disease that harms both humans and livestock. Other African insects include various species of large butterflies, dung beetles, stick insects that resemble twigs or leaves, driver or safari ants that travel in huge columns, and termites that cooperate to build tall earthen mounds. Spiders are plentiful everywhere.

A wide variety of marine life exists off the coasts of Africa, and the continent has more kinds of freshwater fish than any other—about 2,000 species. Some freshwater creatures are ancient varieties that have changed little over millions of years, such as lungfish, lobefins, and reedfish, which can breathe air. Certain types of African catfish not only breathe air but also move across land during rainy weather. Lake Nyasa alone has about 160 species of fish found nowhere else in the world. The waters of southern and eastern Africa harbor the coelacanth, an ancient form of fish thought to have been extinct for over 60 million years until one was caught in 1938. Other coelacanths have been discovered more recently.

Wildlife Preservation. Wildlife numbers have fallen in Africa since the widespread introduction of firearms in the mid-1800s. At first European hunters and colonists slaughtered large numbers of animals. However the greatest decline has come since the 1940s, due to hunting and habitat* destruction by Africans. Some species have been affected more severely than others. The number of African elephants dropped from about two million in the early 1970s to around 600,000 by 1990, mainly as a result of illegal hunting for their ivory tusks. Rhinoceros and gorilla populations were dramatically reduced and the animals became

* **habitat** place where a plant or animal lives or grows

endangered species. In the 1990s experts named Cameroon, Congo (Kinshasa), and Madagascar as the countries in which wildlife species are most threatened.

Most African nations have taken steps to protect and preserve wildlife. One problem is that different countries disagree about how best to deal with the situation. Countries in northeastern and eastern Africa, for example, support a total ban on the Ivory Trade to protect elephants, while those in southern Africa want a regulated ivory trade to continue.

Game Parks. Many African governments have established national parks and wildlife preserves, or game parks, as wilderness areas to be protected from human development. Colonial authorities in the early 1900s created the first parks to provide a safe haven for wildlife, a base for scientific study, and educational and recreational opportunities for both local people and visitors. The oldest of these is South Africa's Kruger National Park.

Africa's protected areas and parks vary greatly in number, size, and quality from country to country. Eastern and southern Africa are particularly well known for their wildlife parks. Tsavo in Kenya and Serengeti in Tanzania are among the continent's largest and most famous parks. Malawi, Namibia, Zambia, and Zimbabwe also boast impressive preserves. However, few countries in western Africa have significant parks.

In Africa's game parks, visitors can observe a remarkable array of wildlife in natural habitats. Here, tourists in the Masai Mara Game Reserve in Kenya view herds of zebras and wildebeests.

Wildlife and Game Parks

See color plate 14, vol. 2.

Several countries of northern Africa, including SUDAN, ALGERIA, MOROCCO, TUNISIA, EGYPT, and MAURITANIA, participated in international talks about preserving wildlife in the 1990s. Since then, they have begun setting aside new protected areas, developing training programs for park managers, and launching efforts to protect certain species, such as endangered seals. Government programs in Morocco have saved the macaco, or Barbary ape, from extinction in the forests of the Middle Atlas mountain range.

Not all of Africa's wildlife parks offer the same level of protection to animals and their habitats. Some governments have completely banned human presence or activity in parks, moving people away from homes that lie within park boundaries. In Tanzania alone, more than 50,000 people have been relocated from parks. Other governments allow people to live in protected areas, but prohibit the use of resources, such as firewood or pasture, inside the parks. Some preserves are designed for multiple use.

In addition to setting aside land, wildlife management in Africa includes efforts to preserve genetic diversity, which means keeping a wide variety of animals in populations large enough to reproduce healthy young. To accomplish this, authorities and park managers work to protect the ECOSYSTEMS in which plants and animals flourish. Although many of Africa's parks are in savannas and rain forests, new parks have been designed to protect areas such as mangrove swamps, deserts, and lakes.

Increasingly, governments and conservation experts are trying to balance the interests of animals and humans. They recognize that Africans will be more likely to protect wildlife if they see the economic benefits of preservation. TOURISM is one source of benefits. However, while wildlife tourism produces significant income for Africans in a few areas, in most regions much of the profit goes to overseas tour operators. Wildlife managers are seeking ways to share that profit with local Africans. At Amboseli National Park in Kenya, people who traditionally used the parkland have been granted a share of the park's profit. Such systems may help stop illegal hunting and farming on park lands. (*See also* **Animals, Domestic; Diseases; Fishing; Forests and Forestry.**)

Witbooi, Hendrik

**1830–1905
Nama leader**

H endrik Witbooi, chief of the Nama people, was a religious leader who fought against German rule in southern Africa. Trained as a carpenter, he became a deacon, an official of the Christian church.

Witbooi was born in Pella, a region south of the Orange River, between the nations of NAMIBIA and SOUTH AFRICA. After nearly dying in 1880 in a confrontation with the HERERO people, he came to believe he had a divine mission to lead his Christian Nama followers north to a new homeland.

About 600 Nama set off with Witbooi in 1885. He was promised safe passage by the Herero and hoped to unite his people with them against the Germans. But the Herero, led by Samuel MAHERERO, attacked the

* **guerrilla** type of warfare involving sudden raids by small groups of warriors

Nama. Witbooi lost two of his sons, several dozen followers, and most of his property in the battle. Witbooi led the surviving Nama to safety in the nearby mountains. From there he waged a successful guerrilla* war against the Herero, who had signed a treaty with the Germans. The Germans responded to the attack and defeated Witbooi's forces in 1894. For ten years he cooperated with German colonial forces in southwest Africa, but in 1904 he led his people against Germany again. He was mortally wounded in an attack on the Germans in southern Namibia. (*See also* **Colonialism in Africa**.)

Witchcraft and Sorcery

Many Africans view both misfortune and spectacular success as unnatural and believe that witchcraft or sorcery causes such events. Individuals referred to as witches or sorcerers—and by various local African names—are said to use secret, magical forces to hurt other people, to bring great success to themselves, or to maintain a powerful position in society. Their activities, which are usually considered destructive, are therefore closely related to jealousy, inequality, and the desire for power.

Witches and sorcerers may be either men or women. In some parts of Africa, people distinguish between witches and sorcerers. They believe that witches are born with supernatural* powers and the ability to hurt others merely by wishing them ill. Sorcerers, however, are thought to be people of normal ability who have learned to use magical substances to harm others.

* **supernatural** related to forces beyond the normal world; magical or miraculous

Some people view witchcraft as the dark side of kinship and possibly the result of aggression and envy within a family. In some African societies it is said that witches have an urge to eat their relatives. Many traditional stories tell of witches who leave their bodies at night and fly off to join others of their kind. At these meetings they turn over their kin, whose vital parts are devoured in cannibal banquets.

Witchcraft in the Modern World. A belief in witchcraft and sorcery exists in modern African cities as well as in traditional villages. Western observers once assumed that as modernization and education spread throughout Africa, these ideas would disappear. In the 1970s European priests in CAMEROON declared that there could be no sorcery where there was electricity. Since then, electrification and other modern developments have gained ground, but belief in witchcraft has not declined. Instead, new ideas about sorcery appear all the time, often with elements borrowed from foreign cultures—such as the notions that witches belong to the Mafia or study with European professors of witchcraft. Rumors about the use of hidden forces are common in African politics, sports, churches, schools, and business.

People in new and unfamiliar social settings, such as urban environments where there is strong competition for jobs and money, often fear that the use of witchcraft is growing. Such views are especially common when new forms of wealth appear. Some say that successful Africans who

Witchcraft and Sorcery

Many Africans consult witch doctors and diviners for protection from sorcery. A witch doctor in Zambia has a collection of gourds and other special items to use in his work.

have become rich have done so by using magic to take advantage of others. In some cases the rich are accused of turning their victims into zombies, or living corpses, who are put to work on invisible plantations. Theories of this sort are used to explain the success of the few and the poverty of the many. They have even inspired attacks on newly rich people.

The views of African governments toward witchcraft beliefs are not always clear. Many governments take sorcery seriously, branding it as a particularly dangerous form of illegal or rebellious activity. Civil servants frequently tell villagers to stop trying to interfere with government projects by using witchcraft. Many educated Africans of the upper classes view sorcery as a real social problem, an obstacle to development and modernization.

At the same time, however, other members of Africa's upper classes, including civil servants and political figures, rely on witchcraft to protect themselves from people who might be jealous of their success. For a high price, wealthy Africans can buy potions, charms, and other witchcraft and sorcery objects.

Protection from Witches. Traditional African defenses against witchcraft include the use of divination* and the services of a witch doctor. Someone who fears becoming the victim of harmful magic may seek the help of a diviner* who calls on special powers to find out what the sorcerer has done. Many Africans say that diviners have "a second pair of eyes"—an extra sense that allows them to "see" witches. The victim may also need a witch doctor to attack or undo the original witchcraft. Respected for their great powers, witch doctors are said to be able to overcome witches and force them to lift their spells. Sometimes called "superwitches," they are feared as well as respected. In southern Cameroon, witch doctors called *nganga* are thought to gain their powers by sacrificing one of their parents. Because of their supernatural powers, witch doctors and diviners are sometimes accused of doing evil themselves.

Throughout history, anxieties about witchcraft running wild have encouraged a search for new forms of protection. During the colonial period, Africans developed a rich variety of anti-witchcraft tools and procedures, including poison ordeals, in which suspected witches were treated with poison. More recently, Christian movements within Africa have led the struggle against witchcraft. A lively debate is taking place within the Roman Catholic Church, for example, about how far priests can go in fighting witchcraft beliefs. Several African priests and even bishops have gotten into trouble with the church because they tried to follow too closely in the footsteps of witch doctors.

African governments are under growing pressure to take action against sorcery. Ever since colonial times Africans have accused state authorities of protecting witches because laws forbid poison ordeals and the execution of witches by chiefs and witch doctors. Some governments have given in to public demand. During the late 1970s the government of BÉNIN launched a radio campaign against sorcery that developed into a witch hunt. Around the same time, the state courts of Cameroon began convicting people of the crime of witchcraft, mainly on the word of witch doctors.

Direct action by the state has led to the appearance of a new type of witch doctor, one who is often interested in publicity. These witch doctors display their importance by wearing modern fashion items, such as sunglasses, by carrying symbols of Christian and Asian beliefs, and by

* **divination** practice that looks into the future, usually by supernatural means

* **diviner** person who predicts the future or explains the causes of misfortune

153

showing off knowledge of medical terms. Above all, they have an aggressive style in finding clients and unmasking witches. Often they approach people with warnings to beware of danger in their surroundings, insisting that "purifications" are needed for protection against sorcery. Such witch doctors or healers play an important role in reinforcing the belief in witchcraft. (*See also* **Divination and Oracles, Religion and Ritual, Spirit Possession.**)

T he Wolof, a western African people, live in the nations of SENEGAL and GAMBIA, mainly in villages between the Senegal and Gambia Rivers. The Wolof number about 4 million. Their language, also called Wolof, is widely spoken in Senegal.

According to tradition, individual Wolof villages combined to create an empire with its center in northwest Senegal sometime in the 1200s. After the Portuguese arrived on the African coast in the mid-1400s, the Wolof formed a trading partnership with them. The Wolof empire developed into a powerful slave-trading state that conquered neighboring kingdoms. Its trading network broke down in the mid 1500s, however, when it lost control of a state that provided access to trading centers along the Atlantic coast. By the mid-1800s the Wolof had converted to Islam*, although some traditional practices and beliefs, including witchcraft and magic, remain.

Wolof society is divided into clearly defined classes: royalty, nobility, warriors, several kinds of commoners, craftspeople, and descendants of slaves. Individuals inherit class membership from their parents, and people tend to marry within their own class or choose a person of equal status. The great majority of Wolof are rural farmers, but some also live in cities and towns where they work as merchants, artisans*, and civil servants. (*See also* **Colonialism in Africa, Ethnic Groups and Identity, Slave Trade.**)

* **Islam** religion based on the teachings of the prophet Muhammad; religious faith of Muslims

* **artisan** skilled crafts worker

D uring the second half of the 1900s, the rise of women's movements around the world brought new attention to the role of women in Africa. Long overlooked by historians and scholars, African women have begun to gain recognition for their contributions to economic and political life as well as to the home and family. Still, African women generally do not receive the same education or employment opportunities as men, and in many cultures they are subordinate* to men.

* **subordinate** belonging to a lower rank, class, or position

Role in Food Production. In the past many scholars regarded men as the principal players in African life. When forming theories about human origins, they focused on the importance of meat eating in human development—and meat eating depended on the male activity of hunting. The female activity of gathering plant food was thought to be of minor significance. Recent studies have shown, however, that gathered plant foods make up 60 to 80 percent of the diet of HUNTING AND GATHERING societies such as the !Kung of the KALAHARI DESERT in southwestern Africa and the Mbuti of the central African rain forest. The same was probably true of prehistoric hunting and gathering groups. These studies places the value of the work of female gatherers in a new light.

Few African societies now live by hunting and gathering, but African women play a central role in agriculture, the continent's main economic activity. Between 60 and 80 percent of all agricultural workers are women. Their work, however, has been undercounted and undervalued in official surveys because such surveys rarely include their unpaid labor on family land under the heading of "economic activity."

Social, Economic, and Political Roles. In some traditional African cultures, particularly those organized in patrilineal* and patriarchal* ways, women had less power, status, and independence than men. This inequality deepened during the colonial era. Colonial administrators' views of family and society were based on a male-centered European Christian model. The laws and economic arrangements that they created in their African colonies imitated those models. Men, for example, were almost always regarded as the heads of households. As a cash economy developed in the colonies, men became the primary controllers of cash crops*, jobs, and money.

Because both traditional and colonial systems often favored men, African men usually received an education, became literate*, and enjoyed employment opportunities earlier than African women did. However, women as well as men have taken part in the movement that has swelled the population of Africa's cities and towns. Beginning in the late 1900s, harsh economic conditions for rural women, together with a growing desire for personal independence, led some young women to move from their villages to the cities. Today women outnumber men in all major African cities except LAGOS, NIGERIA, which is a large industrial port.

The opportunities available to women in African cities often depend on their level of education. Women without education find it hard to get jobs that pay wages and often join the informal labor market, performing tasks that require little training. Many of these women are market traders, bargaining for goods and then reselling them in open-air markets. In western Africa in particular, women dominate the market economy. Other urban women work as domestic servants, makers and sellers of beer, and prostitutes. Since the mid-1900s educated African women have enjoyed more professional opportunities in areas such as teaching and nursing.

Women's political roles are also expanding. In some colonies women made key contributions to the independence movements and the wars of national liberation of the 1960s. By the end of the 1900s, women had begun to appear in some high-level government positions. MALI, for

* **patrilineal** referring to a society in which property and political power pass through the male side of the family

* **patriarchal** describing a society in which men hold the dominant positions

* **cash crop** crop grown primarily for sale rather than for local consumption

* **literate** able to read and write

155

example, had two women government ministers and a woman ambassador in the 1990s.

Education. Unequal education remains a barrier to the full participation of African women in government and economy. In sub-Saharan* Africa, the problem is one of quality. Boys and girls are often educated separately, and girls' schools are not as good as boys' schools. Three-quarters of women cannot read or write, and only between one-quarter and one-third of all girls attend school, compared with more than half of all boys.

The situation is similar in the Islamic* nations of North Africa. Fewer girls receive an education than boys. Women in these countries live with the fact that Islam is often interpreted in patriarchal ways that limit opportunities and privileges for women. However, more and more North African women are learning to read, especially in freer, more modern countries such as EGYPT and MOROCCO. Some go on to study Islamic and state law, often interpreting religious and civil laws in ways that favor women's rights. In recent years some of Africa's Islamic nations have passed laws improving the status and rights of women, including raising the minimum age for marriage, granting women greater rights in cases of divorce, and limiting polygamy* systems. (*See also* **Family, Gender Roles and Sexuality, Kinship, Marriage, Queens and Queen Mothers.**)

* **sub-Saharan** referring to Africa south of the Sahara desert

* **Islamic** relating to Islam, the religion based on the teachings of the prophet Muhammad

* **polygamy** form of marriage in which a man has more than one wife or a woman has more than one husband

WORK

See *Labor.*

World Wars I and II

Although Africa did not play a significant role in either World War I or World War II, the wars had a major impact on the continent. Africans participated in fighting, and African colonies supplied the European powers with food and raw materials. A number of colonies changed hands as a result of the wars, and the wartime struggles inspired Africans to seek their freedom from European domination.

World War I. From the African perspective, the primary aim of World War I was to oust the Germans from their colonies in Africa. Military campaigns took place in four main areas: the German colonies of Togoland, Kamerun (present-day CAMEROON), German South-West Africa, and German East Africa. Africans became involved in these campaigns on the side of the Germans or the Allies (Britain, France, and Belgium in Africa), depending on which European powers governed them at the time.

Encounters between the Germans and the Allied forces in Africa took place over several years. An English and French invasion of Togoland in 1914 removed the German administration in a matter of weeks. The campaign in South-West Africa in 1914–1915 was also relatively brief

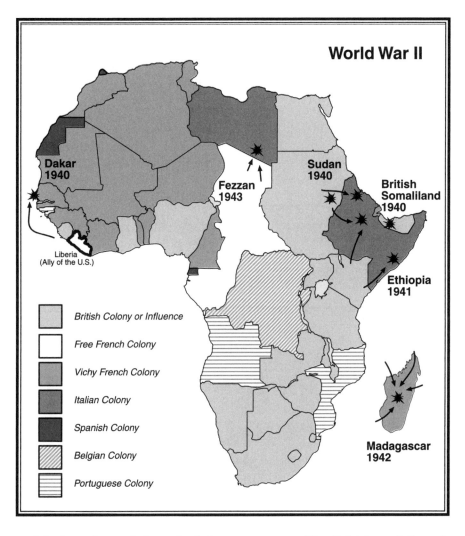

World War II

Dakar
1940

Fezzan
1943

Sudan
1940

British
Somaliland
1940

Liberia
(Ally of the U.S.)

Ethiopia
1941

British Colony or Influence

Free French Colony

Vichy French Colony

Italian Colony

Spanish Colony

Belgian Colony

Portuguese Colony

Madagascar
1942

* **sub-Saharan**   referring to Africa south of the Sahara desert

and led to the withdrawal of German troops. The British and French effort to remove the Germans from Kamerun took longer, some 15 months between 1914 and 1916. The most important conflict, in German East Africa, lasted from 1914 to 1918. This campaign, which involved large numbers of troops and modern military equipment such as trucks and airplanes, most nearly resembled the war in Europe. In North Africa, Britain and France used their colonies mainly as a base of operations for fighting in Europe, the Middle East, and sub-Saharan* Africa.

The immediate impact of World War I on Africans was the transfer of German colonial possessions. France and Britain divided Togoland and Kamerun. Britain and Belgium split German East Africa, while SOUTH AFRICA took control of German South-West Africa. The former German colonies were all placed under League of Nations* mandates, which gave Britain, France, Belgium, and South Africa the right to administer them.

* **League of Nations** organization founded to promote international peace and security; it functioned from 1920 to 1946

During the war Africans participated directly and indirectly as soldiers, supply carriers, agricultural producers, and in many other occupations. Some African troops served in Europe and the Middle East with

157

World Wars I and II

the British and French. For the most part Europeans had to force Africans to serve. African soldiers and laborers in the war effort had poor training and equipment and received inadequate medical care. An estimated 250,000 Africans were wounded or killed in the war.

Many Europeans feared that the war would change political attitudes in Africa, awakening a desire for independence from colonial rule. While the war did inspire some calls for freedom, the European concern was largely unfounded. Africans achieved unexpected gains in employment in jobs previously limited to whites, such as managers and colonial administrators. For the most part, however, such gains were short-lived and the old colonial order was eventually restored.

World War II. Most of Africa's involvement in World War II took place in North Africa, the scene of various battles between German and Italian forces and those of the Allies, which included Britain, France,

Important military action took place in North Africa during World War II. Here British officers lead a line of Indian troops from their camp in Egypt in 1940.

and the United States. The region also served as a base of operations for the Allied invasion of Italy and southern Europe.

Sub-Saharan Africa was not a major center of operations in World War II, with two exceptions. In 1940 the Allies attempted to seize the port of DAKAR in SENEGAL. The following year they liberated ETHIOPIA from the Italians and they freed MADAGASCAR from the Vichy government of France. Nonetheless, the significance of the war for the history of Africa was considerable.

The near defeat of Britain, France, and other European nations in the war, combined with the devastating effect on their economies, ended European claims to "great power" status. Instead, two new superpowers—the United States and the Soviet Union*—came to dominate world politics. Both of these superpowers were hostile to colonialism. In addition criticism of colonialism surfaced in the newly created UNITED NATIONS.

In Africa, World War II unleashed forces of nationalism* that contributed to the rise of INDEPENDENCE MOVEMENTS. Wartime demand for African products and raw materials stimulated economic growth and helped bring about social change on the continent. Many Africans who served in the armed forces acquired literacy* and other skills. Returning to their homelands, these troops often faced low wages, inflation*, and other economic problems. Few felt they had been adequately rewarded for their wartime service.

After the war the colonial powers generally tried to regain their authority over Africans, which had been relaxed during the conflict. However, the Europeans faced a changed atmosphere in which large numbers of Africans saw colonial policies as unfair. Many Africans assumed that the end of the war would bring about reforms and greater freedoms. They expected improvements in housing, education, health care, and employment benefits. They also believed that they deserved the same freedom from oppression* that had been the basis of the war against Germany, Italy, and Japan. Such feelings fueled the movements that eventually led to the independence of European colonies throughout the continent. (*See also* **Colonialism in Africa, Global Politics and Africa, History of Africa, Nationalism, Warfare.**)

* **Soviet Union** nation that existed from 1922 to 1991, made up of Russia and 14 other republics

* **nationalism** devotion to the interests and culture of one's country

* **literacy** ability to read and write

* **inflation** increase in prices

* **oppression** unjust or cruel exercise of authority

Writing Systems

Although there are thousands of African LANGUAGES, most of the systems used to record them originated outside the continent. A number of factors determined the writing system chosen for each language, including which system seemed to fit the language best and various social and political reasons.

Types of Writing Systems. There are two basic types of writing systems: logographic and phonetic. The symbols in logographic systems represent whole words or morphemes, units of language than cannot be broken down into smaller meaningful parts. An example would be "most," such as in the words "mostly" or "almost." Phonetic systems are either syllabaries, in which symbols represent whole syllables, or alphabets, in which each symbol represents a single vowel or consonant. Most African languages use phonetic writing systems.

Roman script, the writing system used by English and many other European languages, is the most common script in Africa. It was spread throughout the continent by missionaries and colonial rule. European missionaries prepared the first written forms of many African languages. Later, European nations established colonies all over Africa and held power there for many years. In most places where the Roman script was introduced, it eventually replaced any previous writing systems. In most cases, administrators, educators, and publishers all preferred Roman script, which in turn influenced the general public. Roman script tends to have fewer and less complex symbols than other scripts, which gives it a real advantage over the competition.

In areas of Africa influenced by Arab culture, Arabic script is often used for writing. The Swahili language, the official language of Tanzania, developed after A.D. 700 when Arab traders mixed with East African populations. Many Swahili-speakers use an Arabic script for writing.

* **indigenous** native to a certain place

Very few indigenous* African writing systems remain in use today. Among the most widely known are alphabets for Somali, Wolof, Kpelle, Mende, Vai, and Bamum. Most of them developed in the late 1800 and early 1900s. According to their inventors, both the Vai and Bamum scripts were inspired by dreams. The shapes of the characters they use are unrelated to either Roman or Arabic scripts. Wolof uses characters similar to Arabic, but some of the pronunciations are different.

Adapting Foreign Systems to African Needs. When Africans embraced foreign writing systems, they adapted the scripts to fit the specific needs of each different language. They had to make numerous adjustments. Many African languages are tonal, meaning that the words must be pronounced at specific pitches to make sense. However, very few writing systems indicate tone. In addition, a foreign script may contain symbols that represent sounds not used by the African language, or it may lack symbols for certain sounds in the African language.

Some African societies have avoided the problem of such symbolic differences by basing their writing on standardized writing systems. These systems are specifically designed to be able to express a wide variety of languages. They include the International Phonetic Association system and the International African Institute's Africa alphabet.

Writing Numbers. While Roman script is most often used for words, the Indo-Arabic system, adopted by Western cultures, is most commonly employed for numbers. It uses only ten symbols (0 through 9) to represent all numbers, which makes it very adaptable and convenient for calculation. Other systems exist, however. The Arabic system has two sets of numbers as well as letters from the Arabic alphabet. The Ethiopian system is based on modified Greek symbols. Both have special symbols for 10, 20, 100, 200 1,000, and so on. (*See also* **Number Systems.**)

Xhosa

* **precolonial** referring to the time before European powers colonized Africa

The Xhosa, an ethnic group of SOUTH AFRICA, mostly live in Eastern Cape province in the southeastern part of the country. Although some groups farther north speak Xhosa, they are not considered part of the cluster of Xhosa chiefdoms.

The language of the Xhosa reveals clues about their history and their connections with other groups. It is very closely related to the language of the South African ZULU people, but it also shows signs of close contact with KHOISAN groups in precolonial* times.

Traditionally the Xhosa lived as extended families in scattered homesteads, farming and herding livestock. By the mid-1800s they had lost most of their livestock and land to British colonists. Today many Xhosa live in the major South Africa cities, supported by wages or social services. As in the past, KINSHIP links remain important in daily life. The Xhosa still practice their traditional forms of ancestor worship, with offerings of livestock and beer. Converts to Christianity have blended many old beliefs and practices into the new faith. Many Xhosa still have a strong believe in witchcraft, traditional healing, and other ancient practices. Through the years, they have maintained a rich oral tradition and also developed their own written literature. The Xhosa arts include colorful beadwork and elaborate clothing dyed reddish-brown with ochre, a pigment made from the earth.

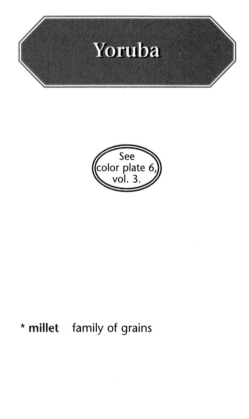

Yoruba

See color plate 6, vol. 3.

* **millet** family of grains

The term *Yoruba* refers to several western African peoples, including the Ife, Ibadan, and Egba. Europeans called all these groups *Yoruba* because they shared commons features of language, political organization, and culture. However, when referring to themselves, the Yoruba tend to use the names of their individual groups. Located mainly in southwestern NIGERIA, BÉNIN, and northern TOGO, the Yoruba number more than 25 million.

The Yoruba are descended from the founders of kingdoms that arose as early as the 1300s, although these kingdoms probably never formed a single empire. The Yoruba have long followed an urban style of life. A typical settlement consists of a densely populated town surrounded by villages, with the palace of the *oba* (king) at the center. In the traditional Yoruba political organization, the king is advised by a council of chiefs, leaders of the smaller villages around his town.

Although the Yoruba are primarily town dwellers, their economy has always been based on agriculture. Farmlands are often at some distance from towns, so the men build dwellings near their fields and travel back and forth between them and their homes in town. Farmers grow yams, corn, and millet* for food and cocoa for export. Women traditionally do not farm but control a complex market system, and a woman's status depends largely upon her skill as a trader. Yoruba arts and crafts—especially masks, pottery, and bronze sculptures—are widely known outside of Africa.

Both Islam and Christianity have a large following among the Yoruba. However, many people maintain traditional beliefs as well.

ZAIRE

See *Congo (Kinshasa)*

Zambezi River

The Zambezi River is the fourth longest in Africa, after the N**ILE**, C**ONGO**, and N**IGER** rivers. It runs for 1,678 miles across the southern part of the continent, from Z**AMBIA** through A**NGOLA**, N**AMIBIA**, B**OTSWANA**, Z**IMBABWE**, and M**OZAMBIQUE** before emptying into the Indian Ocean. Along the river's course are many distinctive natural and human-made features.

For 354 miles from its source in northwestern Zambia, the river is called the Upper Zambezi. This stretch of the river is home to the Lunda people, who once lived by hunting but are now mostly farmers. The Luena and Luvale people, who live between the settlements of Chavuma and Zambezi, fish and hunt, using dugout canoes to carry their goods up and down the river highway. Farther along on the low-lying Bulozi Floodplain is the kingdom of the Lozi people, who build houses out of wooden frames covered with woven reed mats. During the rainy seasons when the river rises and floods the plain, the Lozi migrate outward to drier regions. The Upper Zambezi ends in the Caprivi Swamps.

The section known as the Middle Zambezi begins below the swamps at the majestic Victoria Falls, Africa's largest waterfall. More than 35,000 cubic feet of water cascade over the mile-wide falls every second, dropping more than 300 feet at the highest point. Often called one of the world's seven natural wonders, Victoria Falls attracts tourists from all over the world. Immediately below the falls, the river plunges through a series of rugged and uninhabited gorges. After leaving Botoka Gorge, the last in the series, the Middle Zambezi flows into Lake Kariba. This 137-mile-long lake is formed by a huge hydroelectric dam that supplies electricity to Zambia and Zimbabwe. The lake is also known for fishing and tourist industries.

Another important feature of the Middle Zambezi is the Mana Pools area, which was made into a national park in 1963. Home to a large wildlife population, Mana Pools has been named a World Heritage site by the United Nations Educational, Scientific, and Cultural Organization (UNESCO). Beyond Mana Pools, the Luangwa River flows into the Zambezi from the north. The human population along the river increases at this point.

After the river enters Mozambique, it is known as the Lower Zambezi. It passes through another large lake and dam, the Cabora Bassa. Local warfare has prevented the people of this region from taking full advantage of the dam's potential as a fishing area and for producing electricity. From the dam to the coast, much of the valley of the Lower Zambezi is fertile and densely populated. Some of the oldest towns in Africa, such as Tete and Sena, stand on its banks. In peaceful times, the farmers of the Lower Zambezi produce a variety of crops and fruits for trade in Mozambique's cities and towns.

Zambia

* **urbanized**   concentrated in cities and towns

Zambia, a landlocked country in south central Africa, is known for its spectacular natural beauty and geographic diversity. It is also highly urbanized* and was, until recently, one of the continent's most prosperous nations. Today, however, Zambia struggles with the effects of an economy heavily dependent on mining and years of limited political freedom for its people.

GEOGRAPHY

Located on a plateau between 3,000 and 5,000 feet high, Zambia has a pleasant climate. Heat and humidity are a problem only in low river valleys. The Muchinga Mountains dominate the northeastern portion of the country, sloping down to the Rift Valley along Zambia's eastern border with TANZANIA. Central Zambia is a rolling plateau that gives way to the KALAHARI DESERT on the country's western border. LUSAKA, the capital, lies in this central region.

Zambia's many rivers and lakes provide an ample supply of water. The most important waterway, the mighty ZAMBEZI RIVER, forms a good part of the country's southern border. The river cascades over Victoria Falls, the world's largest waterfall, and then flows into Lake Kariba, one of the largest artificial lakes in the world. Other notable water resources include Lake Mweru and Bangweulu Lake and Swamp.

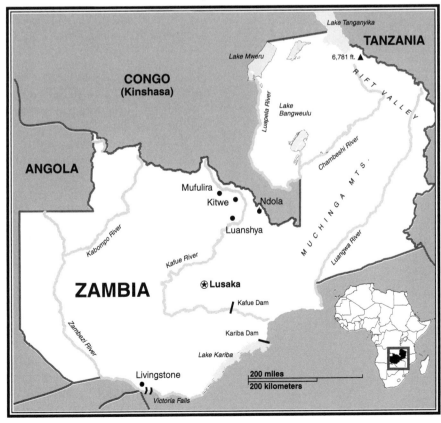

HISTORY AND GOVERNMENT

The first inhabitants of Zambia were the Bantu-speaking Tonga, who arrived around A.D. 1000. Over the next several hundred years, other peoples, including the Luba and the Bemba, migrated there. In the 1820s the Mfecane, a ZULU military movement in South Africa, drove the Ngoni and the Sotho north into the region. By the time Europeans settled in the area, Zambia had a highly diverse population.

Colonial Rule. In the 1890s the British South Africa Company signed treaties with several local chiefs granting the company control over Zambia's land and resources. In the early 1900s extensive copper deposits were discovered in southern Zambia. Copper soon became the mainstay of the colonial economy.

In 1924 the territory became a British protectorate* known as Northern Rhodesia. Meanwhile, in neighboring Southern Rhodesia (now ZIMBABWE), European settlers gained control and established their own government. In the 1940s the white settlers of the two Rhodesias and Nyasaland (now MALAWI) proposed linking the three territories in a federation*. African nationalists* opposed the move, fearing domination by the white racist leaders of Southern Rhodesia. Nevertheless, in 1953 Northern Rhodesia joined with Southern Rhodesia and Nyasaland to form the CENTRAL AFRICAN FEDERATION. Southern Rhodesia dominated the federation, and much of the revenue from Northern Rhodesia's copper mines was used to develop its southern neighbor. Living conditions for Africans worsened as wages failed to keep up with a rising cost of living. Britain dissolved the federation in 1963, and Zambia became an independent republic the following year.

Kaunda's Zambia. Kenneth KAUNDA, head of the United National Independence Party (UNIP), became Zambia's first president. The main opposition party was the African National Congress (ANC). The constitution called for an elected president serving no more than two five-year terms. It also established a one-house legislature.

In 1973 Kaunda outlawed all parties besides the UNIP. He enlarged the legislature and abolished the two-term limit on the presidency. As president, Kaunda had sweeping powers, including appointing almost all the government officials. Under the new system he won every election for the next 18 years.

The Kaunda government nationalized* most of Zambia's major industries, including the copper industry, which accounted for over 90 percent of the country's export earnings. Continuing the policy of the former colonial rulers, Kaunda neglected the agricultural sector*. Prices for agricultural produce were so low that some farmers stopped growing crops to sell. Many abandoned their land and moved to the cities, even though few jobs were available there. Unemployment rose and the country became dependent on imported foods.

Until the mid-1970s Zambia prospered through its exports of copper. However, the price of copper collapsed in 1974 to 1975, cutting average

* **protectorate** weak state under the control and protection of a strong state

* **federation** organization of separate states with a central government

* **nationalist** devoted to the interests and culture of one's country

* **nationalize** to bring land, industries, or public works under state control or ownership

* **sector** part; subdivision of society

164

incomes in half. Forced to borrow heavily from foreign countries, Zambia accumulated huge debts. In the 1980s Zambia agreed to an International Monetary Fund program designed to reduce state spending and balance the national budget. The program produced few results and Kaunda eventually ended it. However, he kept some of its policies, such as devoting a portion of export earnings to debt payment.

Political Change. By 1990 economic hardship had led to political unrest. A group known as the Movement for Multiparty Democracy (MMD) called for an end to single-party rule. After a failed coup* in June, Kaunda agreed to allow multiparty elections. The following October, Frederick Chiluba of the MMD won the presidency and his party captured 125 of the 150 seats in the legislature.

During his first term in office Chiluba privatized* over 140 state-owned businesses. He also ended the government monopoly* on the purchase of food, which increased farmers' incomes and led to agricultural improvements. Although the national debt declined, economic problems such as inflation* and a weak currency, as well as government corruption, still plagued the country.

As the 1996 elections approached, Chiluba feared that Kaunda might attempt a political comeback. To prevent this, he passed a law that allowed only native Zambians who had not served as president to run for the office. Kaunda, of course, had already served as president; in addition, since his parents came from Malawi, he was not considered a native Zambian. Kaunda's angry supporters refused to take part in the election. Nevertheless, about 40 percent of the eligible voters went to the polls, and Chiluba won.

Shortly after the election Kaunda warned of a coming "explosion" in Zambian politics. The next day an army captain made an attempt to overthrow the government. Although the uprising was crushed within hours, Chiluba declared a state of emergency and took complete control of the government for the next several months.

The Chiluba government has faced high unemployment and an economy still heavily dependent on copper. It has also struggled with major health issues. In the late 1990s about 70 percent of Zambians were infected with tuberculosis and about 20 percent had HIV, the virus that causes AIDS. Wars in neighboring CONGO (KINSHASA) and ANGOLA have created ongoing foreign policy concerns.

ECONOMY

Zambia's economy can be summarized in a single word: copper. This resource still provides over 80 percent of export revenues. However, prices have not recovered from their downturn in the 1970s, and production has declined. The industry needs large amounts of money to purchase new equipment for aging mines and to upgrade the country's infrastructure*.

About two-thirds of Zambia's population still practices subsistence farming*. In addition, commercial farmers grow cotton, tobacco, and

* **coup** sudden, often violent, overthrow of a ruler or government

* **privatize** to transfer from government control to private ownership

* **monopoly** exclusive control or domination of a particular type of business

* **inflation** increase in prices

* **infrastructure** basic framework of a society and its economy, which includes roads, bridges, port facilities, airports, and other public works

* **subsistence farming** raising only enough food to live on

Urban Melting Pot

Zambia's busy cities are filled with migrants from the countryside. In these urban areas, rural people sometimes develop new customs and traditions. By the 1950s a number of young men of the Bisa ethnic group had migrated to the copper mining town of Luanshya. Together they developed the Kalela dance, which they performed for audiences in the city. Dressed in European clothing, the dancers sang songs praising the Bisa while insulting other ethnic groups. This mixing of rural customs with new influences is not unusual in Zambia's diverse urban centers.

Zambia

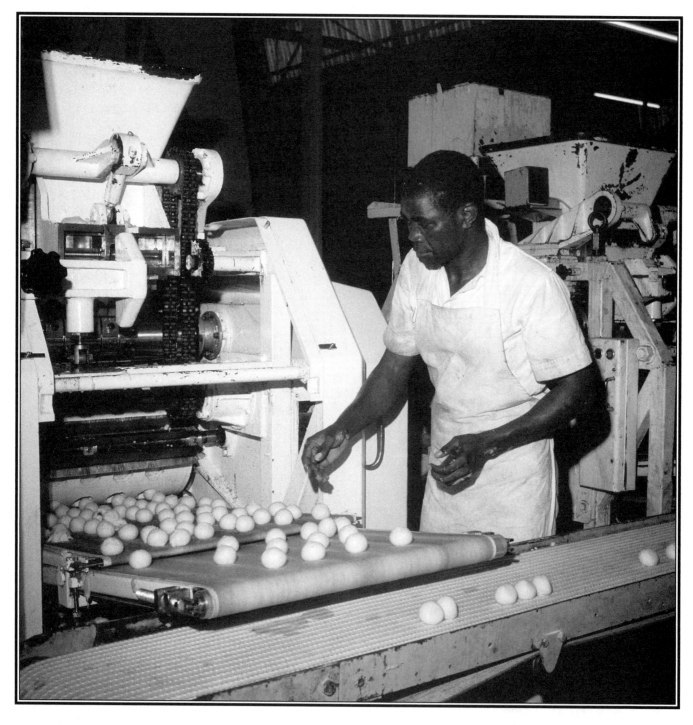

Although copper still dominates the economy of Zambia, food processing, textiles, and chemicals have become important industries. Shown here is a bread factory in the city of Kabwe.

coffee for export. Manufacturing has become a major sector of the economy. Mining of emeralds and other minerals has also been growing.

The country's major economic challenges include finding ways to broaden the economy and to reduce its huge foreign debt. Political problems in neighboring countries also affect Zambia's economy. With no outlet to the sea, it depends on other nations for access to ports. Any

166

Republic of Zambia

POPULATION:
9,582,418 (2000 estimated population)

AREA:
290,586 sq. mi. (752,618 sq. km)

LANGUAGES:
English (official); Bemba, Tonga, Lozi, Lunda, Nyanja, others

NATIONAL CURRENCY:
Zambian kwacha

PRINCIPAL RELIGIONS:
Christian 50–75%, Hindu and Muslim 24–49%, Traditional 1%

CITIES:
Lusaka (capital), 1,640,000 (2001 est.); Kitwe, Ndola, Chingola, Mufulira, Luanshya, Kabwe, Livingstone

ANNUAL RAINFALL:
Varies from 50 in. (1,400 mm) in the north to 20 in. (510 mm) in the south.

ECONOMY:
GDP per capita: $880 (1999 est.)

PRINCIPAL PRODUCTS AND EXPORTS:
Agricultural: cotton, tobacco, coffee, corn, sorghum, rice, cassava, peanuts, sugarcane, livestock and livestock products
Manufacturing: food and beverage processing, textiles, chemicals, fertilizer
Mining: copper, zinc, lead, cobalt, coal, emeralds, gold, silver, uranium

GOVERNMENT:
Independence from Britain, 1964. Republic with president elected by universal suffrage. Governing bodies: 150-seat National Assembly (legislative body), elected by universal suffrage; Cabinet, appointed by the president.

HEADS OF STATE SINCE INDEPENDENCE:
1964–1991 President Kenneth David Kaunda
1991 President Frederick Chiluba

ARMED FORCES:
21,600 (2001 est.)

EDUCATION:
Compulsory for ages 7–14; literacy rate 78% (2001 est.)

disruption in surrounding countries threatens Zambia's ability to export its goods.

PEOPLES AND CULTURES

Zambia's population is mostly made up of Bantu-speaking peoples divided into at least 70 different ethnic groups. The Bemba, who originated in what is now Congo (Kinshasa), dominate the Northern Province. Southern central Zambia is home to the Tonga, while the Ngoni are the primary ethnic group of the southeast. The Lozi are the predominant group in the southwest. Zambia's population is very unevenly distributed. Almost 80 percent of the people live on roughly 33 percent of the land. In the high-density population areas, the residents tend to be better educated than rural dwellers, as two-thirds of them are literate.

Many of Zambia's ethnic groups are matrilineal, meaning that they trace descent through the mother's side of the family. The main exceptions are some Ngoni cattle herders, who are patrilineal (descent through the father's side of the family) and the Lozi, who trace descent through both sides of the family.

About two-thirds of Zambians practice Christianity, which has played a major role in the country's social history. During the colonial era mission schools were important centers of educational as well as spiritual leadership for black Zambians. Many Zambian Christians have held on to various beliefs and customs of traditional religions, including ancestor worship and witchcraft. (*See also* **Bantu Peoples; Cities and Urbanization; Colonialism in Africa; Minerals and Mining; Rhodes, Cecil John** .)

167

Zanzibar

Zanzibar, an island state in the Indian Ocean, lies about 30 miles off the coast of East Africa. Long an Arab stronghold, it became a British colony in the late 1800s. Zanzibar gained its independence in 1963 and the next year joined Tanganyika in forming the United Republic of TANZANIA.

Geography. Zanzibar consists of two main islands, Unguja (also called Zanzibar Island) and Pemba, and several smaller ones. Unguja, the largest, covers an area of 637 square miles. Made of limestone, coral, and sandstone, the islands are fairly flat—the highest point on Unguja is 390 feet above sea level. At one time the islands supported dense forests, but human activity long ago destroyed all but small patches of the original tree cover. Today, mangrove* swamps line their eastern shores.

Zanzibar has two rainy seasons, from March to May and from October to December, and receives about 70 inches of rain each year. The tropical climate and the deep, well-drained soil are ideal for growing clove trees. Cloves, a spice, are one of Zanzibar's major exports. Farmers also raise coconuts and rice, an important local food.

History. Located within reach of Africa, Arabia, and India, Zanzibar attracted colonists from several continents. The earliest inhabitants were BANTU PEOPLES from sub-Saharan* Africa. Migrants from Arabia arrived in the 900s and blended with the African population. Later, Arabs—mostly from Oman, on the Arabian peninsula—colonized the islands.

The Arabs used Zanzibar both as a commercial port and as a base for slave trading expeditions to the African mainland. In the 1500s the Portuguese began conquering many East African coastal settlements, including Zanzibar. However, in 1698 the Omanis drove them out of the region. Under Omani rule, Zanzibar became a center of the IVORY TRADE and the SLAVE TRADE.

In 1832 SA'ID IBN SULTAN, the Omani ruler, moved his capital from Muscat in Oman to Zanzibar. He established a loosely organized state, allowing local groups some freedom to govern themselves. He promoted the development of Zanzibar's clove industry, which depended on slave labor. Meanwhile, he extended the Omani trading network deep into the African mainland. To strengthen the islands' commercial relationships, Sa'id signed trade agreements with the United States, Britain, and France. The merchants of Zanzibar grew wealthy on exports of cloves, ivory, and slaves.

After Sa'id's death in 1856, Zanzibar separated from Oman and became an independent sultanate. In 1890 Britain took control of the islands and abolished the slave trade. Zanzibar became an independent nation within the British commonwealth in 1963. The following year the islanders revolted against the Arab-dominated government, and the sultans' rule came to an end. The uprising led to Zanzibar's union with Tanganyika in the United Republic of Tanzania. Within the republic, Zanzibar maintains some autonomy* concerning education, immigration, and other policy areas. The president of Zanzibar serves as one of Tanzania's two vice presidents.

* **mangrove** tree found in coastal areas that grows in dense clusters

* **sub-Saharan** referring to Africa south of the Sahara desert

* **autonomy** independent self-government

Peoples and Economy. Today's Zanzibaris are a mixture of African, Omani, and other Middle Eastern peoples. Most consider themselves as either Arab or SWAHILI. The language of the islands is Swahili, a Bantu language that has borrowed many words from Arabic, but some recent immigrants from Oman speak Arabic. The great majority of the population is Muslim.

Rural Zanzibaris support themselves through farming, fishing, picking cloves for wages, and small businesses. In the towns, trade is the main economic activity. Merchants sell imported items and locally produced goods in open-air marketplaces. In addition, TOURISM is gaining importance and has brought modern hotels, shops, and restaurants to Zanzibar Town, the islands' capital. Zanzibar Town has two parts: Stone Town and Ng'ambo. Stone Town is a maze of narrow, stone-paved lanes and historic buildings, including the former sultan's palace and a church founded by missionary-explorer David LIVINGSTONE. Ng'ambo is the newer, more sprawling side of the city. (*See also* **Arabs in Africa, Colonialism in Africa.**)

Zara Ya'iqob

**Ruled 1434–1468
Emperor of Ethiopia**

* **theology**   study of religious faith

Zara Ya'Iqob, a powerful and intelligent Ethiopian ruler, was a devout Christian. He sometimes took strong measures to make sure that Christianity remained the dominant religion in ETHIOPIA.

The son of emperor Dawit of Ethiopia, Zara Ya'iqob was educated at his father's royal court. When his father died and his brother became emperor, Zara Ya'iqob was confined in a remote mountain prison. He remained there for more than 20 years until he was called to the throne.

As emperor, Zara Ya'Iqob attempted to improve relations between the Christians of northern and southern Ethiopia. In 1449 he declared both Saturday and Sunday as sabbaths, or holy days, to combine the northern and southern traditions for observing the sabbath. Yet, Zara Ya'iqob was less tolerant of other religious customs. He persecuted certain groups of Christian monks, Ethiopian Jews, and those accused of non-Christian practices. He wrote several books outlining a theology* that became an important part of Ethiopian tradition.

Zara Ya'Iqob built a stone palace in which he lived during his later years. Unlike other Ethiopian emperors of this period, who spent much of their time traveling throughout the empire, Zara Ya'iqob rarely ventured beyond his palace's walls. (*See also* **Christianity in Africa, Ethiopian Orthodox Church, Religion and Ritual.**)

Zimbabwe

Although a powerful and complex kingdom some 700 years ago, Zimbabwe was one of the last countries in Africa to win its independence in the late 1900s. Impressive architectural ruins show glimpses of the nation's past grandeur. From the early civilizations that built these

structures down to the modern day, Zimbabwe has played an important role in southern Africa.

GEOGRAPHY

Zimbabwe is a landlocked country in southeastern Africa, bordered by ZAMBIA to the north, MOZAMBIQUE to the east, BOTSWANA to the west, and SOUTH AFRICA to the south. An elevated ridge known as the highveldt divides the country roughly in two from southwest to northeast. An area called the middleveldt slopes down from either side of the highveldt, covering about 40 percent of the land. The extreme northwest and southeast make up the lowveldt. Mountainous terrain dominates the Eastern Highlands bordering Mozambique.

Most of the country ranges from 1,000 to 4,000 feet above sea level, and this height produces a moderate climate. However, the land is generally better suited to ranching than agriculture because of its thin sandy soils. In addition, rain falls unpredictably, leading to severe droughts that strike the land and people. Although forest covers about one-third of Zimbabwe, forested areas have been disappearing in recent years, which has caused much concern. Savanna* grasslands account for much of the rest of the country. The spectacular Victoria Falls and Kariba, one of the world's largest artificial lakes, are in the northwest.

* **savanna** tropical or subtropical grassland with scattered trees and drought-resistant undergrowth

See
color plate 1,
vol. 3.

HISTORY AND GOVERNMENT

The modern country of Zimbabwe takes its name from the massive stone ruins of Great Zimbabwe that are one of Africa's most impressive archaeological sites. These *dzimba dza mabwe,* or "houses of stone," were built before A.D. 1000 and testify to the rise of the earliest centralized societies in southern Africa.

Great Zimbabwe. The site called Great Zimbabwe was built by the Mashona (or SHONA) people. Its main feature is the Great Enclosure, a circular stone wall over 30 feet high and 800 feet in circumference. Inside the enclosure lie the remains of a cone-shaped tower, as well as other walls and clay building platforms. Glass beads and Chinese porcelain found at the site suggest that Great Zimbabwe was connected to SWAHILI trading networks that stretched to ports along the Indian Ocean coast.

The valleys surrounding the Great Enclosure contain other stone enclosures with similar smaller towers and clay platforms. The remains of clay floors indicate that as many as 10,000 people were living in close quarters in the area. The society featured a complex division of labor between agriculture, pastoralism*, and craft activities. The labor system probably required a highly structured and powerful central authority. Additional walls at the site divided the living areas of the privileged classes from those of the common people.

The rulers of Great Zimbabwe extended their control over a wide area of the surrounding plateau from which they extracted resources and tribute*. The high walls of the Great Enclosure served more as a symbol of the power of the rulers than as a real military defense. Great Zimbabwe was not, however, the only such walled settlement in the region. Some 150 smaller sites have been uncovered in Zimbabwe, eastern Botswana, South Africa, and Mozambique. One of these, Mapungubwe, in South Africa, appears to have been built earlier than Great Zimbabwe. Although not as advanced in its architecture, it too appears to have had a complex division of labor and trading ties with the coast.

The Decline of Great Zimbabwe. The state of Great Zimbabwe dominated its region until the mid-1400s. At that time the rulers began to lose control of peoples living on the edges of their empire. Around 1450 the states of Torwa and MUTAPA (also known as Mwene Mutapa and Munhumutapa) emerged. A Portuguese document dated 1506 contains the earliest existing reference to Mutapa. It, too, held power over surrounding territory and received tribute from weaker kingdoms in the area.

Portuguese traders made contact with Mutapa around 1500 and established trading posts along the ZAMBEZI RIVER and the Zimbabwe plateau. By the early 1600s, they had gained control over the gold and IVORY TRADE with the coast, and the ruler of Mutapa had to obey the orders of the Portuguese. In the 1660s a new ruler became powerful enough to force the Portuguese out of the region. However, internal divisions and

* **pastoralism** lifestyle characterized by herding livestock

* **tribute** payment made by a smaller or weaker party to a more powerful one, often under the threat of force

Reclaiming African History

To justify their colonization of Africa, the British invented the myth that black Africans had no history of advanced civilization or culture. Thus, when British archaeologists discovered Great Zimbabwe in the late 1800s, they did not believe it was built by Africans. Instead they thought it was the remains of an ancient colony of Phoenicians from what is now Lebanon. Only later did other scholars prove that Great Zimbabwe was, indeed, an African creation.

Zimbabwe

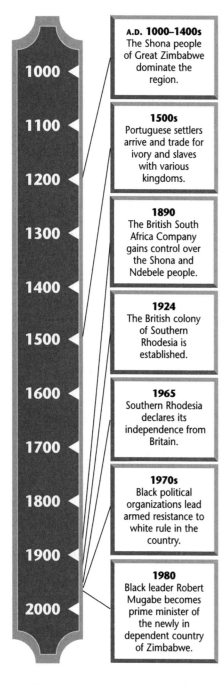

A.D. 1000–1400s
The Shona people of Great Zimbabwe dominate the region.

1500s
Portuguese settlers arrive and trade for ivory and slaves with various kingdoms.

1890
The British South Africa Company gains control over the Shona and Ndebele people.

1924
The British colony of Southern Rhodesia is established.

1965
Southern Rhodesia declares its independence from Britain.

1970s
Black political organizations lead armed resistance to white rule in the country.

1980
Black leader Robert Mugabe becomes prime minister of the newly independent country of Zimbabwe.

* **indigenous**   native to a certain place

* **sanction**   measure adopted by one or more nations to force another nation to changes its policies or conduct

rebellions in outlying areas soon fractured the state and led to its decline.

The Rise of Rhodesia. In the early 1800s the NDEBELE people moved into southwest Zimbabwe from South Africa. They were part of the ZULU nation that had been driven from its land by the eastward expansion of white settlers. Clashes with settlers resulted in the destruction of the Ndebele kingdom in the late 1800s. The displaced Ndebele made frequent raids on the neighboring Shona to obtain food, cattle, and laborers. The ethnic divisions dating from this period have remained an ongoing problem for Zimbabwe.

In 1890 armed troops of the British South Africa Company, a private firm under the leadership of Cecil RHODES, invaded what is now Zimbabwe. Despite fierce resistance from the Shona and Ndebele, Rhodes's army gained control over the region. In 1924 the area was proclaimed a self-governing British colony and named Southern Rhodesia after its leader. Like its neighbor South Africa, the colony practiced racial segregation, denying basic freedoms and civil rights to black Africans. White authorities threw black farmers off their best lands and turned the property over to a handful of influential white settlers.

In 1953 Southern Rhodesia joined with the British colonies of Northern Rhodesia (now Zambia) and Nyasaland (now MALAWI) to form the CENTRAL AFRICAN FEDERATION. The main goal of the federation was to allow Southern Rhodesia access to Northern Rhodesia's abundant copper reserves and Nyasaland's pool of cheap LABOR. During this time the country's leaders took some timid steps toward granting black people a place in government. A new constitution in 1961 set aside about a quarter of the seats in Parliament for blacks.

Most black Rhodesians realized that the new arrangement was only a tactic to delay true majority rule by the indigenous* population. African political groups increased their calls for democracy. In 1962 a right-wing white party called the Rhodesian Front (RF) emerged to challenge those white leaders who approved the 1961 constitution. The RF, led by the openly racist Ian Smith, dedicated itself to total white supremacy.

A year after the founding of the RF, Britain dissolved the Central African Federation and granted independence to Northern Rhodesia and Nyasaland under black majority governments. This move alarmed the RF's leaders, who suspected that Britain supported black rule in Southern Rhodesia as well. In 1965 Smith, by then prime minister, declared independence for Southern Rhodesia. The British passed economic and political sanctions* against Southern Rhodesia, but Smith still hoped that other countries would recognize his nation's independence.

Conflict and Negotiation. In the late 1950s and early 1960s, several black political organizations arose to challenge white rule in Rhodesia. The first group to emerge was the Zimbabwe African People's Union (ZAPU), led by Joshua Nkomo. In 1963 some members of ZAPU split off to form the Zimbabwe African National Union (ZANU) under

172

the leadership of Robert MUGABE and Ndabaningi Sithole. ZANU announced a policy of armed resistance, and a war of liberation against the white government began in the 1970s.

ZANU and ZAPU joined forces in 1976 to form the Patriotic Front (PF), carrying out their anti-government campaign from bases in Zambia and Mozambique. During this time the British attempted to negotiate a settlement between the rebels and the Rhodesian government. This effort resulted in the so-called "internal settlement" of 1978–1979 that put blacks into several high political offices, including president and prime minister. However, whites still controlled the real power in the country, and neither ZANU nor ZAPU accepted the deal.

In 1979 all of the parties agreed to a compromise agreement that called for free elections the following year. To reassure the white minority, 20 seats in the legislature were set aside for whites for a period of seven years. In the resulting elections, ZANU won the majority of seats, and Mugabe became prime minister of the country, renamed Zimbabwe.

Independent Zimbabwe. Mugabe moved cautiously in changing Zimbabwean society. He realized that the Smith regime had developed an impressive industrial infrastructure* to offset the effect of British economic sanctions and boycotts*. As a result, Zimbabwe had a relatively healthy and diverse economy that Mugabe did not want to damage. Although he pledged to resettle black people on land stolen by white settlers, he realized that moving too fast would disrupt the large-scale agriculture that provided the country's main source of export earnings.

Even so, Mugabe did make several important changes. His government turned some white lands over to black people, invested in HEALTH CARE and education, and helped more black Zimbabweans get higher positions in business and civil service. But at the same time relations between ZANU and ZAPU grew worse. In 1982 ZANU accused ZAPU of hoarding weapons for a coup* and fired several ZAPU leaders from the government. The next two years saw a brutal conflict in which ZANU and its followers killed thousands of ZAPU supporters.

Throughout the 1980s Mugabe said that he wanted to turn Zimbabwe into a single-party state based on communist* principles. However, the Zimbabwe Unity Movement (ZUM), a new party headed by former ZANU leader Edward Tekere, emerged just before the 1990 elections. Mugabe won nearly 80 percent of the vote, but only about half of the eligible voters participated.

The fall of the Soviet Union in 1991 led Mugabe to abandon his call for a communist state but not his desire for political dominance in Zimbabwe. A new constitution adopted in 1992 made ZANU the only party eligible for state funding. Mugabe accelerated the land redistribution program in the following year. However, ordinary people found out that some of the first lands taken under the program went to high government officials.

By that time corruption and political mismanagement were ruining Zimbabwe's economy. A catastrophic drought struck in 1992, and poor government planning led to a serious food shortage. In 1996 it was revealed that government officials had stolen money from a fund for

* **infrastructure** basic framework of a society and its economy, which includes roads, bridges, port facilities, airports, and other public works

* **boycott** refusal to participate or buy goods, as a means of protest

* **coup** sudden, often violent, overthrow of a ruler or government

* **communist** relating to communism, a system in which land, good, and the means of production are owned by the state or community rather than by individuals

army veterans. In protest, most opposition parties boycotted the elections that year and less than one-third of the electorate voted.

In 1998 Mugabe made a fateful decision to send troops into CONGO (KINSHASA). Congo's leader Laurent Kabila, who had recently overthrown the dictator MOBUTU SESE SEKO, faced a rebellion of his own. Mugabe hoped to take control of valuable resources such as copper and dia-

Many people in Zimbabwe work in agriculture, an important source of revenue for the country. These women in the fields separate soybeans from their hulls.

174

monds that Kabila's government could not protect. His arms purchases for the war sent the country deeper into debt.

Zimbabwe struggles under a crushing foreign debt, widespread unemployment, and very high inflation*. Mugabe's foreign adventures have bankrupted the treasury. Bands of armed black citizens roam the countryside forcing white farmers off their land and harassing their black workers. Although Mugabe still holds power, most observers believe that a new leader is needed before Zimbabwe can improve its situation.

* **inflation**   increase in prices

ECONOMY

Zimbabwe's economy includes a fairly diverse range of activities and goods. Agriculture provides almost half of the country's export earnings: tobacco is the country's largest agricultural export, followed by cotton and beef. Zimbabwe usually produces enough to feed its people without large imports of food. But droughts in 1991–1992 and 1994–1995 destroyed much of the maize (corn) that Zimbabweans rely on for their own food.

 See map in Minerals and Mining (vol. 3).

Industry and manufacturing, well developed under the Smith regime, contribute a substantial portion of the export revenues. Leading industries include construction equipment, transportation equipment, metal products, chemicals, textiles, and food processing. However, much of the industrial infrastructure has aged and needs to be upgraded. Zimbabwe also has a mining sector* that produces gold and platinum, but foreign companies dominate most mining activities.

* **sector**   part; subdivision of society

Service industries also play a significant role in the economy, with many of them created by government programs. Violence in rural areas has damaged both TOURISM and agriculture. Many experts expect that Zimbabwe's economy will continue to decline for some time.

PEOPLES AND CULTURES

Most Zimbabweans belong to either the Shona or Ndebele ethnic groups. The Shona, made up of six main linguistic subgroups, work mainly as farmers or herders. The Shona forbid marriage between members of the same clan. Marriages usually involve a transfer of wealth from the groom to the bride's family. Married couples often live with the groom's parents. If the groom does not have wealth and gifts to offer, he may perform labor for his father-in-law.

The Ndebele (also known as Matabele) traditionally live as herders with a highly structured social system. In the 1800s they raided Shona settlements and captured Shona as servants. Their social system discouraged marriage between the two groups to ensure the dominance of the Ndebele privileged classes. Ethnic tensions between the two groups still erupt occasionally.

About half of Zimbabweans practice a mixture of CHRISTIANITY and indigenous religions based on reverence for dead ancestors. These religions include SPIRIT POSSESSION, by which religious leaders communicate with the spirit world. Although many Zimbabweans say they belong to the Catholic or Anglican church, their worship often mixes elements of

Zimbabwe

 Republic of Zimbabwe

POPULATION:
11,342,521 (2000 estimated population)

AREA:
150,803 sq. mi. (390,580 sq. km)

LANGUAGES:
English (official); Shona, Ndebele

NATIONAL CURRENCY:
Zimbabwe dollar

PRINCIPAL RELIGIONS:
Syncretic (part traditional, part Christian) 50%, Christian 25%, Traditional 24%, Other 1%

CITIES:
Harare (capital), 1,752,000 (2001 est.); Bulawayo, Gweru, Mutare, Kwekwe, Kadoma, Hwange, Masvingo

ANNUAL RAINFALL:
Varies from 40 in. (1,020 mm) in Eastern Highlands to 15 in. (400 mm) in Limpopo valley.

ECONOMY:
GDP per capita: $2,400 (1999 est.)

PRINCIPAL PRODUCTS AND EXPORTS:
Agricultural: coffee, tobacco, corn, sugarcane, peanuts, wheat, cotton, livestock
Manufacturing: steel mills, textiles and footwear, wood products, cement, chemicals, fertilizer, food and beverage processing
Mining: coal, gold, copper, nickel, iron ore, tin, clay

GOVERNMENT:
Independence from Britain, 1980. Paramilitary democracy with president nominated by the House of Assembly and elected by universal suffrage. Governing body: 150-seat House of Assembly, with 120 members elected by universal suffrage.

HEADS OF STATE SINCE INDEPENDENCE:
1980–1987 President Canaan Banana
1987 President Robert Mugabe

ARMED FORCES:
39,000 (2001 est.)

EDUCATION:
Compulsory for ages 6–13; literacy rate 85% (2001 est.)

indigenous beliefs. (*See also* **Archaeology and Prehistory, Colonialism in Africa, Ethnic Groups and Identity, Harare, Independence Movements, Land Ownership, Southern Africa, History** .)

Zulu

* **hierarchy** organization of a group into higher and lower levels

* **clan** group of people descended from a common ancestor

* **apartheid** policy of racial segregation enforced by the white government of South Africa to maintain political, economic, and social control over the country's blacks, Asians, and people of mixed ancestry

The Zulu, a large ethnic group in SOUTH AFRICA, are based in Natal Province on the country's eastern coast. They speak a BANTU language closely related to that of the XHOSA. Originally one of many small societies in the region, the Zulu grew into a powerful nation in the 1800s.

Traditionally the Zulu were farmers, growing millet, a kind of grain. In addition, the men tended large herds of cattle, which were an important sign of wealth. In the early 1800s a leader named SHAKA ZULU united the Zulu and other neighboring peoples into a well-organized state that dominated the region. Later, European settlers took over much of the Zulu grazing land, causing the great herds to shrink.

The modern Zulu have retained many of the traditional features of their society. In the settlements of KwaZulu in Natal, villages are organized around a hierarchy* made up of older men who serve under the king as clan* chiefs and the heads of clan sections. First created by Shaka Zulu, this form of organization is reflected in the Zulu-based Inkatha Freedom Party, which was involved in the movement to end apartheid* in South Africa.

The Zulu practice polygyny, a marriage system in which a man may have more than one wife. They also follow the traditions of levirate marriage, in which a woman whose husband dies is married to her husband's brother, and ghost marriage, in which a woman is "married" to a dead relative so that her children will carry on the dead man's family line. Early Zulu religious beliefs were based on ancestor worship. Today Christianity is the main religion among the Zulu, with some independent churches organized around PROPHETIC MOVEMENTS. (*See also* **Ethnic Groups and Identity, Southern Africa, History.**)

Suggested Readings

Atlases and Encyclopedias

Appiah, Kwame Anthony, and Henry Louis Gates. *Africana: The Encyclopedia of the African and African American Experience.* New York: Basic Civitas Books, 1999.

Cutter, Charles H. *Africa 2000.* 35th ed. Harpers Ferry, W. Va.: Stryker-Post Publications, 2000.

The Diagram Group. *Encyclopedia of African Peoples.* New York: Facts on File, 2000.

Explorers: From Ancient Times to the Space Age. 3 vols. New York: Macmillan, 1999.

Fernández-Armesto, Felipe, ed. *The Times Atlas of World Exploration: 3,000 Years of Exploring, Explorers, and Mapmaking.* New York: HarperCollins Publishers, 1991.

Freeman-Grenville, G.S.P. *The New Atlas of African History.* New York: Simon & Schuster, 1991.

Middleton, John, ed. *Encyclopedia of Africa South of the Sahara.* New York: Charles Scribner's Sons, 1997.

Murray, Jocelyn, ed. *Cultural Atlas of Africa.* Rev. ed. New York: Checkmark Books, 1998.

Page, Willie F. *The Encyclopedia of African History and Culture.* 3 vols. New York: Facts on File, 2001.

Parker, Sybil P., ed. *World Geographical Encyclopedia: Volume 1, Africa.* New York: McGraw-Hill, 1995.

Ramsay, F. Jeffress. *Global Studies: Africa.* 8th ed. Guilford, Conn.: Dushkin/McGraw-Hill, 1999.

Robinson, Francis. *Atlas of the Islamic World Since 1500.* New York: Facts on File, 1982.

Simon, Reeva S., Philip Mattar, and Richard W. Bulliet. *Encyclopedia of the Modern Middle East.* New York: Macmillan, 1996.

History, General

*Clarke, John Henrik. *African People in World History.* Baltimore, Md.: Black Classic Press, 1993.

Curtin, Philip D., ed. *African History: From Earliest Times to Independence.* New York: Longman Publishing, 1995.

Davidson, Basil. *Modern Africa: A Social and Political History.* 3d ed. New York: Longman Publishing, 1994.

Fage, J. D. *A History of Africa.* 3d ed. New York: Routledge, 1995.

Iliffe, John. *Africans: The History of a Continent.* New York: Cambridge University Press, 1995.

Oliver, Roland. *The African Experience: Major Themes in African History from Earliest Times to the Present.* New York: HarperCollins Publishers, 1991.

Reader, John. *Africa: A Biography of the Continent.* New York: A. A. Knopf, 1998.

Segal, Ronald. *Islam's Black Slaves: The Other Black Diaspora.* New York: Farrar, Straus & Giroux, 2001.

Shillington, Kevin. *History of Africa.* Rev. ed. New York: St. Martin's Press, 1995.

Colonial

Boahen, A. Adu, ed. *Africa Under Colonial Domination, 1880–1935.* Berkeley: University of California Press, 1990.

Pakenham, Thomas. *The Scramble for Africa, 1876–1912.* New York: Random House, 1991.

*Thomas, Velma Maia. *Lest We Forget: The Passage From Africa to Slavery and Emancipation.* New York: Crown Trade Paperbacks, 1997.

*Asterisk denotes book for young readers

Individual Countries

Alie, Joe A. *A New History of Sierra Leone*. New York: St. Martin's Press, 1990.

Berman, Bruce J., and John Lonsdale. *Unhappy Valley: Conflict in Kenya and Africa*. Athens: Ohio University Press, 1992.

Berry, LaVerle, ed. *Ghana: A Country Study*. 3d ed. Washington, D.C.: Federal Research Division, 1995.

Byrnes, Rita M., ed. *Uganda: A Country Study*. 2d ed. Washington, D.C.: Federal Research Division, 1992.

———, ed. *South Africa: A Country Study*. 3d ed. Washington, D.C.: Federal Research Division, 1992.

Fegley, Randall. *The Congo*. Santa Barbara, Calif.: Clio Press, 1993.

Marcus, Harold G. *A History of Ethiopia*. Berkeley: University of California Press, 1994.

Meditz, Sandra W., and Tim Merrill, eds. *Zaire [Congo, Kinshasa]: A Country Study*. 4th ed. Washington, D.C.: Federal Research Division, 1994.

Ofcansky, Thomas P., and LaVerle Berry, eds. *Ethiopia: A Country Study*. Washington, D.C.: Federal Research Division, 1995.

Ruedy, John Douglas. *Modern Algeria: The Origins and Development of a Nation*. Bloomington: Indiana University Press, 1992.

Thompson, Leonard. *A History of South Africa*. 3d ed. New Haven, Conn.: Yale University Press, 2001.

Prehistory and Archaeology

Clark, J. Desmond. *The Prehistory of Africa*. Westport, Conn.: Greenwood Press, 1984.

Hall, Martin. *Archaeology Africa*. London: J. Currey, 1996.

*Haskins, James, and Kathleen Benson. *African Beginnings*. New York: Lothrop, Lee & Shepard Books, 1998.

Leakey, Richard E., and Roger Lewin. *Origins Reconsidered: In Search of What Makes Us Human*. New York: Doubleday, 1992.

Phillipson, David W. *African Archaeology*. 2d ed. New York: Cambridge University Press, 1993.

*Poynter, Margaret. *The Leakeys: Uncovering the Origins of Humankind*. Springfield, N.J.: Enslow Publishers, 1997.

Robertshaw, Peter, ed. *A History of African Archaeology*. Portsmouth, N.H.: Heinemann, 1990.

Early History

Burstein, Stanley Mayer, ed. *Ancient African Civilizations: Kush and Axum*. Princeton, N.J.: Markus Wiener Publishers, 1998.

Gann, Lewis H., and Peter Duignan. *Africa and the World: An Introduction to the History of Sub-Saharan Africa From Antiquity to 1840*. Lanham, Md.: University Press of America, 2000.

Garlake, Peter. *The Kingdoms of Africa*. New York: Peter Bedrick Books, 1990.

*Hart, George. *Eyewitness: Ancient Egypt*. Alexandria, Va.: Time-Life Books, 1995.

*Koslow, Philip J. *Kanem-Borno: One Thousand Years of Splendor*. New York: Chelsea House Publishers, 1994.

Phillipson, David W. *Ancient Ethiopia: Aksum, Its Antecedents and Successors*. London: British Museum Press, 1998.

*Putnam, James. *Life in Ancient Egypt: 3,000 Years of Mystery to Unlock and Discover*. Philadelphia: Running Press, 1994.

Religion and Mythology

Blakely, Thomas D., Walter E. A. van Beek, and Dennis L. Thompson, eds. *Religion in Africa: Experience and Expression.* Portsmouth, N.H.: Heinemann, 1994.

Chidester, David. *Religions of South Africa.* New York: Routledge, 1992.

Gray, Richard. *Black Christians and White Missionaries.* New Haven, Conn.: Yale University Press, 1990.

Mbiti, John. *African Religions and Philosophy.* 2d ed. Portsmouth, N.H.: Heinemann Educational Books, 1991.

———. *Introduction to African Religion.* 2d ed. Portsmouth, N.H.: Heinemann Educational Books, 1991.

*Myths and Legends. 4 vols. New York: Macmillan, 2000.

Ray, Benjamin C. *African Religions: Symbol, Ritual, and Community.* 2d ed. Upper Saddle River, N.J.: Prentice Hall, 2000.

Exploration and Discovery

Brown, Don. *Uncommon Traveler: Mary Kingsley in Africa.* Boston: Houghton Mifflin, 2000.

Dunn, Ross E. *The Adventures of Ibn Battuta: A Muslim Traveller of the Fourteenth Century.* Berkeley: University of California Press, 1986.

Hynson, Colin. *Exploration of Africa.* Hauppauge, N.Y.: Barron's Educational Series, Inc., 1998.

Ibazebo, Isimeme. *Exploration into Africa.* New York: New Discovery Books, 1994.

*McLoone, Margo. *Women Explorers in Africa.* Mankato, Minn.: Capstone Press, 1997.

Park, Mungo. *Travels in the Interior Districts of Africa.* New York: Arno Press, 1971.

Severin, Timothy. *The African Adventure: Four Hundred Years of Exploration in the Dangerous Dark Continent.* New York: Dutton, 1973.

*Worth, Richard. *Stanley and Livingstone and the Exploration of Africa in World History.* Berkeley Heights, N.J.: Enslow Publishers, 2000.

Peoples

Appiah, Anthony. *In My Father's House.* New York: Oxford University Press, 1992.

Bohannan, Paul, and Philip Curtin. *Africa and Africans.* 4th ed. Prospect Heights, Ill.: Waveland Press, 1995.

Gibbs, James L., ed. *Peoples of Africa.* Prospect Heights, Ill.: Waveland Press, 1988.

Kuper, Hilda. *The Swazi: A South African Kingdom.* Prospect Heights, Ill.: Waveland, 1986.

Mirza, Sarah, and Margaret Strobel. *Three Swahili Women.* Bloomington: Indiana University Press, 1989.

*Peoples of Africa. New York: Marshall Cavendish, 2000.

Saitoti, Tepilit Ole. *Maasai.* New York: Abradale Press, 1993.

Shostak, Marjorie. *Nisa: the Life and Words of a !Kung Woman.* New York: Viking Press, 1983.

Thomas, Elizabeth Marshall. *The Harmless People.* New York: Viking Press, 1989.

Suggested Readings

Independence Movements and Independence

Cabrita, João M. *Mozambique: The Tortuous Road to Democracy.* New York: St. Martin's Press, 2000.

Hargreaves, John D. *Decolonization in Africa.* 2d ed. New York: Longman, 1996.

Legum, Colin. *Africa Since Independence.* Bloomington: Indiana University Press, 1999.

Mazrui, Ali A., ed. *Africa Since 1935.* Berkeley: University of California Press, 1999.

*McSharry, Patra, ed. *Apartheid: Calibrations of Color.* New York: Rosen Publishing Group, 1991.

*Meisel, Jacqueline Drobis. *South Africa at the Crossroads.* Brookfield, Conn.: Millbrook Press, 1994.

Ogot, Bethwell A., ed. *Decolonization and Independence in Kenya 1940–1993.* Athens: Ohio University Press, 1995.

Okoth, P. Godfrey, and Bethwell A. Ogot, eds. *Conflict in Contemporary Africa.* Nairobi: Jomo Kenyatta Foundation, 2000.

Osaghae, Eghosa E. *Crippled Giant: Nigeria Since Independence.* Bloomington: Indiana University Press, 1998.

Posel, Deborah. *The Making of Apartheid, 1948–1961: Conflict and Compromise.* New York: Oxford University Press, 1991.

Press, Robert M. *The New Africa: Dispatches From a Changing Continent.* Gainesville: University Press of Florida, 1999.

Arts and Architecture

Africa: The Art of a Continent: 100 Works of Power and Beauty. New York: Guggenheim Museum Publications, 1996.

*Barlow, Sean, and Banning Eyre. *Afropop! An Illustrated Guide to Contemporary African Music.* Edison, N.J.: Chartwell Books, 1995.

Bender, Wolfgang. *Sweet Mother: Modern African Music.* Translated by Wolfgang Fries. Chicago: University of Chicago Press, 1991.

Blier, Suzanne Preston. *The Royal Arts of Africa: The Majesty of Form.* New York: Harry N. Abrams, Inc., 1998.

Cameron, Kenneth M. *Africa on Film: Beyond Black and White.* New York: Continuum, 1994.

*Chanda, Jacqueline. *African Arts and Cultures.* Worcester, Mass.: Davis Publications, 1993.

Clarke, Duncan, and Joann Padgett, eds. *The Art of African Textiles.* San Diego, Calif.: Thunder Bay Press, 1997.

Diawara, Manthia. *African Cinema: Politics and Culture.* Bloomington: Indiana University Press, 1992.

Elleh, Nnamdi. *African Architecture: Evolution and Transformation.* New York: McGraw-Hill, 1997.

Etherton, Michael. *The Development of African Drama.* New York: Africana Publishing Co., 1982.

Garlake, Peter S. *The Hunter's Vision: The Prehistoric Art of Zimbabwe.* Seattle: University of Washington Press, 1995.

Gerster, Georg. *Churches in Rock: Early Christian Art in Ethiopia.* London: Phaidon, 1970.

Gillon, Werner. *A Short History of African Art.* New York: Facts on File, 1984.

Graham, Ronnie. *The World of African Music.* Chicago: Research Associates. Distributed by Frontline Distribution International, 1992.

Kerr, David. *African Popular Theater: From Pre-Colonial Times to the Present Day.* Portsmouth, N.H.: Heinemann, 1995.

Malkmus, Lizbeth, and Roy Armes. *Arab and African Film Making.* Atlantic Highlands, N.J.: Zed Books, 1991.

Monti, Nicolas. *Africa Then: Photographs, 1840–1918.* New York: Knopf. Distributed by Random House, 1987.

Picton, John, Rayda Becker, et al. *The Art of African Textiles: Technology, Tradition, and Lurex.* London: Barbican Art Gallery: Lund Humphries Publishers, 1995.

*Putnam, James. *Egyptian Pyramid.* New York: Alfred A. Knopf, 1994.

Robins, Gay. *The Art of Ancient Egypt.* Cambridge: Harvard University Press, 1997.

Savary, Claude (Ph. D). *The Dances of Africa.* New York: Henry N. Abrams, 1996.

Temko, Florence, et al. *Traditional Crafts from Africa.* Minneapolis, Minn.: Lerner Publications, 1996.

Wilcox, A. R. *The Rock Art of Africa.* New York: Holmes and Meier Publishers, 1984.

Vogel, Susan Mullin, ed. *Africa Explores: Twentieth Century African Art.* New York: Center for African Art. Distributed in the U.S. and Canada by Neues Pubishing Co., 1994.

182

Literature

*Abrahams, Roger. *African Folktales: Traditional Stories of the Black World*. New York: Pantheon Books, 1983.

Achebe, Chinua. *Things Fall Apart*. New York: Anchor Books, 1994.

Brown, Lloyd Wellesley. *Women Writers in Black Africa*. Westport, Conn.: Greenwood Press, 1981.

Cox, C. Brian, ed. *African Writers*. New York: Charles Scribner's Sons, 1997.

*Fairman, Tony. *Bury My Bones but Keep My Words: African Tales for Retelling*. New York: Puffin Books, 1994.

*Halsey, Peggy, Gail J. Morlan, and Melba Smith. *If You Want to Know Me: Reflections of Life in Southern Africa*. New York: Friendship Press, 1976.

*Hayes, Barbara. *Folktales and Fables of the Middle East and Africa*. New York: Chelsea House Publishers, 1994. [New—classified as Young Adult by Barnes & Noble.]

*Leslau, Charlotte. *African Proverbs*. Rev. ed. New York: Pauper Press, 1982.

Okpewho, Isidore. *African Oral Literature: Backgrounds, Character, and Continuity*. Bloomington: Indiana University Press, 1992.

Owomoyela, Oyekan, ed. *A History of Twentieth-Century African Literatures*. Lincoln: University of Nebraska Press, 1993.

*Vernon-Jackson, Hugh. *African Folk Tales*. Mineola, N.Y.: Dover Publishing, 1999.

Biographies

*Andronik, Catherine M. *Hatshepsut, His Majesty, Herself*. New York: Atheneum, 2000.

Aseka, Eric Masinde. *Jomo Kenyatta: A Biography*. Nairobi: East African Educational Publishers, 1992.

Bierman, John. *Dark Safari: The Life Behind the Legend of Henry Morton Stanley*. Austin: University of Texas Press, 1993.

De Klerk, Willem. *F. W. de Klerk: The Man in His Time*. Johannesburg: J. Ball. Distributed by Thorold's Africana Books, 1991.

*Denenberg, Barry. *Nelson Mandela: No Easy Walk to Freedom: A Biography*. New York: Scholastic, 1991.

*Diamond, Arthur. *Anwar Sadat*. San Diego, Calif.: Lucent Books, 1994.

Du Boulay, Shirley. *Tutu: Voice of the Voiceless*. Grand Rapids, Mich.: Eerdmans, 1988.

*Hoobler, Dorothy, and Thomas Hoobler. *African Portraits*. Austin, Tex.: Raintree/Steck Vaughn, 1993.

Ingham, Kenneth. *Obote: A Political Biography*. New York: Routledge, 1994.

*Knight, Virginia Curtin, ed. *African Biography*. 3d ed. Detroit: UXL, 1999.

Leakey, Louis S. B. *By the Evidence: Memoirs, 1932–1951*. New York: Harcourt Brace Jovanovich, 1976.

Leakey, Mary Douglas. *Disclosing the Past*. New York: McGraw-Hill, 1986.

Lovell, Mary S. *A Rage to Live: A Biography of Richard and Isabel Burton*. New York: Norton, 1998.

Mandela, Nelson. *Mandela: An Illustrated Autobiography*. Boston: Little, Brown, 1996.

Morell, Virginia. *Ancestral Passions: The Leakey Family and the Quest for Humankind's Beginnings*. New York: Simon & Schuster, 1995.

Nkrumah, Kwame. *Ghana: The Autobiography of Kwame Nkrumah*. New York: Thomas Nelson & Sons, 1957.

*Rasmussen, R. Kent. *Modern African Political Leaders (Global Profiles Series)*. New York: Facts on File, 1998.

Shillington, Kevin. *Ghana and the Rawlings Factor*. New York: St. Martin's Press, 1992.

Soyinka, Wole. *The Man Died: Prison Notes of Wole Soyinka*. New York: Noonday Press, 1988.

Thomas, Antony. *Rhodes*. New York: St. Martin's Press, 1997.

Vaillant, Janet G. *Black, French, and African: A Life of Léopold Sédar Senghor*. Cambridge: Harvard University Press, 1990.

Other

Harris, Jessica B. *The Africa Cookbook: Tastes of a Continent*. New York: Simon & Schuster, 1998.

LeVine, Robert A., et al. *Child Care and Culture: Lessons from Africa*. New York: Cambridge University Press, 1994.

*Scoones, Simon. *The Sahara and Its People*. New York: Thomson Learning, 1993.

Toulmin, Camilla. *Cattle, Women, and Wells: Managing Household Survival in the Sahel*. New York: Oxford University Press, 1992.

Suggested Readings

On-line Resources

Africa Daily. *Provides daily news reports for entire African continent, as well as several links to other African web sites.*
www.africadaily.com

Africa: South of the Sahara, Stanford University. *Contains a multitude of links to web sites concerning African issues and individual country information.*
http://www-sul.stanford.edu/depts/ssrg/africa/guide.html

African Information Centre. *Provides web site links to academic centers, governmental information, and current events.*
http://www.africainformation.co.uk/index.html

African Policy Information Center. *Discusses political, economic, racial, and health struggles in Africa, and promotes positive change.*
www.africapolicy.org

African Studies Center, Michigan State University. *Provides various resources of information on Africa, including access to the University's Africana library.*
http://www.isp.msu.edu/AfricanStudies/

African Studies Center, University of Pennsylvania. *Contains country-specific data and information on African organizations in the U.S.*
http://www.sas.upenn.edu/African_Studies/AS.html

AllAfrica Global Media. *Provides daily news reports from over 80 media organizations on events occurring throughout Africa.*
www.allafrica.com

CIA World Factbook 2000 online. *Provides updated statistical information on each country.*
http://www.odci.gov/cia/publications/factbook/index.html

New Africa. *Contains information on business, economy, news, and tourism.*
www.newafrica.com

The Story of Africa: African History From the Dawn of Time, BBC World Service. *Provides a detailed historical account of the continent.*
http://www.bbc.co.uk/worldservice/africa/features/storyofafrica/index.shtml

U.S. Aid in Africa. *Discusses the actions the U.S. has taken to improve the political and economic situations in Africa.*
http://www.usaid.gov/regions/afr/

U.S. State Department—Bureau of African Affairs. *Provides country and regional information on U.S. involvement in Africa, particularly sub-Saharan.*
http://www.state.gov/www/regions/africa/

World Atlas. *Provides maps of Africa and individual nations, plus some statistical information on each country.*
www.worldatlas.com

Photo Credits

Volume 1

Color Plates for Peoples and Cultures
1: Corbis/Peter Johnson; 2: Corbis/Paul Almasy; 3: Corbis/Michael and Patricia Fog; 4: Gallo Images/Corbis; 5: Corbis/Dave Bartruff; 6: Corbis/Earl and Nazima Kowall; 7: Corbis/David and Peter Turnley; 8: Gallo Images/Corbis; 9: AFP/Corbis; 10: Laure Communications/Jason Laure; 11: Reuters NewMedia Inc./Corbis; 12: Corbis/Howard Davies; 13: Reuters NewMedia Inc./Corbis; 14: Corbis/Mohammed Al-Sehiti; 15: Corbis/Jeremy Horner

Black-and-White Photographs
2: AP/Wide World Photos; 7: Corbis/Vince Streano; 11: Global Learning Inc./David Johnson; 12: United Nations; 20: UPI/Corbis-Bettman; 29: Corbis/Francois De Muller; 33: Photo Researchers, Inc./The National Audubon Society Collection/Leonard Lee Rue III; 34: Cory Langley; 39: Corbis; 44: Vanni Archive/Corbis; 52: AP/Wide World Photos; 56: Corbis/Margaret Courtney-Clarke; 57: Corbis/Christine Osborne; 58: Cory Langley; 63: Corbis/Lindsay Hebberd; 66: University of Iowa Museum of Art; 68; Cory Langley; 72: Corbis/Richard List; 75: Gallo Images/Corbis; 82: Corbis/Owen Franken; 85: Corbis/Tiziana and Gianni Baldizzone; 89: Corbis; 100: Corbis/Charles and Josette Lenars; 106: Corbis/Howard Davies; 111: AP/Wide World Photos; 116: Corbis/Patricia Fogden; 121: Corbis/Dave G. Houser; 129: Cory Langley; 133: Corbis/Dave Bartruff; 134: Corbis/Dave Bartruff; 137: Corbis/Caroline Penn; 140: Corbis/Roger Wood; 141: Wolfgang Kaehler; 145: Corbis/Sharna Balfour; 149: Gallo Images/Corbis; 154: Archive Photos Inc. 161: Corbis-Bettman; 165: Corbis/Jan Butchofsky; 170: Granger Collection Ltd.; 182: Corbis/Roger De La Harpe; 184: Corbis/Liba Taylor; 189: Corbis/Marc Garanger; 193: Papilio/Corbis; 197: Cory Langley; 200: Corbis/Caroline Penn; 205: British Library; 209: Archive Photos Inc.; 216: United Nations; 219: Corbis/Charles and Josette Lenars; 223: Wolfgang Kaehler

Volume 2

Color Plates for The Land and Its History
1: Gallo Images/Corbis; 2: Gallo Images/Corbis; 3: Corbis/Roger Wood; 4: Cory Langley; 5: Corbis/Paul Almasy; 6: AP Wide World Photos; 7: Corbis/Nik Wheeler; 8: Hulton-Deutsch Collection/Corbis, painting by Richard Caton Woodville; 9: AFP/Corbis; 10: Ecoscene/Corbis; 11: Corbis/Kevin Schafer; 12: Corbis/Nik Wheeler; 13: Gallo Images/Corbis; 14: Gallo Images/Corbis; 15: Cory Langley

Black-and-White Photographs
3: Corbis/Wolfgang Kaehler; 6: Laure Communications/Jason Laure; 12: Cory Langley; 17: Corbis-Bettman; 23: Corbis/Lowell Georgia; 25: AP/Wide World Photos; 31: Corbis/Caroline Penn; 34: Reuters NewMedia Inc./Corbis; 41: Global Learning Inc.; 45: Corbis/Anthony Barrister; 59: Cory Langley; 62: Laure Communications/Jason Laure; 63: Carolyn Fischer; 67: Cory Langley; 72: Phototake/Marco Polo; 77: Corbis-Bettman; 80: The Purcell Team/Corbis; 84: Corbis/Liba Taylor; 86: AP/Wide World Photos; 91: AP/Wide World Photos; 95: Milepost 92 1/2 /Corbis; 105: Reuters/Bettman; 117: Susan D. Rock; 122: Corbis/Liba Taylor; 126: Underwood & Underwood/Corbis; 130: Archive Photos Inc.; 135: AP/Wide World Photos; 139: United Nations; 145: Photo Researchers, Inc./Science Photo Library/John Reader; 149: Corbis/David Turnley; 156: Public Domain; 160: Corbis/Paul Almasy; 164: Kenneth Decker; 169: Corbis-Bettman; 173: Corbis/Charles O'Rear; 177: Corbis/O. Alamany and E. Vicens; 182: The Purcell Team/Corbis; 185: AP/Wide World Photos; 190: Gallo Images/Corbis; 200: Laure Communications/Jason Laure; 206: Historical Picture Archive/Corbis; 212: Corbis/Paul Almasy

Volume 3

Color Plates for Art and Architecture
1: Gallo Images/Corbis; 2: Corbis/Roger Wood; 3: Corbis/Wolfgang Kaehler; 4: AFP/Corbis; 5: Corbis/Fulvio Roiter; 6: Bowers Museum of Cultural Art/Corbis; 7: Laure Communications/Jason Laure; 8: Corbis/Lindsay Hebberd; 9: Laure Communications/Jason Laure; 10: Seattle Art Museum/Corbis; 11: Corbis/Peter Johnson; 12: Laure Communications/Jason Laure; 13: Corbis/Georg Roth; 14: Corbis/Daniel Laini; 15: Laure Communications/Jason Laure

Black-and-White Photographs
3: Archive Photos Inc.; 5: Public Domain; 10: Public Domain; 15: Corbis/Roger Wood; 21: Archive Photos Inc.; 29: Cory Langley; 34: Corbis/Caroline Penn; 40: Reuters NewMedia Inc./Corbis/Bobby Yip; 49: AP/Wide World Photos; 53: Corbis/Charles and Josette Lenars; 59: Granger Collection Ltd.; 64: Corbis/Robert van der Hilst; 66: Corbis/Paul Almasy; 71: Corbis/Nik Wheeler; 79: Corbis/Eldad Rafaeli; 83: Corbis-Bettman; 88: Corbis/Charles O'Rear; 94: Corbis/Carmen Redondo; 100: Archive Photos Inc.; 109: Jack Vartoogian; 112: Jack Vartoogian; 118: Archivo Iconogafico, S.A./Corbis; 123: Corbis/Peter Johnson; 128: AFP/Corbis; 136: Corbis/Yann Arthus-Bertand; 142: Corbis/Daniel Laini; 152: Cory Langley; 156: Corbis/Robert Holmes; 162: AP/Wide World Photos; 169: Corbis/Wolfgang Kaehler; 179: The Gamma Liaison Network; 183: Laure Communications/Jason Laure; 188: Corbis/Daniel Laini; 195: AP/Wide World Photos; 199: Laure Communications/Steve Hall; 202: Corbis/David and Peter Turnley; 205: Corbis/Liba Taylor; 208: Corbis/Daniel Laini; 219: AP/Wide World Photos

Volume 4

Color Plates for Daily Life
1: Corbis/Richard Bickel; 2:C/Charles and Josette Lenars; 3: Corbis/Charles and Josette Lenars; 4: Laure Communications/Jason Laure; 5: Laure Communications/Paul Joynson-Hicks; 6: Laure Communications/Jason Laure; 7: Corbis/David and Peter Turnley; 8: Gallo Images/Corbis; 9: Corbis/Nik Wheeler; 10: Laure Communications/Jason Laure; 11: AP Wide World Photos; 12: Laure Communications/Jason Laure; 13: Corbis/Roger Wood; 14: Corbis/Bojan Breceji; 15: Corbis/David and Peter Turnley

Black-and-White Photographs
3: Corbis/Andrea Jemolo; 16: David Johnson; 25: Corbis/Jon Spaull; 31: Granger Collection Ltd.; 38: Granger Collection Ltd.; 44: AFP/Corbis; 49: Gallo Images/Corbis; 51: Hulton-Deutsch Collection/Corbis; 57: AP/Wide World Photos; 62: Reuters NewMedia Inc./Corbis; 68: Corbis/Bojan Breceji; 84: JLM Visuals; 88: Laure Communications/Jason Laure; 95: Cory Langley; 102: Corbis/Catherine Karnow; 110: Laure Communications/Jason Laure; 115: Public Domain; 118: Laure Communications/Jason Laure; 124: Corbis/Inge Yspeert; 131: AFP/Corbis; 142: AP/Wide World Photos; 149: Gallo Images/Corbis; 152: Corbis/Paul Almasy; 158: Hulton-Deutsch Collection/Corbis; 166: Corbis/Paul Almasy; 174: Corbis/David Reed

Index

Page numbers of articles in these volumes appear in boldface type.

Index

Index

Bornu, **1:90–91**, 2:178, 4:36
Botha, Louis, 4:48
Botha, Pieter W., 4:53
Botswana, **1:91–94** *(map)*
    AIDS in, 1:14
    famine relief program in, 2:149–50
    geography and economy of, 1:91–92
    hereditary rank in, 1:147
    history and government of, 1:92–93
    Khama, president of, 1:92, **2:185–86**
    peoples and cultures of, 1:93–94
Botswana National Front (BNF), 1:93
Boudiaf, Mohammad, 1:22
Boukman, 1:207–8
Boumédienne, Houari, 1:21, **1:94**
Boundaries in Africa, **1:94–95**
Bourguiba, Habib, **1:95–96**, 1:161 *(illus.)*, 4:123
Bouteflika, Abdelaziz, 1:22
Braide, Garrick Sokari, **1:96**, 3:189
Brazil
    African population in, 1:207
    architectural influence of, 1:59
Brazza, Pierre Savorgnan de, 1:97, 175 *(illus.)*, 176, 2:74, 81, 4:117
Brazzaville, **1:97**
Bread, 2:66
Brewing, 2:68
Bridewealth, 2:194, 3:63–65
Brink, André, **1:97**
Britain. *See* Great Britain
British colonialism, 1:156–60
    architectural influence of, 1:59
    Asante attacks during, 1:15
    and Asante Union, 1:69
    in Bornu, 1:90–91
    in Cameroon, 1:114, 116
    and Cetshwayo, 1:126
    in Egypt, 2:18
    and Fante state, 1:15
    in Ghana, 1:108, 2:94
    in Kenya, 2:180–81, 3:120
    languages during, 2:207–8
    law in, 2:211
    Lugard, administrator during, **3:31–32**
    Mau Mau opposition to, 3:67–69
    in Mauritius, 3:74
    myths justifying, 4:171
    in Nigeria, 3:140–41, 141, 143
    and the Nile, 3:149
    and political freedom for colonies, 2:155
    Rhodes, Cecil, **3:212**
    Saint Helena, **4:5–6**
    and "scramble" for Africa, 1:153
    in South African Republic, 1:5

    in Sudan, 4:67–68
    in Tanganyika, 4:82–83
    Thuku, Kenyan political leader, 4:90
    in Togoland, 4:93
    in Uganda, 4:129–30
    in Zambia, 4:164
British Creoles, 1:185
British Somaliland, 1:158
Broad-leaved savannas, 2:3, 4
Brong people, 2:98
Brotherhoods, Islamic, 4:15
Bruce, James, 4:115
Bubi people, 2:26
Buganda, 4:129, 130
    Kagwa, prime minister of, **2:176**
    Mutesa II, ruler of, 3:115, **3:115**
Building materials, 1:54, 2:138
Bulsa people, 2:97
Bunyoro, 4:129
Bunyoro-Kitara, 2:175
Burial, 1:191–93 *(illus.). See also* Funerals
    in ancient Egypt, 2:11–12
    of Malagasy people, 3:39
    pole sculptures, 1:64
    in pyramids, **3:196–97**
Burkina Faso, **1:98–102** *(map) (illus.)*, 4:96
    cultivation in, 1:11 *(illus.)*
    geography and economy of, 1:98
    history and government of, 1:99–102
    Mossi people, **3:96**
    peoples and cultures, 1:100 *(illus.)*, 102
Burton, Sir Richard Francis, **1:103**, 3:149, 4:116
Burundi, **1:103–8** *(map)*
    geography and economy of, 1:103–4
    history and government of, 1:105–7 *(illus.)*
    peoples and culture of, 1:104–5
    and Rwanda, 3:218
Bushman (San) people, 2:186
Busia, Kofi A., **1:108–9**, 2:95
Buthelezi, Gatsha, 4:54
Buyoya, Pierre, 1:106–7
Buzzer instruments, 3:113
Bwiti cult, 3:208 *(illus.)*
Byzantine Empire
    in Egypt, 2:15–16
    Ethiopian monks from, 2:38

C

Cabinda, 1:25, **1:109**
    art of, 1:28

    forestry in, 1:27
    petroleum in, 1:27
Cabora Bassa, 3:103, 4:162
Cabral, Amílcar Lopes, **1:110**, 2:110, 111, 3:172
Cabral, Luis, 2:111
Caesar, Julius, 1:147
Caillié, René, 4:116
Cairo, **1:110–11** *(illus.)*, 2:140
Cairo Declaration on Human Rights in Islam, 2:141
Calendars and time, **1:112–13**
Calligraphy, 1:68–69 *(illus.)*
Camara Laye, **1:113–14**, 3:25
Camels, 4:42
    dromedaries, 1:32, 33 *(illus.)*
    race, camel, 1:85 *(illus.)*
Cameroon, **1:114–18** *(map)*
    as British colony, 1:156
    folk dance masks of, 3:66 *(illus.)*
    as French colony, 1:162
    geography and economy of, 1:114–15
    as German colony, 1:163
    history and government of, 1:115–18
    maize grown in, 1:12 *(illus.)*
    peoples and cultures of, 1:116 *(illus.)*, 118
Cameroon National Union (CNU), 1:117
Camp David Accords, 3:93
Canary Islands, **1:119**
Cancer, 1:217
Candomblé, 1:208, 209
Cape Colony, 1:158, 4:137
Cape Coloured People, **1:119**, 1:185, 2:48, 4:49
Cape Malays, 1:185
Cape Town, **1:120**, 4:102 *(illus.)*, 138
Cape Verde, **1:120–22** *(illus.)*
    and Guinea-Bissau, 2:110, 111
    Pereira, president of, **3:172**
    as Portuguese colony, 1:165
Capitalism
    as development model, 1:199
    and labor organization, 2:197
Caravans, 3:29 *(illus.)*
Cardoso, Mãe Julia da Silva, 1:180
Carnivals. *See* Festivals and carnivals
Carthage, **1:122**, 3:214, 215, 4:123
Carved figures, 1:61, 62
Carving, 1:183, 184
Casamance (Senegal), 4:15
Casbah, 1:143
Casbah of Ait Benhaddou, 3:94 *(illus.)*
Casely-Hayford, Joseph, 3:23
Cash crops, 1:10–11
    labor needed for, 2:199
    and shortage of food crops, 1:13

Index

Index

Index

Index

Index

of Mali, 3:52–54
of Mauritania, 3:70–73
of modern Egypt, 2:15–20
of Morocco, 3:91–93
of Mozambique, 3:98–102
of Namibia, 3:121–23
of Niger, 3:133, 134
of Niger River and Delta, 3:136–37
of Nigeria, 3:139–44
of North Africa, 3:153–60
and oral tradition, **3:165–66**
of pastoralism, 3:29–30
of plantations, 3:176–77
prehistory to Iron Age, 2:123–25
of Réunion, 3:211
roots of colonialism in, 2:131–33
of Rwanda, 3:216–20 *(illus.)*
of Sahara desert, 4:2
of São Tomé and Príncipe, 4:7
of Senegal, 4:12–15
of Sierra Leone, 4:21–26
since independence, 2:134–36
    (illus.)
society, trade, and urban develop-
    ment, 2:125–27
of Somalia, 4:41–44
of South Africa, 4:48–54
of Southern Africa, **4:56–59** *(illus.)*
of Sudan, 4:66–70
of Swaziland, 4:77–78
of Tanzania, 4:82–83
of Togo, 4:92–95
of Tunisia, 4:121–23
of Uganda, 4:128–32
of Western Sahara, 4:145, 146
of Zambia, 4:164–65
of Zanzibar, 4:168
of Zimbabwe, 4:171–75
The History of the Yorubas (Johnson),
    2:174
HIV, 1:14, 215, 4:55, 165
Hodgson, Sir Frederick, 1:70
"Homelands" (South Africa), 1:37
Hominids, 2:142–45
Homo erectus, 2:144–46
Homosexuality, 2:89–90
Horn of Africa, 1:164, 2:29, 30, 32,
    4:40, 41
Horses, 1:32
Horton, James Africanus, **2:137**,
    3:126
Horus (Egyptian god), 3:118 *(illus.)*
Hospitals, 2:120, 121–22
Houphouët-Boigny, Félix, **2:137**,
    2:166–69 *(illus.)*
Hours, 1:113
Households
    as family units, 2:57–58
    slaves in, 4:13
    in small villages, 2:103

Houses and housing, **2:138–40**
    in Bénin, 1:82 *(illus.)*
    Islamic laws for, 2:210
    for migrant workers, 2:200–1
    rural, 2:138
    urban, 2:139–40 *(illus.)*
Hova people, 2:51
Human rights, 1:36, **2:140–42**
Humans, early, **2:142–47** *(map)*
    ancestors of, 2:142–45 *(illus.)*
    archaeological evidence of,
        1:48–51
    emergence of modern from,
        2:146–47
Hunger and famine, **2:147–50** *(illus.)*
Hunger season, 2:69
Hungry rice, 1:9
Hunting and gathering, 2:87–88, 102,
    2:150–51
Hut Tax, 4:23
Hutu people, 1:104–7 *(illus.)*, 2:92,
    3:216–20 *(illus.)*
Hydatid disease, 1:217
Hydroelectric power, 2:21, 22

I

Ibadan, **2:151**
Ibibio people, 2:50
Ibn Battuta, Abu Abdallah
    Muhammad, 2:133, **2:151**, 3:85,
    4:90, 113
Ibn Khaldun, 4:125
Ibo people, 2:50
Ibrahim, Abdullah, 3:110
Identity, sense of. *See also* Ethnic
    groups and identity
    and age, 1:5
    Diop's work on, 1:212
Idiophones, 3:114
Idris I, 3:14, 92, 197
Idris II, 3:92
Ifni, 1:167
Ifriqiya, 4:121–22
Igbo (Ibo) people, 2:50, **2:152**, 3:137
    gender roles in, 2:88
    masks of, 1:65
    scarification among, 1:87
Igbo Ukwu (archaeological site), 1:46
Igboland, 1:2, 3:139–40, 140
Ijaw people, 2:50
Ijo (Ijaw, Kalabari) people, 2:50
Ile-Ife, 1:139
Illegal housing settlements, 2:140
Illnesses. *See* Diseases
IMF. *See* International Monetary Fund
Imhotep, 3:196
Imperialism, 1:153. *See also*
    Colonialism in Africa

In Darkest Africa (Stanley), 4:64
In the Fog of the Season's End (La
    Guma), 2:197
Inan, Abu, 3:159
Indentured labor, 2:198
Independence movements, **2:152–56.**
    See also Nationalism
    in Afrikaner Republics, 1:5
    in Algeria, 1:20–21, 78–79
    in Angola, 1:28–29
    in Belgian Congo, 1:174–75
    in Botswana, 1:92
    of Cape Verde, 1:120
    Chilembwe's activities in, 1:131
    Diop's influence on, 1:212
    early roots of, 2:152–53
    in Egypt, 2:19–20
    ethnic cooperation/conflict related
        to, 2:91
    in Ghana, 2:94–95
    in Guinea-Bissau, 1:110
    and independence era, 2:154–56
        (illus.)
    and Indian communities, 2:157
    in Kenya, 2:180–83
    in Mali, 3:52–54
    Mau Mau role in, 3:67–69
    in Mauritania, 3:71
    missionaries, role in, 3:84
    in Morocco, 3:92–93, 105
    in Mozambique, 3:86, 101–2
    in Namibia, 3:122
    and neocolonialism, 3:130–31
    Nkrumah, leader of, 3:149
    in Senegal, 4:14
    in Sierra Leone, 4:23–24
    in Sudan, 4:68–69
    Tshombe, leader in, 4:119
    and unions, 4:134
    and World War II, 4:159
Independent ICU, 2:176
Indian communities, **2:157**
Indian Ocean, coastline of, 2:1
Indigenous government, 2:102–6
Indirect rule, 1:156, 157, 159
Indo-Arabic number system, 4:160
Industrial and Commercial Union
    (ICU), 2:175–76, 4:49, 50, 134
Industrial Revolution, 2:131–32, 4:32
Industry, *For specific countries, see
    under* Economy
    fuel used by, 2:22
    labor, industrial, 2:200
Infancy, 1:128, 129 *(illus.)*
Infectious diseases, 1:213–17, 2:119
Informal labor, 2:201
Inheritance
    Islamic law related to, 2:165
    of kingship, 2:190
Initiation rites, 1:130, **2:158–59**

Index

Index

Index

Index

Pyramid Age, 2:11
Pyramids, 1:53–54, 2:12, **3:196–97**

Q

Qaddafi, Muammar al-, 3:13, 15–16,
    3:197–98, 4:44
Quaque, Philip, **3:198**
Queen of Sheba, 3:20
Queens and queen mothers,
    3:198–200 (illus.). See also specific
    queens
A Question of Power (Head), 2:114
Qwi languages, 2:205

R

Race. See Ethnic groups and identity
Race issues
    and African archaeology, 1:41
    apartheid. See Apartheid
    and Central African Federation,
        1:122–23
Radama I, 3:38, **3:200**, 3:203
Radama II, 3:39, 203
Radio and television, 3:182, **3:201–2**
    (illus.)
Raffia art, 1:183
Rahab (instrument), 3:113
Rai music, 3:107
Railroads, 4:107 (map), 110–11
Rain forests, 1:54, 149 (illus.), 150
Rainlaiarivony, 3:39
Rakoto, 3:203
Ramadan, 2:61
Ramaema, Elias, 3:5
Ramanantsoa, Gabriel, 3:41
Ranavalona I, 3:38–39
Ranavalona, Mada, 3:200, **3:203**
Rand. See Witwatersrand
Rand (currency of South Africa), 3:88
    (illus.)
Rassemblement Démocratique
    Africain (RDA), Burkina Faso, 1:99
Rassemblement du Peuple Togolais
    (RPT), 4:94
Ratsimilaho, 3:38
Ratsiraka, Didier, 3:41, 42
Rawlings, Jerry J., 2:96, **3:203–4**
Raya people, 2:36
Red Hand, 4:134
The Reds (SFIO), 4:14
Reform programs, 1:199–201
Refugees, **3:204–6** (illus.), 4:136
    camps of, 4:44 (illus.)
    in Djibouti, 1:220
    Hutu, 3:219 (illus.)
    from Rwanda, 3:217

Le regard du roi (Camara Laye), 1:114
Regional organizations, 2:100
Relief agencies, 2:99, 100, 149
Religion and ritual, **3:206–10**. See also
    Ethnic groups and identity;
    Festivals and carnivals
    of Africans in Americas, 1:208–9
    of ancient Egypt, 2:11–12
    animal symbolism in, 3:210
    animal worship, 1:32
    body painting as part of, 1:87
    Christianity in Africa, **1:132–36**
    in construction process, 1:55
    dance in, 1:188
    elements of, 3:207–9 (illus.)
    funeral, 1:191–93
    and Galawdewos, 2:83
    of the Hausa, 2:113
    health and, 2:115
    initiation rites, **2:158–59**
    Islam, **2:162–65**
    Judaism, **2:174**
    and kingship, 2:189
    Mami Wata, **3:56–57**
    marriage, 2:158
    masks used in, 1:65
    missions and missionaries,
        3:81–84 (illus.)
    in modern Egypt, 2:15, 16
    personal identity and, 1:192
    practices and prohibitions,
        3:209–10
    prophetic movements, **3:187–92**
        (illus.)
    and rank of leaders, 1:147
    respect for elders in, 1:6
    roots of colonial education in, 2:5
    royal, 2:61
    sins in, 4:79–80
    spirit possession, 4:60–61
    therapeutic, 2:117, 118
    of Tunisia, 4:126
    Vodun, **4:139–40**
Religious leaders
    Kimbangu, Christianity, **2:187**
    Kimpa Vita, Antonianism,
        2:187–88
    Mahdi, Islam, **3:44**
    Maranke, Apostolic Church of
        John Maranke, **3:61**
    Tutu, Anglican, **4:126–27**
    Umar, Islam, **4:133–34**
RENAMO (Mozambique National
    Resistance Movement),
    Mozambique, 3:102
René, France Albert, 4:18
Reptiles, 4:148
Republic of Congo. See Congo
    (Brazzaville)
Research, African, 1:4

Resettlement of Africans, 1:210–11
Resources, redistribution of, 1:199
Respect
    age and, 1:6
    for elderhood, 1:144, 145 (illus.)
Réunion, 1:163, **3:211**
Revolutionary United Front (RUF),
    Sierra Leone, 4:24, 25
Rhodes, Cecil John, 1:5, 159, 2:185,
    3:31, **3:212**, 4:59, 172
Rhodesia, 1:92, 4:53, 172
Rhodesian Front (RF), 4:172
Rhythms, dance, 1:188, 189
Rice, 1:10, 13, 3:40 (illus.), 42
Riddles and proverbs, **3:192–93**
Rif tribe, 1:84
Rift Valley, 2:179, 180, 4:83, 163
Rites
    initiation, **2:158–59**
    puberty, 94
Ritual sacrifice, 2:174
Rituals. See Religion and ritual
River blindness, 1:214, 216 (illus.)
Robeson, Paul, 1:136
Rock art, 1:19, 47, 67, **3:212–14**
Roman Africa, **3:214–15**
Roman Catholic Church, 1:133,
    135–36, 156, 209, 2:38
Roman Empire, Africa in, 1:19, 122,
    2:15–16, **3:214–15**
Roman script, 4:160
Rome, ancient, 1:56
Rotimi, Ola, 4:88
Rotse people, 2:51
Royal dances, 1:187–88
Royal rituals, 2:61
Royal slaves, 4:13
Rozwi people, 1:55
Ruanda people, 2:52
Ruanda-Urundi, 1:105, 156
Rundi people, 2:52
Rural areas
    housing in, 2:138
    labor systems in, 2:197
    spread of AIDS to, 1:14
Rwanda, 1:105, **3:215–21** (map)
    economy of, 3:220
    ethnic rivalries in, 1:107
    genocide in, 2:92
    geography of, 3:215–16
    history of, 3:216–20 (illus.)
    peoples and cultures of, 3:220–21
Rwanda (Ruanda) people, 2:52
Rwandan Patriotic Front (FPR), 3:218,
    220
Rwandese Alliance of National Unity
    (RANU), 3:218

Index

S

Sacred Hope (Neto), 3:131
Sacrifice, 2:174, 3:209
Sadat, Anwar al-, 2:19, 3:104, 125, **4:1**
Safaris, 4:99
Sahara desert, 1:196, **4:1–4** *(illus.)*
  Algerian, 1:18
  cultivation in, 1:12
  formation of, 1:19
  herding in, 2:124
  historic climate change in, 1:45, 47, 2:124
  rock paintings of, 1:67
  Tuareg people of, **4:120**
  zones of, 2:2
Saharan Atlas Mountains, 1:18, 71
Sahel, 1:196–98, 3:166, 4:2, **4:4–5**
  French colonialism in, 1:162
  and slavery, 4:36
  in Sudan, 4:65–66
  as zone of Sahara desert, 2:2
Sahir, Murad, 1:204
Saïbou, Ali, 3:133
Sa'id ibn Sultan, **4:5**, 4:91
Saint Antony, 1:179
St. Frumentius of Tyre, 2:38
St. George church (Ethiopia), 1:133 *(illus.)*
Saint Helena, **4:5–6**
Saint-Louis, Senegal, 4:16 *(illus.)*
St. Paul's Cathedral (Abidjan), 1:1
Salad Hassan, Abdikassim, 4:44
Saladin, 1:110, 2:16
Salazar, Antonio, 3:101
Sallah festival, 2:61
Salt, 3:87, 89, 4:2
Salt lakes, 1:17
Salt marsh ecosystems, 2:1
Samba, Chéri, **4:6**
Samba wa Mbimba-N'zinga-Nuni Masi, David, 4:6
Sambizanga (film), 1:138
Samburu people, 4:118 *(illus.)*
San people, 2:186, 3:125
Sande societies, 2:158, 4:10–11
Sanhá, Malan Bacai, 2:111
Sankara, Thomas, 1:101
Sankoh, Foday, 4:25
Sankore Mosque, 4:90
Santería, 1:208, 209
Sanyang, Kukoi Samba, 2:85
São Tomé and Príncipe, 1:166, **4:7–8**, 4:30
Sara people, 2:52
Sarafina!, 4:89
Sarakole people, 2:53
Sarbah, John Mensah, **4:8–9**
Sassou-Nguesso, Denis, 1:171

Savannas, 1:11, 17, 25, 26, 2:3–4 *(illus.)*
Sawyer, Amos, 3:11
Sayfuwu dynasty, 1:90
Scarification, 1:87
Scarlet Song (Bâ), 3:28
Schistosomiasis, 1:214
Schools
  art, 1:64
  colonial, 2:6–7
  Islamic, 2:7, 9
  Muslim, 1:39 *(illus.)*
  segregation in, 2:6
Schreiner, Olive, 3:24, **4:9**
Schweitzer, Albert, 3:83
"Scramble" for Africa, 1:94–95, 153, 162, 163, 2:55
Sculpture, 1:62–64 *(illus.)*, 182, 183
Seaports, 4:109–10
Seasons, 1:112–13, 2:69
Secret societies, 1:130, 2:158, 3:209, **4:10–11**
Segregation. *See also* Apartheid
  in colonial cities, 1:141
  educational, 2:6–7
Sembène, Ousmane, **4:11**
Semetic language group, 2:203
Semideserts, 2:1–2
  Kalahari Desert, **2:176–77** *(illus.)*
  in Namib Desert, 2:1
  in Sahara desert, **4:1–4**
  Sahel, **4:4–5**
Senegal, **4:11–17** *(map) (illus.)*
  classes of slaves in, 4:13
  confederation with the Gambia, 2:85
  Dakar, capital of, **1:187**
  decorative arts of, 1:68
  Diagne, politician in, **1:202–3**
  economy of, 4:15
  as French colony, 1:162
  geography of, 4:11–12
  history and government of, 4:12–15
  as part of French West Africa, 2:76
  peoples and cultures of, 4:16, 17
  Senghor, president of, **4:17–18**
Senegal River Development Organization, 2:161
Senegalese Democratic Party (PDS), 4:15
Senegambia, 2:85, 4:12–13
Senghor, Léopold Sédar, 3:25, 130, 4:14, **4:17–18**
Sennar Dam, 2:161
Senufo people, 1:65, 2:52, 171
Septimius Severus, 3:214, 215
Servitude, 1:144, 145
Sesotho language, 3:6
Sets, age, 1:7, 8

Setswana language, 3:175, 176
Settlements
  early European, 2:55
  early urban, 2:126
  villages, 2:102–3
  West African trading, **4:144–45**
Sèvi Iwa, 1:208
Sexuality, 2:89–90
Sexually transmitted diseases (STDs), 1:14, 217
Seychelles, 1:157, 158, **4:18–19**
Shaaban, Robert, 3:21, **4:19**
Shagari, Shehu, 3:144
Shaka Zulu, 1:211, 3:119, **4:20**, 4:58, 176
Shamans, 2:115
Shantytowns, 1:139, 142, 2:139 *(illus.)*, 140
Share contracts, 2:199–200
Shari'a, 2:209–10, 4:69
Sharmarke, Abdirashid Ali, 4:42
Sharp, Granville, 4:21
Sharpeville (South Africa), 3:57–58, **4:51** *(illus.)*, 52, 139
Shawn (instrument), 3:113
Sheep, 1:33, 4:42
Shells, 3:87, 89
Shembe, Isaiah, **4:20**
Shifting cultivation, 1:11–12
Shi people, 3:200
Shisima, 4:63
Shluh tribe, 1:84
Shona people, 2:47, 52, 3:204, **4:20–21**
Shrimp, 3:103
Shrines, 1:194, 218, 2:189
Sidamo people, 2:36, 53
Siddis, 1:204
Sidewalk radio, 3:182
Sierra Leone, **4:21–27** *(map)*
  as British colony, 1:156
  economy of, 4:26
  founding of, 1:210
  Freetown, capital of, **2:73–74**
  geography of, 4:21
  history and government of, 4:21–26 *(illus.)*
  masks of, 1:65
  on misery index, 1:199
  peoples and cultures of, 4:26–27
  secret societies in, 4:10, 11
Sierra Leone People's Party (SLPP), 4:24
Simba: The King of Beasts (film), 1:136
Simbi and the Satyr of the Dark Jungle (Tutuola), 4:127
Singobile Mabhena, 3:129
Sinkofa (film), 1:138
Sins, 4:79–80
Sirocco, 1:18

210

Index

Index

Index